WOMEN OF THE UNDERGROUND: MUSIC

CULTURAL INNOVATORS SPEAK FOR THEMSELVES

EDITED BY

ZORA VON BURDEN

MANIC D PRESS
SAN FRANCISCO

For Michael Slavinsky
a talented musician, the love of my life, my inspiration,
and whose unending support made this book possible

Disclaimer: Opinions and statements made by the interview subjects herein do not necessarily reflect the views of the editor or publisher, nor have any statements by the interview subjects been verified for accuracy.

Photo credits: Cover photo of Kembra Pfahler by Katrina del Mar. All photographs courtesy of the musicians, with known photographers credited as follows: Pam Tent photo by Clay Geerdes; Laurie Anderson photo by Maggie Soladay; Lydia Lunch photo by Marc Viaplana; Adele Bertei photo by Johnny Rosza; Ana Da Silva photo by Shirley O'Loughlin; Patricia Morrison photo by G. Silva; Nina Hagen photo by Amber Gray; Jarboe photo by Jill Williams; Teresa Nervosa photo by Geoff Cordner; Kembra Pfahler photo by Katrina del Mar

Library of Congress Cataloging-in-Publication Data

Women of the underground : music cultural innovators speak for themselves / edited by Zora von Burden.
    p. cm.
  ISBN 978-1-933149-19-6 (trade pbk. original : alk. paper)
  1. Women rock musicians--Interviews. I. Burden, Zora von, 1968-
  ML82.W683 2008
  781.66092'273--dc22
  [B]
                                2007052510

CONTENTS

INTRODUCTION

Several years back I was going through some turbulent times, desperate to connect and find inspiration from other women who had been through the same and were not afraid to face their fears. I found that inspiration in the work of these women musicians, many of whom greatly influenced me in my formative years. These are women who celebrate pushing the boundaries of not only their own abilities but those of the world around them. There was solace and strength in what they presented as their art. They are outsiders who have successfully drawn strength from the challenges of living on the edge of cultural norms and safe zones, champions of individual thought and expression.

This book is a record of amazing reflections from these creative women who, despite their brilliant and prolific careers, have remained on the periphery of the mainstream, never fully acknowledged for their achievements yet garnering large, cult-like followings. These are women who have never compromised their integrity, and in doing so were consigned to creating their works in a realm classified as the 'underground'—never sacrificing the quality for quantity, or catering to the propensities of the masses. When searching for books relating to this genus of woman, there isn't much out there.

The women included in this book are originators—insurgents—whose work as incendiary revolutionaries and cultural engineers has influenced subsequent generations. In the underground, these artists are free to roam through sound and body, mind and spirit. They are brave, risk-taking, autonomous sensory explorers who travel into unexplored territory. These interviews give credit to the women themselves, these daring and groundbreaking artists who also happen to be female.

The genius and cultural engineering through their various sounds has left an indelible mark on music history, stemming from the counterculture in which they thrive and play. It is now slowly filtering through into society in every aspect of conceptual thought in mass media, be it literature, fashion, or technology. Their musical visions have become the foundation for much of today's artistry, and yet they remain in the background. Often those who emulate their work are unaware that they are a direct result of the evolutionary processes the women in this book provoked.

Slowly, though, these women are becoming more and more appreciated for their importance and impact on modern works. Within, you will find an oral history that offers a glimpse into the world of female musicians across the decades and across the world, from LA's Laurel Canyon and New York's Lower East Side to Germany and the UK, with many stops in between.

Because we live in an intensely technology-driven era, it has never been easier to navigate globally through endless, overwhelming collections of information which can inspire us in vast and various ways. There were several male publishers who rejected this project, and I found myself disillusioned and intimidated. I finally found the woman who could recognize the importance of this book, a publisher who shared the same passion for the underground that I do, via a social networking website that I had felt was totally useless and narcissistic. But if I had not had the ease and anonymity of this type of networking tool, I may have never had the nerve to approach Manic D Press. Thanks to the help of my publisher, I now have the chance to inspire others with the words and accomplishments of the artists I have interviewed in this book. They have all reached far beyond the societal confines of their gender and their art to create bodies of work that have had a great impact on subsequent generations, within one of the most influential of all media: music.

Zora von Burden
San Francisco

WANDA JACKSON QUEEN OF ROCKABILLY

Wanda Jackson was born in Maud, Oklahoma, on October 20, 1937. In her teenage years, she became known for singing country and rock'n'roll, and was one of the first female rock'n'roll singers. During these years she toured with Elvis Presley, and togther forged the new sound of Rockabilly. She started recording in 1954. Her early hits were "Let's Have a Party" and "Fujiyama Mama." Her early performances were considered risqué, and were condemned for being wild and energy-fueled, earning her the nickname "Hurricane Wanda."

In the '60s, Jackson started to move away from rock'n'roll towards country music again and continued to release numerous albums. In the 1970s she became a born-again Christian and with husband Wendell Goodman, she became an acclaimed gospel singer. She has been a successful gospel singer ever since, though she never completely left country or rock music behind. She and her husband continue to be active in the evangelistic ministry.

In the '80s, her music was rediscovered in Europe, and then in the '90s in the US, thanks to an emerging rockabilly scene. Wanda feels that a big part of this is due to her recording two songs with Rosie Flores, released on Flores' album *Rockabilly Filly*. Thanks to renewed interest in her work, Jackson has been re-releasing and performing her classic albums in the US and around the world, including *Rockin' in the Country* (1990), *Right or Wrong* (box set, 1993), *The Vintage Collection* (1996), *Queen of Rockabilly* (2000), *Rockin' with Wanda* (2002), *Wanda Rocks!* (2002), *Live and Still Kickin'* (2003), *Heart Trouble* (2003), *Heartache* (2004), and *I Remember Elvis* (2006).

Wanda has been nominated for two Grammy awards and has been inducted into more than a dozen Rock and Roll Halls of Fame internationally. She is widely recognized as an originator, singer, and songwriter, and is known as the First Lady of Rock and Roll, and the Queen of Rockabilly. In May 2009, Wanda Jackson was inducted into the US Rock and Roll Hall of Fame.

When did you first start singing?

Let's see... Well, I've always sung, you know, with my dad at home. My mother used to have me sing while I was in the bathtub when I was about five and she'd tell me to sing so that she could go ahead and fix supper but not worry about me. I was okay as long as she could hear me singing. (Laughs) I had to sing loud, so she could hear me! Other than that, I started singing on the radio, a little program here in Oklahoma City, on this program that devoted the last fifteen minutes of an hour show to local talent. You'd go up and try out and I guess see if you could carry a tune, and, well, they'd let you sing for fifteen minutes. Through that little show I won a contest that they had for your own radio show. I'm not sure how long they gave it to me, maybe a month. It was five days a week. They had a way of telling that I had quite a few listeners and so they told me I could keep that time slot if I could keep the sponsor, because they couldn't give me the time anymore. So I found a sponsor or they had one for me, and I just worked really hard to keep that little show sponsored because I loved doing it. I was about fourteen, and it was just me and my guitar. I'm sure it couldn't have been real good. (Laughs) But I had my share of listeners and everything.

Are there any recordings of this show that exist?

Not to my knowledge; they didn't do much of that. It wasn't convenient in those days. That little show became the actual catalyst for my whole career. A very popular Number One western swing bandleader in our nation at the time, Hank Thompson (who also happened to be my favorite singer) lived in Oklahoma City at the time. I didn't know this, of course, but after my show one day they told me that I had a phone call. I said, "Well, who is it?" They said, "Oh, we don't know, it's a man." I said to myself, "Well, it's probably Daddy, I better talk to him." Lo and behold, it was Hank Thompson. I nearly fainted right there on the spot. But he told me he had been listening to my show and wanted to know if I'd be interested in singing with his band that coming Saturday night at the big ballroom downtown, the Trianon Ballroom. It was probably the most popular ballroom in the Midwest at that time for country and western music. So I said, "Well, I sure want to, Mr. Thompson, but I'll have to ask my mother." I knew I couldn't get in those places at fourteen, but you could if you were accompanied with a parent. So naturally, they were thrilled for me.

I sang with Hank that Saturday night, scared to death, breaking meter. I was just so scared. For some reason he had confidence in me, and he had me sing each time that he and the band played there in the coming year or whatever. Then somewhere in that time, I guess maybe after about a year, he got a television show. It was just local, but it was a very popular show, and he had me as his featured girl singer. So through that I got a lot of recognition locally. Then, at age sixteen, Hank got my first recording contract for me with Decca Records, a major company. My first time to sign with anybody, so I thought that was pretty amazing. He let me come out to his home and he had a full room of recording equipment just like a commercial set-up. He brought his band in and I did a demo record and he sent it to Decca and they signed me. Ever since then, Hank has just been such a special person to me. He's still a dear friend, and we got to work together quite a bit throughout the years. And, as it turned out, I actually wanted to go with Capitol Records. I set my sights pretty high, I guess. They were the largest recording company in the world in 1956. Hank helped me to get that contract as well. So, I was a junior in high school and I was with Decca Records for two years, then I signed with Capitol and I was there for eighteen years, until I asked for my release in the 1970s. Hank has been very instrumental in my career—that's how I got started.

What kind of vocal training did you have? Any formal training?

Just singin' in the bathtub. (Laughs) No, I didn't ever take voice lessons. No, most country singers haven't.

Was the signature style from your early records a technique that came naturally, or was it consciously developed?

It was really just my natural voice, you know. Depending on what type of song I was singing, it could sound a little different on a ballad than it could on a growlin' rock and roll song. Yeah, I just sang them however I felt them... that's all any of us do, actually. Maybe some work purposefully on a style, I don't know. I never did.

What did your parents think about you becoming a performer at sixteen?

I wasn't a rock and roll singer in the very beginning, of course. I did country music. Well, I'm an only child and they were so proud of me. It was really like a family affair. My dad had been a professional singer back in the thirties. He had a little band and he'd play on Saturday nights in little towns around Oklahoma. That's how he met Mother, at one of those dances. They were married and the Depression was on, times were hard, and then I came along. It just wasn't payin' for him to try and continue to sing, so he had to get a real job. He never really got his dream fulfilled of being a star, but I thought it was wonderful that he was able to live that dream vicariously through my career. He traveled with me, he was such a big part of everything I did. It was a real blessing to have him. He quit his job so that he could drive and help me with all the stuff that required help on the road, especially as a woman, a young girl. I couldn't have done it by myself.

My mother stayed home, so they gave up their lives, so to speak. They invested their lives into me. My mother, who was a professional seamstress, made all of my clothes—my stage clothes and most of my street clothes. She'd always sewn for me, and my dresses fit like a glove. She and I worked out the style—with the silk fringes, lower-cut necklines, a very glamorous, sexy style, with high heels—when I was about seventeen. You have to remember, at that time there were only about four girls in country music. I was about the third one to come along, so there was maybe about five of us.

Who were the other ones at that time?

Well, there was Kitty Wells, Jean Shepard, and myself. They were kind of like the main ones that were on major companies. There were a few other girls recording yodel songs or polkas or specialized music. But all of them up until this point wore cowboy boots, a full skirt, a little vest with maybe some leather fringe, and a western tie around your neck, and a hat. I never did like all of that. I was a young lady, and I realized that dressing in the standard style was hiding a lot of my assets. (Laughs) So Mother and I discarded those and came up with our designs, and consequently, I changed the look of women's dressing in country music.

What kind of reactions did you get at first to that style?

Everybody thought it was great. They may have been a little shocked, but I always like to shock a little bit. It was just fine with my folks, so that gave me the freedom to say, "Hey, other people can take it or leave it but this is the way I'm going to dress." It did make changes in our music. So

I'm really proud I did that.

Were you able to remain in school when you were touring and recording?

Oh yeah, I didn't begin touring until I graduated from high school. My sessions would just amount to maybe every three or four months to go into a studio and record. Either Nashville or Hollywood. So I was able to manage that fine.

When my first record came out, our principal got on the intercom system in all the classroom homerooms, and he announced that I had signed with Decca Records. You could hear applause throughout the whole school. All the rooms were applauding. I had so much support and so much help. It was wonderful.

Did you write any of your own music?

Yeah. On the Decca label you'll see that I wrote songs in those young teenage years, and then with Capitol Records in 1956. I started working with Elvis in 1955. He encouraged me to stretch myself to try to do this new music he was doing that all the young people loved. He was very wise. He said, "It's always been an adult audience buying our records and coming to our performances, but that has changed. Now it's the young people buying our records, they're the ones coming to our shows, they've got money to spend now." Of course, *he* was the one who changed it. So he said, "You need to tap in on that." It convinced my dad and me. I said, "Okay, that's what I'll do." We tried it. Oh, I got a song from a lady here in Oklahoma City that was actually my first rockabilly song. It was called "I Gotta Know." It was actually a song that started off with a country melody. Can I just sing it to you?

Please.

(Sings softly) "If our love's the real thing, where is my wedding ring?" Then it goes into the rock beat, "Well, you used to dance and go around..." (snaps fingers and hums rhythm).

So it was a good segue way for me, 'cause it had that little country sound with the fiddle and everything. That proved to be a good one. I found songs in movies, [like] "Hot Dog, That Made Him Mad." That may have been the first one I released in the rock vein. I saw a movie that was starring Betty Hutton, I think she was on Capitol, and she sang this song.

So I got the record, it was easy to find it. I recorded my version of that and then I found that I was running out of places to find this rock material for girls. I found one other that's proven to be my biggest song in rockabilly and rock and roll, and that's "Fujiyama Mama." I found that Annisteen Allen, I think was her last name, had the original record. I heard it on the jukebox. I just flipped and said, "I've got to find that record! I've got to record that." So it was one of my first ones. But then, there just wasn't any coming in to me. I couldn't find any. So my dad, being the encourager, said, "You've been writing country songs; why don't you start writing some of these?" I said, "Well, they are real simple, I bet I could write them." So that's when I started writing quite a few of the rockabilly songs.

So what was the first rockabilly song that you wrote?

I think it was "Mean, Mean Man."

Your songs had subject matter that was risqué, confident, and aggressive, dealing with issues like love, independence, sex, loss, and even prison.

Kind of far-out stuff for the 1950s, you know.

What was the reaction to a young lady singing about such things?

Well, in the industry it was fine, it was acceptable. I didn't hear that many comments about it. On personal appearances—they went over fabulously. 'Cause I knew how to sing them and I was dressing different. I was making a statement, I was making an impact. So I was very well accepted. Even on television they'd want me to do these rock songs. Well, the only problem was I couldn't get airplay. For some reason, it was just like a boycott. So what we began doing is putting a country song on one side of our single and rock on the other, hoping we could at least get airplay on one side or the other. It just never did happen in America.

"Fujiyama Mama" became number one in Japan in 1959. But in America, I still had not had a hit in rock music. After all this time, I finally gave up, you know. I said, "Well, I'll go back and just do country." Which I started doing on my sessions. By golly, it was right at that point when "Let's Have a Party" became popular at a radio station up in Iowa. They called my producer Ken Nelson and said, "You're gonna miss the boat if you don't pull this out of the album and release it." "Let's Have A Party" was my first rock and roll hit, and it didn't come until 1960. About four years there. I had recorded quite a bit of material, so that's why I have a good amount of these songs recorded, because I was trying so hard to produce a hit. "Let's Have A Party," of course, was one Elvis had sang in his second movie *Loving You*. I had also heard it on the Collins Kids; they had it recorded. I started doing that song just as an opening song with my band. I think I had a band at this time. And the people really liked it. On my first album recording session with Capitol, I did eleven country songs, pure country. But you had to have twelve songs on the record. So I told my producer, "I've been doing this little thing people just love and it's not really country but I want to put it on this album." So I did and it was the last song on the first album. It was a couple of years later that it was pulled out of the album into a single. It was first a hit here in America, and it certainly didn't become number one or anything, but on the country charts it got up—maybe in the top ten. In the rock charts it wouldn't have been all that high, probably in the top twenties. But it became my signature song throughout the world. "Let's Have A Party" and "Fujiyama Mama" are signature songs. This would have been in the '60s, 1961.

My next hit after "Let's Have a Party" was "Right or Wrong." It was what we called then a crossover song. It was aimed at country, but country had already started changing; they were using violins and the arrangements were being done by professional arrangers using vocal background voices and things. So I thought that "Right or Wrong" will fit right into this groove with what's happening now. It was my next hit, which threw me really back into country, so I more or less stayed there. But on my first, people pretty well know me as a rockabilly singer.

You've been called the Queen of Rockabilly. How do you feel about that?

It's right. I'm flattered, I like it very much. Well, if Elvis is King, I don't mind being the Queen. (Laughs) He was the one that taught me how to do it and he had the confidence. He said, "You've got the voice for it and the feel." So it was with his confidence that I was the first one to record anything like this. That's why it was shocking and it took awhile for them to accept me, you know, radio people and things like that.

How did you meet Elvis?

I went on tour with him. I'd never heard of him at the time.

This was while you were doing country?

Oh yeah, 'cause it was 1955. I was still with Decca Records. I'd had a couple of those country songs with Decca that had gotten on the *Billboard* country charts. I was building my name up pretty well through the nation. So my dad again came to my rescue, he said, "Well, I don't know anything about booking but let's see if we can find somebody that does," because when I graduated, I was ready to go on tour. He'd quit his job so he could do it with me. So he found Bob Neil's name. It was really just a blind guess, you know, he just called and told Bob Neil that he represented me and would like for him to set some dates. He said he would like to do that and was familiar with me, and he'd like to use me on some of the package shows and tours. He was promoting this young man called Elvis Presley, who was getting very popular very fast. He said that it would be a good show for me to be on and there would be large audiences everywhere. So that's how I met Elvis—the afternoon of the first show that I worked with him. I met him at a radio station where we went out for interviews.

You have been called the First Lady of Rock and Roll. Did you realize at the time the enormity of what you were involved in?

No, of course you don't have any idea of that. You're just struggling, trying to put out a good record and get a hit, then perform it at places so that people will buy the record. No, I didn't know. The First Lady of Rock and Roll is also a title that is true and correct. I was the first. This was the first rock and roll. It was kind of called rockabilly at the very beginning. You wanna know why? Elvis was called the Hillbilly Cat from the very beginning, and hillbilly was the word that they used for anybody that sang this country-style music. If you played that guitar or if you sang this type of music, you were a hillbilly singer. Later it went to country-western, and then they dropped the western, and it's just country music now. But that's the evolution of it. So the Hillbilly Cat, when he started getting real popular with this new stuff he was doing called rock, well, then it became rockabilly and that set phrase was short-lived. Yet it's the style that this new generation of fans just love, they love the rockabilly and it turned [into] a whole lifestyle. It's really a phenomenal thing. We were the first rock and roll people. Every kind of music will evolve from one kind into something else a little different, but it's all under the banner of country music or gospel. As it changed, early rock and roll emerged. So, I was the First Lady of Rock and Roll and the Queen of Rockabilly.

In the 1970s, your music changed, you began performing gospel music.

Big change in my life. I became a Christian, as did my husband. We were very enthusiastic about what God and Christ had done in our lives, and we still are. It was just so important to me not to preach to people, I don't mean it that way. I just wanted my fans—I wanted the whole world to know how wonderful it was to be in Christ, to give your life to Christ. So it became the most important thing to me. I recorded one gospel album on Capitol called *Praise the Lord*. The next year I wanted to do another one because I was beginning to be invited to a lot of churches. Word got around and my name was still a big name in country music then, so everybody wanted me to come to all their meetings, revivals, and conferences to sing. So that became the biggest part of my career. A ministry actually evolved out of that. I didn't ever mean or intend in any way to divorce country music. I just wanted to add the gospel and have material out there—product that people could buy in stores. Well, it just didn't work out that way. So I asked for my release from Capitol. They didn't put any importance on gospel singers. They had Tennessee Ernie Ford and they said, "That's all that we want. He sells a lot of gospel music and that's all that we need." So I got off of Capitol and went with a Christian label that was the biggest one nationally at the time. It was called Word Records. I recorded with them a good while. Then I asked to get out of that deal because they were sold to some big conglomerate. I got lost in the shuffle. I said, "Just let me out of here, I'll record independently for awhile." We did ministry work and gospel music for about fifteen years and I did some television appearances. I even did some country concerts during that time. It was primarily ministry, with my husband and I together. He was being used greatly in that type of ministry because, as we found out, he was a very good speaker. We didn't even know, but he began giving testimony and he was just marvelous. We were a real popular team at the time.

When did you learn there was a renewed interest in your early music?

Well, there again, it was just kind of put in my lap. Here's how it came about: out of the clear blue sky we hear from a man in Sweden, who owned a record company and happened to be a big fan of mine. When he found out that I was still performing and touring and everything, even though I was doing gospel (we still did one-night things mostly, my husband and I), he wanted me to come to Sweden and record an album of rockabilly and country songs—even if we put some gospel in it. Just kind of a showcase album. We thought about it. I began getting excited. I thought, "Gosh, I would love to sing that music again." If it was okay with the Lord, we had to make sure of that and we got real peace about it.

Yeah, we went over there and recorded, did a three-week tour in Sweden and Norway, and found all these fans that I had no idea I had in Scandinavia. I wound up touring Sweden, well, all of Scandinavia, every year for twenty-one years now. I spent as much as two months at a time in that area. Shortly after that, the other European countries saw that I was still alive, singing and touring. They wanted me to come to their festivals and do a concert tour. So all of Europe opened up and for about at least ten years, 90% of my work and my income was made in Europe. I was a bigger star than I had any idea I was, and I had never really toured overseas. I'd done some military bases with my band. I had recorded for the German Capitol Records—the mother company is EMI out in Germany. I had a number one song in the German language in 1965, but I never really worked it or took advantage of that. Now I was popular again. So I started touring Germany a lot and then France. Found out that I have a real big fan base in France, Switzerland, Belgium, Holland, Denmark, and now even Spain has opened up to me. So I go there every year. I was making four to five trips a year to Europe and Scandinavia for ten years. That's very hard on you.

In 1995, America discovered me again and I discovered them. They were out there, fans of mine, and I didn't even know it. That came about by a recording I did with Rosie Flores, another rockabilly singer from this newer generation. She wanted me to do a couple of songs on an album of hers, which I did. She was quite popular, so through that they found that I was still singing and started asking for me. Rosie and I wound up doing a five-week tour here in the United States from San Diego and San Francisco to New York City. Zigzagged up and down and all across the United States, where I found all these fans. I just couldn't believe it! These young adults knowing all these old songs that I had recorded and struggled so hard with to get a hit. And here they were—just loving them and they were singing along with me. They knew the songs; it was really thrilling. That's what's been happening now since 1995. I've got all these new fans here in America as well as Europe, Australia, and Japan. I'm going to Australia soon, looking forward to a two-week tour over there where I have a lot of fans, and I haven't been there in ages. So all these countries are opened up to me. I'm hoping that as long as my health will allow that I'll be able to do this. Until they get tired of me, I guess. (Laughs)

Do you ever feel that you might have been ahead of your time?

Absolutely, I sure was.

Do you think that was primarily because you were a female singing rock and roll music, as opposed to Elvis that had bigger hits during that time?

I'm sure you've read or seen documentaries on the trouble that Elvis had just being accepted by the adults. Of course, the young people... well, that was another story. The things that were being said about him: that he was singing the Devil's music and corrupting young people, teenagers and stuff like that. It just really broke his heart. He said, "What are they talking about? I'm just singing a song, I'm not..." Anyway, that's what I was doing. It took them that long to accept him, well, it just took a little longer for them to accept a girl, a young girl, you know, singing that stuff. By today's standards it's laughable, there's nothing suggestive about my performance. I had a lot of fun. I was just different from everybody else since I was very lively and said whatever I wanted to in my new way of dressing and new kinds of songs.

Did you consider censoring your material or the way that you dressed?

No, the only time that I had any problem at all was the story that most everybody wants me to tell. It may have been '55 or '56, I was asked to come sing a song on the Grand Ole Opry, on the Ernest Tubbs portion. Of course, the thrill of any country singer was to be on the Grand Ole Opry. I was so excited, Mother and I designed a new dress that was white with red fringes and rhinestones. It was really pretty. That's what I wore. I was ready to go on stage and Ernest Tubbs came back and said, "Are you Wanda Jackson?"

I said, "Yes."

He said, "Well, honey, you're up next."

I said, "Yeah, great, I'm ready."

He kinda stepped back and looked at me and said, "Well, you can't go on the stage of Grand Ole Opry like that."

I said, "I beg your pardon, what do you mean?"

He said, "Well, you can't show your shoulders. A woman can't show her shoulders on stage." I never heard the like, of course. I'm a Westerner, you know. He said, "Well, you can't go on like that so get a coat or sweater or something and you better do it fast because you're up after this song."

My heart was just broken. You can imagine, I was in tears. I went back and my daddy tried to help me calm down. I put on my leather western jacket. I wore the white leather jacket on the stage and sang my song practically in tears. I was mad, I got so mad at myself because when I get really mad, I start crying. I just get that upset—I can't really express myself, I start crying. Well, that's the point—that I tried to sing and it was real hard. I didn't like anything about being on the Grand Ole Opry. Not just for that incident, but everybody was upstaging you, behind you. It was just very unorthodox and I knew stage manners, things you're supposed to do and not do. They were doing all the wrong things. That made me mad, so I got off of there, I grabbed Daddy and I said, "We're getting out of here and I'm never coming back."

I learned later that Elvis had the very same experience there. They invited him to come, and when he started singing in his gold lamé suit, they actually booed him. I got a nice reception from the audience, but they booed him. When he walked off, he said, "I'll never come back here," and he didn't. I haven't either. That was just one incident. That's about the only censoring or problems I've had. They asked me to join the Grand Ole Opry and I just laughed and said, "No way." Right after that, I signed with the first country music television network show on ABC. I was a regular on it, which did a lot more for me nationally than the Grand Ole Opry ever did. It was called *The Ozark Jubilee*, out of Missouri. Red Foley was the head man, master of ceremonies. He was the most popular and loved man in country music, probably. So that was really a good deal for me.

When you're performing currently, what venues do you like to play? And what songs are most popular with the newer generation?

Well, let's see. For the most part I'm doing rockabilly shows, as the headliner. If there's a package show, I'll headline. There are a lot of smaller-type theatres, where it's more of family-oriented Saturday night regulars who perform there all the time. They bring in guests. So I do a lot of those, mostly just my own one night stand. On those, depending on how it's advertised, if it's a country show, well, I do mostly country, but I still do my big rockabilly. And they love it. Country and rockabilly are first cousins, and most people, if you like one, you'll like the other. If it's a rock and roll festival, I do almost all rock, except "Right or Wrong." I also do one gospel song, "I Saw the Light," a Hank Williams song. I only do a couple of country on those.

What aspects of your career are you most proud of? And what would you most like to be remembered for?

Well, probably the things that we've talked about. I did change some things for the women in country music, also in rockabilly, and even rock and roll. I think that would be appropriate. The accomplishments? Well, just the fact that I've had such a long-lived career. You see, I've never quit performing and touring. I did have a one-year hiatus, or two-year I guess it was, where I was kind of forced to for a little while. But then I went right back, so that's all I've ever done and I think it's quite an accomplishment to be able to do that for your whole life. From thirteen until now, and I'm going on seventy. All I've ever done to make a dime was to sing and perform, and to keep crowds coming back. That's a pretty good trick.

One thing I was very proud of is that I was the recipient of the National Endowment for the Arts award in 2005, and that is the most prestigious award that can be bestowed on anyone in the arts. I was chosen because of my contribution to music in the country, rock and roll, and gospel fields. It's a Presidential award, and I was the first girl in country music to receive it and the only rock and roll singer that has ever received it. Not Elvis, not anyone, and that was really a shock. I'm in the German Country Music Hall of Fame, the International Rockabilly Hall of Fame, the International Gospel Music Hall of Fame, the Oklahoma Music Hall of Fame, it just goes on and on.

Will you talk about Wanda Jackson Day?

It kind of grew out of the fact that they named their main highway through my hometown Wanda Jackson Boulevard, in Maude, Oklahoma. About sixty-five miles out of Oklahoma City—a very small town. One thing led to another and we decided that we should have an official day to let everybody know and celebrate the name of the street. It began to take on a life of its own, you know—in a little town people grab something and run with it. I had a cousin that lived there at the time and she and her husband spearheaded the whole thing. It became an annual event. We had a parade, kiosks or street vendors, different foods and things—eventually a small carnival came in and set up the grounds there. Then we had a car show and we had some nice prizes and trophies and things. I would put on a benefit concert in the evening and bring in other known artists from Nashville to do the show with me. The proceeds from those concerts really helped the town; they got new paving for their main street. Everybody started dressing up their storefronts and cleaning up the messes around them and really brightened the town up. They were very proud of that. At some point, a talent contest started, about a month before the Wanda Jackson Day. We had as many as seventy-five contestants on that show one time. If I was in town I would be one of the judges. We picked out people who knew something about entertaining and singing, you know, people in the business, for the other judges. My husband got together a lot of very nice prizes for a newcomer. So that grew and grew. They made money from the entry fee. It was an annual event that lasted for thirteen years. One of the girls that was a real big help got sick and her doctor said she would just have to stop doing it. One of the other key ladies' son was killed or died, I'm not sure, and she didn't feel like doing anything. It kind of began to fizzle, but we got a pretty good run out of it, because originally it was just going to be for one day. It became very well known; one time the Governor of Oklahoma made that the official Wanda Jackson Day in Oklahoma. People just from all around came. The winners of the talent contest were in the parade and they got to perform that evening with the stars. I had another day named for me when I received the National Endowments for the Arts award.

With the new generation of young people playing rockabilly music today, how would you compare the new music to the old stuff?

Actually, I think they're doing a real bang-up job of writing songs that could have been done in the '50s. They've got that music down really good. I use a lot of these bands around the country and around the world to back me, and they do an excellent job. I think that rockabilly is still in real good hands so it will live on.

Where do you find your backup bands?

Sometimes the people that bring in the shows, whether it be a festival or just an evening in concert or even a nightclub, know the bands in that area. So we start from there, with a recommendation of a band that can play my kind of music the best. I don't need fiddles or steel guitars for rockabilly songs, so that starts narrowing it down. That's how we find our bands. Now I've worked enough that if I'm in the northeast part of the country, I have the Luster Kings. On the West Coast I have a recording band now that I use, but for a long time I used a group called the Cadillac Angels. I can't think of the names of the other ones—but all different locals from around the country. Then I've had my bands that work with me each year when I tour in Europe.

Any new artists you listen to playing this type of music?

Kim Lenz is very good. Marti Brom is really about my favorite, I guess. She's a recording artist. They were on the tribute CD. Blood Shot Records out of Chicago did a tribute album for me featuring twenty-one different artists who chose any song that I had done in my whole repertoire. So the album is all my things but includes cover songs that I'm known for, like "Stupid Cupid." I've done that ever since. A lot of fans think I had a hit with that, but I didn't. They were all real good on this CD; I've enjoyed listening to it through the years. It was done five or six years ago. There's some real fine girl singers doing rockabilly. I don't know all of them, of course.

Another name is Rosie Flores, she's just a super talent. She plays excellent lead guitar, writes a lot, and sings real fine. I credit her for giving me my career back. I'd been doing rockabilly for several years in Europe and Scandinavia, but I didn't know all these venues were here in America—didn't know about all the festivals. The kids that go to them didn't know that I was still performing. So when I did a five-week tour and recorded with her on a new CD of hers at the time, in 1995, that's the first time that this new generation here in America knew that I was still alive, still singing and working. So it's been just really great that I can stay in America a lot more now the last few years, because of that exposure. I got so much publicity. I've never had so much press and radio and interviews or books, just like you're doing. I have more now than I've ever had in my whole career. It's really something.

Maureen "Moe" Tucker was born August 26, 1944, in Levittown, New York. She's best known as the drummer of the influential '60s rock band, the Velvet Underground. The band, which was formed in early 1965 and lasted until 1971, was considered ahead of its time for its highly unorthodox and complex sound. The Velvet Underground's music was dark, intellectual, and licentious with subject matter rooted in a harsh urban realism.

The Velvet Underground is considered a precursor to many musical genres, including punk, new wave, goth, experimental, and noise music. The band was embraced by Andy Warhol and included in many of his performance art projects with *The Exploding Plastic Inevitable*, which existed from 1966 through 1967. They also appear in a 1967 documentary about *The Exploding Plastic Inevitable*, directed by Ronald Nameth.

In the Velvet Underground, Moe Tucker played an upturned bass drum and tom toms, and performed standing part of the time to fully facilitate manipulating her drums. She joined the band in 1965, replacing Angus MacLise. She stayed with the band until she became pregnant with her first child and took a brief hiatus in 1970, but promptly returned later that year. The Velvet Underground had its final reunion tour in 1993, and was inducted into the Rock and Roll Hall of Fame in 1996.

Moe began her solo career in the 1980s, playing guitar and singing. She recorded and released many singles, and her first album, *Playing Possum*, was released in 1981. She has also contributed to others' recording projects, including Lou Reed's *New York* (1988); John Cale's *Walking On Locusts* (1996); *EAT/KISS: the Music of Andy Warhol's Films* (1997); and recording with the bands Paris 1942, the Kropotkins, Magnet, and Half Japanese. She appeared with Half Japanese in their 1993 documentary *The Band That Would Be King*.

How old were you when you first had the inclination to become a musician?

Actually, I've never considered myself to be a musician, but my first interest and love of rock and roll began when I was about twelve.

Why have you never considered yourself a musician?

I guess because I never set out to be a musician and considered my association with the Velvet Underground as fun and lucky!

When did you first decide drumming was your interest?

I had a guitar and was learning chords, having fun doing that, and then realized when I was about nineteen that a drum would really be fun, bought a snare drum and had a great time playing along to my favorite songs.

Who were you listening to at the time?

Little Richard, Chuck Berry, Bo Diddley, girl groups, Stones, Beatles, all the *good* stuff!

Did you play any other instruments?

In elementary and junior high I played clarinet, and my brother gave me a guitar for my eighteenth birthday.

Being that you began playing drums and seemed to have mastered them during a time when there were really no other women doing this, who did you look to for inspiration musically?

Thankfully, I certainly have not mastered drums. My influences were Olatunji, Bo Diddley, and Charlie Watts.

Why do you say thankfully you have not mastered the drums? Because it's too constructed?

Yes, it's so easy to do a roll or a cymbal crash at every opportunity if you're trained to do so. In fact, it's difficult *not* to do so, and I would have to think of different ways to accent.

How did you learn to play drums? Any lessons, or were you self-taught?

No lessons, just playing along with records.

Did the environment you grew up in influence your decision to become a musician?

I don't think so.

Were you encouraged by your parents?

My father had passed away by the time I started floundering around with guitar. My mom was great! I'd run downstairs and say, "Listen, Mom," and play some very, very simple little thing I'd learned, and she'd smile and say, "That's nice," or whatever. I'd run back upstairs, turn on the record player, and continue playing along. She never complained.

In fact, as a surprise, she bought my first drum set. Fifty dollars! Bass drum, pedal, tom, one wrecked cymbal. She also let me use her car to drive to shows in and around New York at the Bizarre, the Dom, etc., because her car was more reliable then mine.

Drums are often considered a masculine instrument. How did you overcome the stereotype and get people to take your playing seriously?

It was never an issue for me.

Did you find playing such a physically demanding instrument difficult?

Nope.

Did you encounter difficulties due to sexism or criticism about your playing?

Believe it or not, no.

What musical projects had you worked with before joining the Velvet Underground?

I played with a cover band for a month or so. We practiced a lot, played one job at a bar on Long Island, and then the lead singer got uppity and we just kind of all said the hell with it.

What cover band was that?

As I recall, we were called The Intruders, after an airplane that Grumman manufactured.

Were you with the band before they became the Velvet Underground, and how many incarnations did they have before deciding on the name?

They had taken the name before I joined, but not much before. In fact, maybe the show in New Jersey was the first where that name was used. I'm not really sure. The only other name that I think they used was the Falling Spikes.

You were asked to join the Velvet Underground after your brother introduced you?

Right. My brother and Lou [Reed] became friends at Syracuse University. My brother and Sterling [Morrison] had been best friends since they were twelve, and my brother introduced Sterl to Lou at some point. They had been booked to play the Summit, New Jersey high school, and their drummer, Angus MacLise, quit because he didn't think you should be paid to play music. They desperately needed a drummer and Sterl said, "Tucker's sister plays drums."

Lou came out to Levittown to see if I actually could play and was satisfied that I could play the show. I went into the city a few times to learn the three songs we would play. As a result of that show, we were booked at The Bizarre in the Village. They didn't allow drums, so the guys said come along and play tambourine. I was still not officially in the band—that just sort of happened because things kept coming up and apparently they were content with what I was doing.

What interested you in joining the Velvet Underground?

The songs! I was amazed when I first went to the city to practice. Sterl had told me a little about the band but I hadn't heard anything, and I was really thrilled at what I heard.

How did the formation of the Velvet Underground first come about?

John [Cale] and Lou used to play in the streets of New York to get money. Sterling had met Lou through my brother, and one day bumped into Lou in the subway. Lou mentioned that he was doing music with Cale, who Sterl didn't know yet, and invited Sterl to come hear them and jam. I hate that word, "jam."

Apparently, Sterl liked what he heard and so did Lou and John, who invited him to join them. I'm not sure if Angus was working with them at this point. I think he lived next door to Cale and would come over and play sometimes when they were working on songs. Anyway, it became Lou, John, Sterl, and Angus. When they got their first paying job, Angus quit because he didn't think you should get paid to play music. They were desperate to have a drummer and Sterl mentioned Tucker's sister plays drums. I did that first show with them. I just sort of melted in and there I was!

What was a typical Velvet Underground rehearsal like?

We never really rehearsed—sometimes we would before recording, but we didn't rehearse between shows. Early rehearsals were really mostly improvising. When Lou had a structured song, chords, and lyrics, we would work on it until we liked it, but those were the only actual rehearsals. We didn't rehearse for no reason, only to learn new songs.

How did the Velvet Underground creative process work? How was the first album made?

Lou would have a structured song that he'd present and we'd just keep playing it until everyone was happy with what they were doing. The first album was made very quickly: eight hours in the studio. And when MGM bought it and signed us, they paid for another four or so hours for us to tweak it if we wanted to.

How much were you allowed to improvise during recording and shows?

I approached what I would do for a particular song according to what I thought would fit. Is this song sad? Is it angry? etc. I also felt my role was to keep everything together, especially early on when we did a lot of improvising in shows. Lou and John would go off on a tangent and it was up to me, and Sterl somewhat, to keep something steady so that it didn't sound like just noise. At least that's how I felt about it. It would depend on the song. "Sister Ray" or "European Son," for instance, would allow for anything goes, just about.

How much creative freedom and input did you have with the band?

No one in a band really hears or cares what the drummer is doing unless he or she totally screws up or suddenly does something really clever. I played what I wanted to play. I did what I wanted to as far as drums or percussion goes. I made a few suggestions about other things here and there. Some were used, some weren't. Not knowing what chords go with what, I couldn't make those kinds of suggestions, but I did, for instance, suggest that we don't resolve the progression at the end of "White Light."

Your band was known as one of the first and most profound experimental rock bands. Did you see yourself as that?

Correctly or not, I never thought of us as experimental. Then again, I was just having fun. My drumming is what you'd call totally untrained, and I couldn't do a roll for a million dollars. That was perfect for what we were doing. I always hated busy drumming!

What were the Velvet Underground's interpersonal dynamics like?

Sometimes dynamics were very touchy, mostly between Lou and John, but on the whole we all respected each other and enjoyed each other's company. I remember only one actual yelling argument.

You're known for using all types of objects to create sound, like mallets and steel drums. What are the different tools you have used during your time with the Velvet Underground?

No, I never used steel drums; I used garbage pails for a week or two when my drums were stolen. I played some songs using one mallet and one drumstick, some using two mallets, some using two drumsticks.

How did you develop your signature style?

By not learning how to play properly! I played by instinct, and as I said, I couldn't do a roll to save my life.

What was your experience singing on some of the albums?

The experience was very, very nerve-wracking. I was very uptight about wasting time trying to sing. When I did "After Hours," I finally asked everyone but Lou, who was playing guitar, and the engineer, to leave. They were laughing at me in the booth! I also sang on "I'm Sticking With You" and "Murder Mystery."

What was your first Velvet Underground show like?

We played at Summit High School in New Jersey. We were allowed to play three songs and were not a hit with the teens!

How did the early shows differ from the later ones?

A lot of improvising early on, and more structured later.

How many shows did you play before joining the Warhol crowd?

Two! Summit High School and Café Bizarre.

What was The Exploding Plastic Inevitable?

It was music, lights, dancers, movies, all at once.

What do you remember most about the Warhol days?

The fun we had, especially at Max's, and sitting around the Factory. I just really enjoyed the people we hung around with, and we always had a good and interesting time, whether sitting in Max's or lying around the Factory.

Was the Warhol atmosphere comfortable? Did you appreciate his contributions?

When the atmosphere became uncomfortable, which wasn't often, I would simply leave. I don't really think he contributed to the music in any way, but you would also need Lou and John's thoughts on that.

What was the strangest show you performed at during this period?

Probably the Mod Wedding in Detroit. I believe the bride and groom had won a contest, and their prize was a wedding at the State Fair. I don't know how or why we wound up participating.

That was in 1966, with the Exploding Plastic Inevitable. *How did you feel about Nico becoming a part of the band?*

She was never really a part of the band, more of a guest singer. I love her renditions of the four or five songs she did with us.

Do you have any regrets from working with the Velvet Underground?

Not one!

Do you feel you get the recognition you deserve for your pioneering work with the Velvet Underground?

I think so. The main reason I'm aware of recognition is that when I had my own band and toured, I would hear it from fans. Was quite surprised, to tell you the truth.

What solo work have you done?

With my band I've done four or five studio albums: *Playin Possum* ('81), *Life in Exile After Abdication* ('89), *I Spent a Week There the Other Night* ('91), *Dogs Under Stress* ('94), and a few live ones: *Oh No, They're Recording This Show* ('92), *Moe Rocks Terrastock* ('02). I've produced a few albums for other groups. I've guested on a number of records.

Playin Possum was recorded in my family room. I played and sang everything and had a great time doing it! *Life in Exile*, Penn Jillette (of Penn and Teller) put up the money for me to record an album. We did it in New York and once again I had a great time and lots of help from friends: Lou, Sonic Youth, Daniel Johnston, and of course, Half Japanese.

How did your work with Half Japanese come about?

Jad Fair had sent me a rehearsal tape and I was immediately hooked! We started corresponding and he would send me tapes, tapes, and more tapes. When I had the opportunity to play live again, Half Japanese offered to be my backup band. When I played with them, I played drums for most of the set, and played guitar and sang for just a few songs. I was a nervous wreck but, happily, the fans enjoyed it.

What are you doing now?

Mostly babysitting my grandson, Holden. He and his mom have been with me for a year, and although the job takes most of my time and energy, I'm crazy about him and very glad he's here.

Will you talk about the Velvet Underground reunion?

We did a reunion tour in 1993. Can't be another without Sterl. [Sterling Morrison passed away in 1995.]

What would you best like to be known for?

Being a good parent.

Did you have any idea at the time you would be so revolutionary in your work with the Velvet Underground?

I always loved our music but never thought it would become what it has.

How do you think you have influenced bands today?

I know we have with some hundreds of bands, each in a different way, I suppose. Hopefully some because of the feel of our music and some because of the lyrics, some because of the drums and some because of the viola...

Miss Mercy (Mercy Fontenot) was born in February 1949 in Burbank, California and raised near San Francisco. She's best known as a member (with six other women) of The GTOs, or Girls Together Outrageously, a band that existed from 1969 to 1971. Originally called the Laurel Canyon Ballet Company (after the LA neighborhood they frequented), the women danced on stage in nightclubs with many bands, including Frank Zappa's Mothers of Invention. Tiny Tim added the "Miss" before their first names. At the time, Zappa had his own record company, Bizarre, to promote non-mainstream acts like Wild Man Fischer, Captain Beefheart, and Alice Cooper.

The GTOs included Miss Mercy, Miss Cynderella, Miss Christine, Miss Lucy, Miss Sparky, Miss Sandra, and Miss Pamela. Zappa named the band and produced their only album, *Permanent Damage* (released in 1969, reissued in 1989). On the album, the GTOs were backed by musicians from the Mothers of Invention and others including Ry Cooder, Jeff Beck, and Rod Stewart. Friends of the GTOs, like DJ Rodney Bingenheimer and Cynthia Plaster Caster, also appeared on the album. Songwriting contributions came from Little Feat's Lowell George, Jeff Beck, and the Monkees' Davy Jones. The album mixed music with spoken word/conversation, and included Miss Mercy's "The Eureka Springs Garbage Lady" and a song about Beefheart's shoes entitled "The Captain's Fat Theresa Shoes." Their only known performance was in 1968 at LA's Shrine Auditorium, and featured music, dancing, and theatrics.

Miss Mercy also sang backing vocals on the song "Hippie Boy" on the Flying Burrito Brothers' *The Gilded Palace of Sin* (1969), and on Wild Man Fischer's *An Evening With Wild Man Fischer* (1969). She graced the cover of *Rolling Stone* in its early years, and appeared in the films *Rainbow Bridge* (1972), *Plaster Caster* (2001), and *Mayor of the Sunset Strip* (2003). Much of the GTOs' story can be found in Miss Pam's published memoirs, *I'm with the Band* (1987) and *Let's Spend the Night Together* (2007). Mercy was married to Shuggie Otis, the musician son of rhythm and blues legend Johnny Otis, and became the proud mother of Lucky Otis, another great musical talent.

Are you a native San Franciscan? What were you doing early on?

I was born in Burbank but I was raised in San Francisco. What happened was I had a beatnik girlfriend in '65 about, and I went over to hang out in North Beach—City Lights bookstore, Kesey, all that whole thing. All the beatniks in North Beach at that time basically moved over to get away from the commercialism... oh, and the mob. Two things in there they didn't like, really. So they moved over and they got a coffee shop called the Blue Unicorn in Haight Ashbury. So I started going to it, which was a coffee, beatnik hangout, poetry and all that.

What kind of happened there is (this is the honest-to-god truth) that Bob Dylan plugged in his guitar and that's when everything basically changed and the hippies started. With the electricity, everything changed. The beatniks were an influence, but they were introverted. Hippies were extroverted. I think what happened was Hollywood had movie stars, New York had Broadway, and San Francisco only had, like, Alcatraz and North Beach, and didn't have a tourist trap. So the media came in and said, "Let's use these flower people," and totally blew it up into a tourist trap.

It's too bad. Seems like that happens with every new scene. They move in, turn it into a commodity, and it becomes generic and mainstream.

Yeah, I think that's what happened. The media got ahold of the Haight Ashbury. It got overblown, just like North Beach became overblown from the beatniks. FM radio had come in with Tom Donahue. The exposure to music was growing. The beatniks were smaller, but after FM radio came in, it got bigger exposure for the hippies' music. Where you didn't before, now you had a format; they only played three-minute songs on AM radio. Then Tom Donahue brings in FM and you get the format changes and really there's nobody owning the radio stations. They're telling you what you can play and the music got longer, it got more bizarre, now that I think back. Hippies, I don't even know where the word "hippie" came from. I know the beatniks used to say "I'm hip..."

So you were a hippie at one point?

I was on, like, the sixth cover of *Rolling Stone* as a hippie, and a year later I was on the back cover as a GTO. It happened just like that. I had to run away from the juvenile authorities, they were after me because I put myself in juvenile hall and was made a ward of the court. They were looking for me in San Francisco, so I had to run down here. That's how I got back to LA. I couldn't go home.

What was the catalyst?

I was incorrigible. I went up to Haight Ashbury and I went home; I had taken LSD and had become incorrigible. I said, "Well, just take me to juvenile hall," and my mother did. I got signed up to the courts because I thought I was so cute, and they don't let you go. I had to get out of there, so I ran. They were going to send me to juvenile hall down here, to the youth authorities. I think I was about seventeen.

Your image was very different from the rest of the GTOs. Your image was darker... very...

Gothic?

During an interview you said you were the Theda Bara in the group....

Actually, I was like a gypsy. I also did a lot of speed, so I would put on ten dresses at one time. (Laughs) No, really. (Laughs more) And fifteen belts, thirty-five bracelets, and whatever else. And I left the eye makeup on, that kohl black around my eyes. Like Vali, Vali Myers. They did a movie about her called *The Witch of Positano*. She's dead now. When you see her you'll flip. She's got a tattooed face, it's amazing. She's so stunning, she's like a Fellini character. She had all that gypsy stuff on and the heavy black kohl eye makeup. Tennessee Williams based one of his characters on her in the '50s. She really was underground, really big in the '60s underground.

You know, I've got to say something about clothes: the hippies did not just wear one flower in their hair. We dressed in velvet dresses, mostly from thrift shops in the Fillmore district. Beautiful, beautiful long dresses in San Francisco. Down in LA they cut them all off and made miniskirts, it was fabulous. Everybody was fabulous. At first I didn't like LA when I was in San Francisco 'cause I had this whole thing about LA, just like SF doesn't like LA today. There were a lot of people that were influenced by us because we were in *Rolling Stone*. *Rolling Stone* was very popular at that time. I mean, with the underground. I can't say it was with the overground because it wasn't.

How did you meet up with the other GTOs?

I followed a boyfriend down here [to LA]. He lived with some beautiful hookers that worked the street; they were beautiful girls. They happened to know some guy named Vito. Vito was famous in the '60s here. He was like an artist, surrounded by people, actors and such. In the house where all these crazy beautiful girls were, there was a girl named Miss Christine who became one of the GTOs. She had become Zappa's nanny. There was also the Laurel Canyon Ballet Company. That was a bunch of girls that would just crazy dance like Vito with Zappa, just show up at a club and dance. I went over to Frank's house 'cause Christine lived there and we did speed together, something we loved to do. I went over to visit and there was Frank. I never really had a big thing for Frank at all. I didn't like Frank. I'm into soul music, black soul music, and that kind of thing.

Frank had the idea for the GTOs, I think he had got the name the GTOs at this point. There was also a boy named Jobriath, an underground star, he was in *Hair*. *Velvet Goldmine* was based on him and Paul Morrisey's *Crazy*; I was running around with him. Frank said to him, "The only way this girl group is going to be put together is if you have Cynderella and Mercy." So then he decides he's going to cut an album with us, and that's what he did. Very quickly we got well known. It happened very fast. It was all Frank's idea to put this girl group together. We all had pretty individual ideas and stuff. He didn't write any of the songs; we wrote them and we sang them. We tried to sing them, anyway. You know, it was mostly theatre art, like the Cockettes. I was friends with them, too. In other words, if you went to see the GTOs perform, it would not be straight singing, it would be dialogue running into songs. Almost like a play. We only did one show; it was at the Shrine. That was it. Then we folded after that.

When you had released your album, how did people hear about you?

We just started getting a reputation, and people like the Stones and Zeppelin wanted to meet us. It wasn't the album. It's hard to answer this. When Pamela went over to London in '69, our album was released all over; a whole store window was done in it. It got released in Europe, but we didn't get airplay because there really was no airplay. We got advertising on *Record World* pick-of-the-week, something like that. It would be really very hard to put anything out as a single from that album. They tried to put mine out as a single—that's me and Rod Stewart and Jeff Beck.

We had such a reputation, it went from people that just wanted to meet us to all types. It was by word of mouth more than commercialism. People would come over, "Oh, you're a GTO, I've gotta meet ya, gotta meet ya!" and all this. David Bowie did that (who I didn't meet because I didn't really care to meet him). When we met George Harrison (we got introduced to him on that *Rolling Stone* shoot), we were at A&M Records. Our secretary at the time took us over there and said, "Well, these are the GTOs," and he said, "Oh, now I believe what I've heard," something like that. It was all verbal reputation is what it was.

Did you go to London, too, as promotion?

Instead of going to England, I went to Memphis. I was never big on London. I was really big on our music. I particularly didn't care for English [music] except for a few of the Stones and Zeppelin and maybe the Yardbirds. I ended up married to Shuggie Otis, who was supposed to be the new Jimi Hendrix, and his father is Johnny Otis—he started rock and roll. So I met all the people that started rock and roll in my backyard, recording with Johnny Otis. This was in LA. I actually married into the real foundation of rock and roll.

What were you listening to back then?

Basically roots music... soul music. I was crazy about Stax, went to Memphis and went to Stax, where they cut a lot of Sam and Dave, Isaac Hayes, and all that. That's where I met Al Green; I went out with him. The last performer that moved me was a couple of years back, the great Duke of Earl Gene Chandler, who at seventy-five is remarkable and still has the ladies reacting to "Rainbow," one of the great R&B singles of all time. Gene was never given the credit he deserves.

Where did you meet Shuggie Otis?

I met him in a dream, I really did. It was in Los Angeles. I met him in a dream and they said you're gonna marry this person and I did. It was crazy. His father started rock and roll in the '40s. He's responsible for the hand jive. He discovered Jackie Wilson. The kid I married was half black, Shuggie Otis. You'll really trip on him, he had a huge afro. They asked him to be in the Rolling Stones and he turned them down. He had his own things going. His album, his stuff that he did in '69, came out again five years later. He's the one Prince and a lot of these people base their stuff on.

So I had everybody in my backyard: Johnny Otis, Big Joe Turner, Louis Jordan, all the people that started rock and roll, but I didn't know who these people were. This was 1970. I didn't know that because they didn't really let us know. Their stuff, by the time we hit the '60s, had been taken off the radio, most of it. Because they were black artists, they had been removed. It's just a real trip and Frank was very into that stuff, too. He had my husband at the time on *Peaches en Regalia*. He had brought Johnny Otis back out of retirement. So I have a 33-year-old son, Lucky Otis, who has all their talent. My deepest love was for Shuggie, who gave me the most unique child, Lucky, who is traveling this planet with burdens and celestial gifts from his two parents. I did marry my dream, even though it didn't survive the youthfulness of it all.

Did the GTOs or Frank ever intend for more than one album?

We were going to be part of his whole roster until we got the drug thing started. Three of us were junkies.

Was this related to why the GTOs ended?

We fell to pieces 'cause of drugs. I mean, like, Frank just flipped. The FBI was investigating Frank. He was in trouble for drug use and people affiliated with him. He was getting some heat from that so he folded the GTOs up.

What drug was prevalent with the group back then?

Speed and some heroin. I got it through my doctors. I actually met the guy that was Kennedy's doctor. He's in a lot of books, you know... *Ciao Manhattan*, Edie Sedgwick, and all that. It started out as vitamin shots that had methamphetamine in them. Speed was not really a big, popular drug like it is today. Drugs were very prevalent in LA back then, even in San Francisco. The CIA brought in all sorts of drugs. They put it in the punch backstage, that's why that Monterey Pop Festival was so darn crazy, because the government had a drug called STP that they were lacing everything with. The footage from Monterey Pop Festival is much groovier than Woodstock, believe me. Everybody was just stoned out of their gourds. Hendrix, the Who, even Otis Redding was high.

How long did it take you to put together and record that album?

That album, he said, "Go right to the songs," and we did. I rehearsed with Lowell George and then we went into the studio. That was for "I Have a Paintbrush in My Hand to Color a Triangle," that was Lowell George and me singing.

"Shock Treatment" was actually Rod Stewart singing. We had Jeff Beck and Nicky Hopkins as musicians on it, and they were part of the Jeff Beck Group at the time, which was with Rod Stewart. So two of them were hired and Rod just happened to come along and ended up (we had never heard him sing) singing my song. Once he started singing, I said, "You know what? Just let this guy sing, this guy sounds great."

Despite the end of the group, did you lay down any ideas for new songs, album concept, anything like that for a second album?

No, nothing. The diaries were gonna come out. My husband Shuggie tore mine up, though. That's how Pamela's book *I'm With the Band* got written. They were gonna print our diaries but everything stopped.

That would have been interesting. Was that with a musical concept?

Just as diaries, books. But my husband got very jealous of Al Green or Chuck Berry or something like that. He flipped out and tore it all up.

Would you talk about your friendship with the infamous Jobriath?

He was a real love of mine, aside from the sex we didn't have. Clearly one of the most talented and unique people that lived on this planet. He was the first celebrity to die of AIDS, really. He was sick with it back when no one knew what it was, in the 1970s, way before Warhol was calling it the gay cancer. When he would get sores all over him from AIDS, he would think he was possessed by the devil, and that he was being punished by God for being gay. People were still very ignorant about homosexuality, even back then, that he would develop guilt about being gay. At one point he was so delusional, I witnessed him chopping up a grand piano with an axe. He died of AIDS in 1982.

In the Bay Area, until the late '60s, it seemed like big name musicians sometimes performed free in the park—what happened to end it?

The promoters and the record companies came in. It all became about making money, and heavy drug use. It was just bad. The record companies, boy, if you get on drugs they'll come knockin' and send the pusher right to your door. Because what they wanted to do was they give you your advance money and then they get it all back. Come on. You see what I'm saying. Not us but the big groups. No, seriously, I'm not kidding. Then they'd write about it when they got busted, then the records would sell more. They'd off them and the records would sell more. If you think about any artist that died, Hendrix and Janis (she died about a block away from me), Morrison or Brian, any of them, right before they died they all get busted. Everybody knows they're on drugs, then they're dead, and then the records sell a lot, they make a lot of money. Because the artists are so strung out at that point that they aren't going to make or show up to their gigs anymore, so [the record companies] make more money by offing them. This is my conspiracy theory that I've had for years. It's terrible. All the way up to Tupac, Biggie, Kurt Cobain. He's made more money than anybody, but he would have never made that much money if he was alive. He made more money being dead than he would have alive because he was in no condition to go gig and he probably would have said "Fuck you" and never gigged anyway. They died in their heyday. The only one that isn't is Dylan. You can't kill Bob. Bob and Keith. You can't off 'em. (Laughs loudly)

Musicians are a type of creative genius, and genius often coincides with mental instability, and people who suffer often self-medicate with drugs.

My ex-husband is a prime example of that. He's an extreme genius and he's gone underground for years. Right now he's mixing his album down for the first time in years. Beyoncé said nice things about Shuggie Otis on this TV show I was watching. She did his song. One of the songs he wrote but she put her words to it. She's brought him up. She did another one of his songs, too. I mean, the man lives off the royalties of the hit that he wrote called "Strawberry Letter 23" that the Brothers Johnson did. He is a genius and like you're saying, he's a recluse and he's mentally challenged. My boyfriend that just died, Arthur Lee from the group Love, he's a black guy that crossed over to the whites and he was another one. He just died of leukemia. He was doing Europe five years ago but got very, very sick. He was a strung-out, absolute genius, but mental problems beyond. Beyond, beyond.

Was Frank Zappa as appreciated back then as he is now?

People idolized him. You know, he was there. It took me a long time to really respect him because I thought he was dingy. I found out his roots were in soul, R&B, and classical. He was very, very hip. I didn't know that at the time with the Mothers of Invention. I didn't know. He grew on me.

What was a typical day like at his house? Did you spend any time there?

I went and stayed with him for three days with just me and my baby and the family. He was nice; he was really sweet. He was a great guy, he was a little dingy but a great guy. But really quite brilliant.

What was behind the Frank/Captain Beefheart scene?

Oh, Captain Beefheart, he was dark—he was a beatnik, a jazz beatnik, that was before the GTOs. Frank, he had a sarcastic view towards everything. He was just sarcastic, even though he admired it all, he loved it, believe me. He was sarcastic like the Fuggs from New York. Even though he was from here, he came out of New York as the Mothers of Invention. It was very odd. He had been married to a very straight woman from Pacoima, I think. But Pamela never went against the hippie movement. She loved Lenny Bruce during that period. I did a movie called *Rainbow Bridge* during that time. If you've seen *Factory Girl*, there's a guy named Chuck in that movie; the guy was named Chuck Wein and he was with Andy Warhol, he had done the original *Ciao Manhattan* with Edie. When he got here, I met him and we went over to Hawaii and did the movie *Rainbow Bridge* with him and Hendrix. I introduced her to Chuck Wein, who was a very spiritual person. She called him "the wizard." He did a movie called *Arizona Slim* after *Rainbow Bridge*. It was after that Pamela met her husband Michael Des Barres, he played the rock star in *Arizona Slim*.

How did all the artists end up in Laurel Canyon?

Laurel Canyon was just a fun place to be. A lot of people lived in Laurel Canyon. It was a hip place to be, like Topanga Canyon, only it was right by Hollywood. It was fun, we used to just hang out there... and just sit on the road, crazy. It was that fun.

At the time you put out your album, did people see you as a feminist?

I doubt it. Not really. We didn't try and do that. We just wanted to say girls could hang out with each other. But we didn't think that far ahead. I don't think it was feminist. It was just an early version of the girl power. You know the only thing I can think of to compare it to were Spice Girls. (Laughs) Like a girl power trip, but two decades later. (Laughs again)

The press reported that you were lesbians. Was that the case?

We said we were lesbians. Most of us were bisexual. No one was really lesbian because we liked the guys. I'd say we were all, except for Sandy, a little bisexual, but we weren't dykes. It's hard to explain.

So you just fully enjoyed each other's company?

Oh yeah. Two of them were hanging out together like that. I had a couple girlfriends, but they weren't GTOs.

Will you say something about each band member?

All the girls except for Pamela, Sparky, and me, are all dead. Miss Christine killed herself in about '74. The beautiful one with the big hair, on the cover of *Hot Rats*.

I had thought it was scoliosis-related.

You know what? It may have been. She had gone to London and got her back done. She was in such great pain after the operation. They screwed her up.

Well, Miss Christine, who I loved dearly, she was such an innovator. She's on *Hot Rats*, that's her on the cover. She found Iggy Pop before he became famous.

I heard she discovered Alice Cooper.

Well, he copied my makeup. We influenced him a great deal. His name was Vince when we met him. She dressed him and he copied my eye makeup, you know. He changed his whole thing from when we met him. He came out here from Arizona. But that was her boyfriend and she influenced him. She lived with Todd Rundgren. One strange memory was I went out to Woodstock with her and Todd, and I was there, I was sitting with The Band, some of the greatest musicians who ever lived. She was a beautiful thing. She was just too frail to be here. Couldn't take it. Very inventive person. She was a young girl when she died, at twenty-five.

What was the average age of the GTOs?

Eighteen was the average age. I was about nineteen. The youngest one was Cynderella, she was eighteen. Miss Sandy died of cancer when she was very young. She got married, had a couple of children.

Miss Pamela has been my mainstay on this planet. I've been the closest with Pam. Anytime that I've been through all of my problems, she's been there. She's always kept me in some kind of limelight with her. She's always shared stuff with me, like, "Okay, Mercy, come along. Let me put you in my book and make you well-known that way." When we do interviews, she makes sure I am there. When we did the E! *True Story*, she made sure I was in it. Pamela and I are still really close, I just lived with her for a year. I left my husband, so I moved in with her and now I'm over here working. She's just too much, she's an amazing woman.

Miss Cynderella, I loved her. I loved all of them. We had a lot of good times together, we shot a lot of dope together. She was married to John Cale of the Velvet Underground. She was with him after the band. He was an established artist, but all I saw was a junkie. When Pamela was with Michael, the GTOs were guests on this Silverhead bill, that was his group, it was at the Palladium. I couldn't go because I was married to Shuggie and he didn't want me to go. I was living at Johnny Otis's house. I snuck out, I was doing heroin with Cynderella and I snuck out the door. I looked really great at the time, I was really skinny, I had this black Puerto Rican wig on and this cinched waist, you know, this whole look going. We hadn't rehearsed, we were doing "Mr. Sandman," the old song, and they were doing "Jailhouse Rock" with Michael. The Dolls were on the bill and a whole bunch of people. I'm really, really stoned when we get on the stage. At the end of the night I threw up, I was so loaded. When I went home, Johnny Otis meets me at the door and says, "How could you do that to us, go on stage like that?!" We were on the news, and I had told him we were going to a movie. He was really embarrassed.

I remember that, a Cynderella trip. It was a GTOs reunion. We weren't supposed to, but we came anyway. She said at one time, "Have you heard of this actor called Robert DeNiro?" I said, "No." She goes, "That's the only person I cheated on my husband with." Later in New York, I thought, oh my god. She lied all the time, first she had a London accent, then she got this New Orleans accent later which I thought was funny because nobody knows a New Orleans accent better than me since my mother was from outside New Orleans and I'm a Fontenot. I guess Cynderella wanted to be, too. She had these fake accents and she made up these insane stories; it was great. Both Pamela and I love her, we really loved her. Cynderella died around '98.

Miss Sparky, she was a nice girl. She doesn't talk to Pamela anymore. She's fine, she's still alive. She's got a kid named Santa, married to an actor, Alan Bronstein. I always got along with her. She was a pretty little thing. She was not a junkie. She became a Disney artist. She broke away from us. She really doesn't relate to this whole thing.

Miss Lucy, Lucy is very dead, she died from HIV. She died about ten years ago, when I was going out with Arthur Lee. She was wonderful. She was a hooker, too. She was a great chick, a Puerto Rican. Her and I had the same boyfriend, Bernardo. That's how we met each other. Throughout the years, we were friends. She's just a real strong personality. She's in *200 Motels*, if you want to see her. She's really cool, the pretty one with black hair. We were friends up until she died.

When did you start using the "Miss" in front of your names?

I think Tiny Tim did that. He started the "Miss" stuff. He was going out with Cynderella. I mean, they just had a platonic relationship. He called her "Miss Cynderella" and we just all picked it up. We got called "Miss Christine," "Miss Mercy."

How did you get your name?

I had that name since I was about fifteen. I just heard it one day and I loved it. It kind of related to "Have Mercy" by Don Covay, and a Stones song later. It's just a black name and I related to black people. I heard it and wanted to be that person. I took it and I never looked back.

Because the GTOs were named for being outrageous, are there any specific memories that made the news back then?

I got mentioned in *Rolling Stone* a lot. That was the news of the day because I kept getting in trouble and busted. Even when I worked. I worked for a lady manager for the Stax people like the BarKays and Rufus Thomas and all that. Everything I did basically ended up in *Rolling Stone*. They picked me as their favorite girl that year. What I did always ended up in the random notes.

I made the *Times* down here when I popped out of a cake for Alice Cooper's birthday in '69. The Cockettes were the waitresses at this party. From a big cake, I was supposed to pop out nude. I took some angel dust and was in the pantry of the Ambassador Hotel and I thought, this is where Bobby Kennedy was shot. Then I just flipped out, I was so high. Then when I popped out of the cake, I had all my clothes on. I took the cake and threw it. I hit people like Richard Chamberlain and some writer. But he wrote a letter thanking me, and that showed up on the front page of the calendar in the *Times*.

What are you doing now?

I work with a charity thrift store as a production lead for one of the stores. You have to know antiques. I deal with vintage stuff and pop culture and stuff like that. Because I know what's worth money from when I was homeless. I learned how to make money from the trash. I was homeless and a drug addict. You know, I went through all that. I learned how to turn things out. So I got my knowledge there.

Pam Tent, AKA Sweet Pam, was born in Detroit on October 20, 1949. She was one of a few women to work with San Francisco's campy, gender-bending, psychedelic theater group, the Cockettes. She joined the predominantly gay male Cockettes in 1969, when she dropped out of college and moved to San Francisco from suburban Detroit. The Cockettes' first performance was on New Year's Eve when Hibiscus and friends attended a show at the Palace Theater and ended up on stage doing a kick line to the Rolling Stones' "Honky Tonk Woman" during intermission. Their first real show as a performance troupe happened at the Palace Theatre in San Francisco's North Beach, during the Nocturnal Dream Show's weekly midnight film series.

With stage show titles like *Tinsel Tarts in a Hot Coma* and *Journey to the Center of Uranus*, they also created the films *Luminous Process* (1970), *Palace* (1971), *Elevator Girls in Bondage* (1972), and *Tricia's Wedding* (1971)—a parody of Tricia Nixon's wedding with drag caricatures of Mamie Eisenhower, Eartha Kitt, and Lady Bird Johnson—which was shown the same day as the actual first family nuptials and got an almost equal amount of press coverage. Pam played Israeli Prime Minister Golda Meir in the film. Many underground celebrities, such as disco star Sylvester and Divine, the drag queen superstar from John Waters' classic films, performed as Cockettes.

The Cockettes became nationally famous with the help of a review in the *Chicago Tribune* by Rex Reed and the praise of other celebrity fans, from John Lennon and Janis Joplin to Truman Capote and Gore Vidal. The worlds of music, film, theater, and fashion were inspired by the Cockettes, as evidenced by the glitter rock movement and *The Rocky Horror Picture Show*. The Cockettes worked together from 1969 to 1972.

The release of the documentary film *The Cockettes* (2002), which won an award at the Sundance Film Festival, renewed interest in the group. In 2004, Pam's memoir, *Midnight at the Palace: My Life as a Fabulous Cockette* was published.

What was it like being the only female involved in the group? Did you ever feel a sense of loneliness or being left out at times?

Actually, there were five women (regulars) in the Cockettes and any number of walk-ons. The female cast members were: Sweet Pam, Dusty Dawn, Fayette, Harlow, and Marquel. All of the Cockettes lived together, ate together, got stoned together, and a number of us slept together. The only time I ever felt left out was at The Stud, when all the guys would find dates and us women weren't always so lucky.

How long were you around before the Cockettes got noticed in the press?

The Cockettes only staged a few shows before the local press started coming around. Everyone was flattered at first, although after things got out of control and the *Rolling Stone* photographers and the European press flocked to the Palace, some Cockettes felt that we were being contaminated. As Fayette said, "We hadn't had enough time to define ourselves as a group."

What type of press did the group get initially? Did you ever receive any negative reviews? Did this affect you?

Journalists were extremely enthusiastic and delighted to write about the Cockettes. The entire culture was expanding and experimenting and at the time, we were riding the crest. It wasn't until the New York tour bombed that we got any bad press, and then it was big time—*the Washington Post, the Village Voice*—all the majors. After we came back to the West Coast, the *Berkeley Barb* greeted us with an exposé, then reversed itself completely after the next show, "Kockettes Kick Gotham Kritic Kurse." No one ever worried about reviews or took them seriously. We did love to read them. In fact, we ate them up no matter what they said, especially if our pictures were in the paper.

What was the first spark that ignited this whole concept and how did it come together for the very first time in rehearsal stages? How did the audience respond on opening night?

Hibiscus was the spark that ignited the shows. He'd been living at Kaliflower Commune with writer Irving Rosenthal (a friend of Jack Smith's, who made the film *Flaming Creatures*). Hibiscus had been singing show tunes and dancing in Golden Gate Park for months, doing what amounted to free shows. He collected people wherever he went and included them in his troupe. That's where I met him. I awoke to find him up in a tree singing "Tropical Heatwave." There were no rehearsals for that first Palace Theatre show. The Cockettes commandeered the stage during the intermission of the Floating Lotus Opera—a Berkeley performance commune—and did a spontaneous kick line dressed in layered costumes from Irving's drag room. It was totally unexpected and the midnight movie crowd went ballistic. The applause was thunderous and as Scrumbly later said, "We thought it was a one-time thing. The audience made us think again."

What was the typical hippie's attitude at the time towards the Cockettes?

We were embraced by the entire hippie counterculture because we came out of it. People didn't label themselves like they do today: gay, straight, hip. We were all freaks, no matter what our sexuality.

Was there ever a time when the city tried to censor the performances for obscenity or public indecency? How did the group get around these laws?

Oddly enough, obscenity was never an issue. Well, it was an issue... only tongue-in-cheek in Herb Caen's column [in the *San Francisco Chronicle*]. Although we sometimes performed in various stages of nudity, we were hardly erotic. The police did give the theater owners a hard time about stage permits. I believe that a tidy sum changed hands to grease the wheels and keep the doors open. Also, there was much made about getting us offstage by 2 a.m., as it was a citywide ordinance and one we flaunted continually. The theatre was raided one night for overcrowding, and Mr. Chew and our manager Sebastian were arrested.

It's been noted that the group performed while high. What happened if there was a shortage of these drugs on show night?

There was never a shortage of pot, and that was a mainstay. People always turned us on. And of course, most of us drank wine as well. Lack of drugs—or stimulation—was never an issue.

Who was in the Cockettes' audience and how did this change over time?

The audience was originally longhairs of every type who enjoyed the eclectic midnight movies that Sebastian showed on weekends. Eventually, we drew parties of socialites and old ladies in mink coats with blue hair. We were aiming to have a good time and party with our friends in the audience. Everybody else was secondary.

How did the queer community react to you being a heterosexual woman?

The queer community wasn't as divisive as it is today, nor were there the labels. People weren't hung up about that. Most of us were coming from a psychedelic experience and open to knowing all types of people.

Was this a queer experience or were straight men experimenting, too?

Many of the Cockette men were gay and many more were bisexual. Cockette Marshal was straight—married with a daughter—and other straight guys sometimes made appearances with us on stage and experimented without the rigid role stereotypes. They would do drag and makeup. No one worried about who was sleeping with who.

What films, literature, or art inspired you the most? How did you react when it became evident that your work was being imitated?

We adored songs and movies from the '30s. Hibiscus and his entire family had a background in New York musicals, and he brought the drama of the stage with him. We were flattered when we heard there was a company in Brazil imitating the Cockettes.

How were jobs allocated for props, direction, scripts, etc.? How were things organized so they didn't get totally out of control?

Things *did* get out of control, on a regular basis. In one rare event, we actually had a director [for *Hollywood Babylon*], but cast members ignored him and stumbled on stage to do their numbers completely out of sequence. Luckily the lighting crew knew what to do, once they recognized who was on stage.

The organization and direction of the shows was nothing less than a free-for-all. Everyone had their strengths, like Nikki and Bobby were really good at makeup. But we all helped each other with our drag and wrote the shows collectively, for the most part, with the exception of

Pearls Over Shanghai and *Hot Greeks*, which were written by individual cast members.

How did you acquire the necessary paraphernalia with no money? How were the shows able to run without funds, and was there ever a dilemma over whether to charge admission?

We threw the shows together with very little money. Cardboard for the sets was usually donated, and most of us rummaged through thrift stores and dumpsters for bits of costumes and old flowers. The audience was charged $2 for the midnight movies and the Cockettes were just an added feature.

Eventually, after the shows were successful, Sebastian began to dole out about $20 to each of us for a three-week run. And that was all the money any of us ever saw. It was usually enough to buy a pair of eyelashes for the next show and some new makeup or something. Everything we had we shared, and some things we found in "free boxes," which littered the Haight Ashbury.

Later, there was some dissension from Jilala over performing "art for money," even though we went hungry, as none of us had a job and only Hibiscus had a welfare check. After much drama, this became a sticking point for Hibiscus, who felt Sebastian was a profiteer. It eventually led to his forming the Angels of Light.

How did you manage to get the venue at the Palace?

We didn't "get" the Palace. Sebastian realized he was drawing a lot more people into his midnight movies if he advertised the Cockettes on the bill, so he let us perform there during intermission. Later we became the headliners, although the movies were always a big part of the evening's entertainment.

Where did the group get its ideas? How much was simply sexually fueled? How much importance was placed on social or political commentary?

Everyone came up with ideas and everything was encouraged. A lot of it was sexually fueled. We came out of the '60s, and everybody wanted to have a good time. Most of what we did was social commentary, but that was because of the times, the beginning of all the movements—gay lib, women's lib, civil rights, ecology, the end of the Vietnam War, etc. We were trying to change everything.

Did you mainly operate as a group or as individuals that just happened to work the same stage? Did any of the members act differently offstage?

There were factions of the Cockettes who always performed "solo." Sylvester was always a star, as was John Rothermel. The rest of us enjoyed performing as a group, although everyone wanted to sing at least one song, even if they couldn't carry a tune. Hibiscus was larger than life and was always on stage. The only person I remember behaving differently offstage was Divine. He was so brazen up there, so funny and outrageous, but offstage he was the sweetest man in the world, very sensitive.

How much of John Waters' work was inspired by your shows? What was it like working with Mink Stole and Divine?

John Waters has told me he was influenced a lot by the Cockettes, although he had already started making movies on the East Coast. We loved his brand of humor and did a benefit to raise money to bring Lady Divine to San Francisco. It was wonderful working with Divine and Mink Stole. Mink and I became friends and even attended French classes at City College together, dressed very French in neckerchiefs and berets.

Why were the Cockettes such a success? How did it change attitudes towards the gay/lesbian community?

The Cockettes lived out their fantasies, on stage and off. We broke a lot of ground for the Gay Rights movement, which was in its infancy. I mean, there were even laws against dancing in bars and same-sex touching still on the books. We opened things up with a bang. Back then, we spearheaded the movement. I think now there are some factions of the gay/lesbian community who are more serious. Perhaps they don't appreciate that particular brand of in-your-face outrageousness. They want to tackle other issues.

Of all the shows, what were some of the most memorable moments?

Each show had its own magic. Some were filled with our *Little Rascal* attempts at Busby Berkeley production numbers, and others were more audience involved. In fact, at the end of *Les Ghouls*, our 1970 Halloween production, we dragged as many audience members up on stage for the finale—a kick line to the song "Monster Mash"— that we could fit.

What were some of the group's most powerful or elaborate shows?

Our most elaborate show was probably *Les Etoiles du Minuit*, where the stage floor was the top of a vanity table and all the Cockettes were dressed as perfume bottles with huge headdresses.

It's said that the Cockettes influenced glitter rock as well as The Rocky Horror Picture Show. *What other scenes do you feel it has influenced?*

The Cockettes ushered in the glitter rock era, including the likes of David Bowie and Elton John. We were the first to explode onstage with outrageous drag, and when I say "drag," I mean we mixed time periods, cultures, genders... and wore it all at the same time. We used everything in our "art." We pulled it off the walls and wore it. Nikki once looked out the window to see Hibiscus walking down the street wearing the pink satin sheet off his bed. Last year, the Cockettes were credited by both John Galliani and Marc Jacobs for their recent fall and spring lines.

Were the Cockettes influenced by any particular artists or productions?

One early influence was the Living Theatre's 1968 performance of *Paradise Now*. The Living Theatre—Julian Beck—wrote the primer on audience participation. In addition to every musical ever made, we loved the early Warhol films and the Theatre of the Ridiculous. I believe filmmaker Jack Smith started everything with his film *Flaming Creatures*.

Who was your favorite person to perform with?

I loved performing with Link and Harlow. Link was so much fun, and Harlow and I were cast in a lot of duets in the early shows. Also Hibiscus, because he had a way of encouraging you and bringing out your potential. You felt so safe on stage with him.

What was the main element that made the Cockettes so unique?

The Cockettes were unique. We lived our art every day. Most of us had little theatrical training, but we got on stage and did just what we did at home—sang, danced, and entertained each other. Basically, our lifestyles just spilled onto the stage. Humor was a big part of our shows, intentional and otherwise. Sets were always toppling over, but it was never a calamity because the audience was in on the joke.

How much of it was scripted as compared to improvised?

Only two shows were ever scripted; we all helped write the others. There was a lot of improvisation and a lot of part-padding, which went on all the time. We interacted with the audience and played off of them, so the show was never the same on any given night.

How did the Cockettes influence mainstream culture?

The Cockettes directly led the way for *Beach Blanket Babylon*, which has been running ever since. Its founder, Steve Silver, came to a number of our shows and married the idea of outrageous costuming and large hats with performers who could actually sing. Every time I see someone on the street with pink hair or wildly inappropriate drag, I'm looking at a potential Cockette. The look is so mainstream and accepted that it's become part of the culture. Back then, we were barred from places because we actually disgusted and shocked people. The culture is virtually shockproof anymore.

What was the closing night like? What brought about the group's demise?

We never realized the *Miss Demeanor Beauty Pageant* would be our last show, and it really wasn't. Most of us were performing our solo acts around town by this point, and we still continued to do shows at the Palace with Divine and Mink Stole for a couple of more years—only we didn't bill them as Cockettes shows. We finally split as a group for artistic reasons. We all needed to grow in different directions.

Did you know at the time you were creating history?

We never considered posterity. We were too busy living in the moment.

What was the main intent for the group, if you had to pinpoint an underlying message? Was it art? Or a movement?

The Cockettes put the '60s ideals into practice... we went the next step. We brought the sexual and gender revolution to the stage and broadened the scope to include everybody. Happily, this "movement" included a huge dose of laughter and art.

Why did you wait so long publish your memoir, Midnight at the Palace? *Do you have many mementos? Was this book a collaborative effort?*

I always knew I'd write about the Cockettes one day, and I'd saved every scrap I could in boxes in my closet. After the documentary, *The Cockettes,* was released, we were all reunited after a twenty-five year period. The time was right. This was definitely a collaborative effort. I couldn't have done it alone. We were all so much a part of each other's lives, and the film and this book have rekindled those old friendships. I've never felt closer to people in my life. I probably have enough material for a couple more books, but we had to cut it off somewhere. Luckily, I had an intuitive editor with enough distance to guide me and to set some limits.

With the knowledge that the Cockettes will remain an important part of history, how would you best like to be remembered?

Most of all, I'd like people to re-experience the magic and the freedom before AIDS and today's negative climate. To appreciate what some art school dropouts did to open up the culture to possibilities... to go beyond stereotypes and nurture a world where everyone is free to love whomever they please.

LAURIE ANDERSON

Laurie Anderson, born June 5, 1947, in Glen Ellyn, Illinois, is an experimental avant garde musician, inventor of instruments, performance artist, composer, filmmaker, sculptor, and art instructor. Her career began in 1969 as a performance artist working solo on symphonies of sound. In the 1970s, she also worked as a teacher and an art critic for *Artforum*.

She has created instruments such as the Tape Bow Violin, a violin with a tapehead in place of strings and magnetic tape in place of bow hairs, as well as the Talking Stick, a six-foot-long MIDI controller, which replicates sounds and rearranges sound fragments. These instruments have been heralded as revolutionary experimental sound achievements.

Her songs "New York Social Life" and "Time to Go" were included in *New Music for Electronic and Recorded Media* (1977). In the late 1970s, she began working with New York poet John Giorno on his Giorno Poetry Systems label. Her best-known work, "O Superman," was released as a single in 1981, and was included on her first album *Big Science* (1982). It was originally part of an eight-hour live performance piece, *United States*, which included "Language is a Virus," based on a William Burroughs quote. This performance piece would become her third album, *United States Live* (1984), a five-LP box set which consisted of music, sound clips, and spoken word about life in America, recorded at a two-night performance in Brooklyn, New York. Her second studio album, *Mister Heartbreak*, was also released in 1984. In 2003, she was artist-in-residence at NASA, which resulted in the work "The End of the Moon," and, in 2008, released the album *Homeland*. Anderson was awarded the 2007 Gish Prize for her "outstanding contribution to the beauty of the world and to humankind's enjoyment and understanding of life."

Among other projects, she released the compilation *You're the Guy I Want to Spend My Money With* (a two-LP set with John Giorno and William Burroughs, 1981), and the concert film, *Home of the Brave* (1986). Her voice appears in *The Rugrats Movie* (1998). Laurie and her partner Lou Reed have collaborated on many albums, including *The Raven*. She has also collaborated with Arto Lindsay, Bill Laswell, Peter Gabriel, Nona Hendryx, Brian Eno, Bobby McFerrin, and Andy Kaufman.

What was your upbringing like? Were there any influential experiences?

I had a lot of music around when I was a kid, and my mother was a violinist, several people in my family played music. I played the violin pretty seriously, then stopped completely when I was sixteen. The big influences were when I was at music camp, Van Cliburn played with our [youth] orchestra. I had a huge crush on him and I also thought he was just so deeply musical. He was the first adult I saw up close who was really emotional about music and I thought, *That's how I want to be.* Not just working on chops, but dive into how it feels.

What were your first performances likes? How has your music changed?

The first ones were in art galleries and they were always in the context of some kind of visual show. That's how I got into combining visuals and music, because often I was making little films and music was more or less the soundtrack.

In many ways that's been a thread throughout my work because the most prominent thing in all of the shows starting from the mid-1970s to now—thirty years of stuff—has been the stories. So the music tends to support it by making some kind of either musical counterpoint or a soundtrack that supports it in terms of some kind of propulsive rhythm that moves it along or something for the rhythm of the spoken words to go against. I tend to use the stuttering, repeating patterns of real language against these loop-like structures that give it that kind of coherence. That's been something that's been the same throughout all this.

The ways that they differ have been various ways that I've used different systems, from homemade jerry-rigged things to more sophisticated things, but those are not a straight development, those come and go. Now I'm using something that's very sophisticated but it's all invisible stuff, you know, it's software. But similar in the sense that there's one person and a bunch of electronics, that's one of the threads.

What prompted you, and when, to start inventing your own instruments?

I was a sculptor, so I made a lot of different kinds of talking boxes; there's a talking table that I made for the Museum of Modern Art as a project that worked by a bone conduction. There are a number of violins that I made into self-playing things. Partially, it was a way to change the violin, could be a bit of revenge in that package of things, because when

I stopped playing when I was sixteen it was partially because I wanted to learn to do other things. But at the bottom of that was, really, I knew I wasn't going to have a solo career, I would probably be in an orchestra. Basically, I wasn't that good. So that was a realization that made me stop for a while. When I went back to the violin, I used it almost like a kind of prop, so it became a way to do sculpture, a way to shape the voice into different things. I'd put that into all sorts of instruments, like there was a talking pillow and various ways for the voice to be in various types of boxes.

Can you explain what the talking pillow was?

That was just some stories that were in a speaker inside the pillow so that you could hear things as you drifted off to sleep.

You're known for your solo work, but you also tour with a band.

Right now I'm working with some musicians who are really great improvisers and that's really exciting. So we don't play the same show every night. We're in the middle of developing all these pieces, so I've asked a bunch of people to come in and play, and I just give them the bare bones of how it should go, and then they contribute a lot to how it sounds. Then, as I collect these ideas, I work with some and throw some of them away. It's a really interesting project because I have a lot of flexibility in the software, so that it's not a linear set-up anymore. I can go from any point to any point at any point. In terms of this, there's a bunch of foot petals that trigger things, and in other systems I've had to do a step-through pattern. Now I can just go anywhere at any time and that makes improvisation really, really fun. I'm not stuck with certain sounds.

How do you decide with whom to collaborate?

I just try to think of whose music I really like and who has an interest in collaboration. Because sometimes people who make music that I just love have no interest in something improvised or collaborative. That's cool, I'm not really a great collaborator myself, I don't do it that often. Often I'm just working things out on my own and then presenting them. Highlights have definitely been Brian Eno, who I've really enjoyed working with probably more than anyone else because of the way he solves problems. In fact, the way he welcomes problems, he's like, "Great, couldn't be more exciting!" He's happy to see a problem because it gives him a chance to think on his feet. I love that because the world is full of problems. Our lives are is full of problems, you know, they happen all the time. If you run into them and go, "Oh, a problem," then it becomes just a series of grinding responses instead of something that can make you rethink things. I love that attitude. Whenever I get depressed I try to think of that: What's in here, what's bothering me, what's the problem? because if I find that, then I can change it. So it's a great way to get out of your misery, if you can just find what it is that's really bothering you. If you can do that, then you're probably smart enough to change it.

Can you define what "experimental" means to you in regards to music?

For me, it means harmony now. In working with the violin instead of the keyboard, which I'm doing, I'm trying to get into more adventurous harmonic realms. That really is exciting. I don't know if it's experimental, I don't really care so much anymore. I'm not really sure and I haven't been sure for fifteen years what it means to be avant garde because of the timeframes. Especially when you have, for example, so many people who are artists and musicians, and so much acceleration that you see something in a gallery on Saturday and by Monday it's in an ad. Principally because there're so many artists who are on their way to becoming an artist working in ad agencies. That's kind of a great plus because the commercials look a lot better, they're more artful and with that sense of design. Things looking a lot better, I think, is the result of a lot of art students. People who've decided, "Yeah, I'll try to be an artist." So we have an awful lot of young artists now, which is really exciting.

What about the collective dream you wish to reach during your shows?

That's a little harder to talk about. I do have that as a goal, and it means that if the story is good enough, you can drift into a place where you're not constantly looking at your watch, and if you start realizing that things aren't making sense in a normal way, that this isn't developing in a normal way, the story isn't being told in a normal way, it's kind of sometimes going off onto tangents, but you think, Okay, I'll go off on a tangent. That's, in a way, the associations I'm trying to make; they really are ones that are hopefully not as obvious, but also things that make people say, "Oh, I know what you're talking about." I'm not really trying to invent a fantastical language or something. I'm trying to connect some things that are really common experiences that maybe haven't been put into words in that way.

What was it like being the first artist-in-residence at NASA?

They told me on kind of a bad day in the studio, we were having some frustrating experiences. This person said, "I'm from NASA and we'd like you to be the first artist-in-residence here." I thought, Come on, you're not really from NASA. That's the kind of call you would dream of getting but you'd never get. So finally I realized they were from NASA. So I said, "Well, what do you mean? What would I do?" They said, "We don't know what you'd do. What do you think you should do?" I thought, Oh brother. So I think in the end... I did this for two years. I thought, What a great way to invent jobs. I went around to all these places: Mission Control, Hubble Space Telescope in Maryland, Jet Propulsion Lab in California, and so on. I just looked at things and then I wrote a long poem. I think that when they asked me, they had another idea about what I should do. I think that on some level they thought I'd do a big, sexy techno project. When I told them I was doing a long poem, you could see the disappointed look on their faces, they were like, Why would you do... ? That became "The End of the Moon," which was just a description of the things I saw.

What about the content of your works' themes draws you to your observations and provokes you to share this with the audience?

I think that it centers on its everydayness, that it's not things that are wildly from another planet but things that people can say, "Oh, I know what you're talking about." That to me is the biggest compliment, in a way. "I didn't put it that way but I know what you mean."

What is the ultimate goal that you wish to provoke with your music?

When you mentioned this kind of dream state, that's the ultimate goal, but of course along the way I like it if people can feel rhythm in a way that makes them want to dance, that they can feel joy in a way that makes them in this inexpressible... "whoa."

I guess mostly a certain kind of freedom by bending a lot of rules. I'm hoping to get to a more flexible place, not just for myself, for other people. That said, I think that's about the limit of what art can do: just free things up little bit, because I don't think it can teach things that well. It's just not set up that way. It's also that teaching I find a little bit oppressive, you know, "Here's the fact and just learn it." As opposed to art, which goes, "Here's the way it could be, what do you think?" That's always been the way I've wanted to live, not that I do that all of the time. I wish I could claim that I did; there's a lot of times I get trapped in my own preconceptions and sit there in misery not knowing how to get out of them.

What made you put stories to music rather than another medium?

I put them to pictures, too—I do a lot of different things. One of the projects I did recently was a big film, which was really visual fables, and the stories were written in it, not spoken. They were part of a big silent world. I mean, there was music, but it was very in the background. It was made for Expo in Japan. So sometimes it's part of a visual thing as well.

What is your favorite subject to use as content?

Strange adventures and true-life stories. So I try to put myself in situations where I don't know what to say or do, and then see what happens. That's one way. And another way in terms of songs is to try and invent imagery that's really vivid, that you could really, really see and feel, not abstract. So I try to make as many nouns as possible.

What are your feelings about your mainstream recognition?

That was quite a long time ago. I was, at the time, working as a downtown underground artist, and the last thing I wanted to do was work in the mainstream or pop culture. First of all, we had no interest in that, and we were snobs. We just thought that's idiotic stuff. I made a record that by chance reached the charts in England and I was sending it out mail order from my house, and suddenly instead of one order I got a phone call one day saying we need forty thousand records by Friday and forty more Monday and forty more by Wednesday. I thought, Okay, no problem, eeh. So I called the record company, Warner, that had been coming to my shows and I said, "Can we press some records?" They said, "That's not the way we do it at Warner Brothers; you sign an eight-record deal." I thought, Eeh, I don't think I have enough ideas for eight records or interest in doing eight records. So I got a lot of flak from other artists and then, really, a couple years later a lot of people in that scene thought it was a good idea to sign with a major label. I was kind of identified as this first

traitor, or then it was called 'first crossover.' The hit was "O Superman."
Why did it become a hit?

It's hypnotic. That's the only reason. It's hypnotic and it pulls you into its world through repetition that sounds, feels, like your breath and your heartbeat. It's also about a big system that can't protect you and it pulls on that feeling, that nothing can save you, and people know that. But that song was very pointed in that direction.

Was there any pressure for you to replicate that commercial success?

Yeah, but they didn't know what to say or do. I didn't have any bass lines in these things. Usually the A&R person would come in and say, "More bass," and sit in the studio. I had a lot of things like birds, so I think they felt stupid saying, "More birds," you know, so they stopped trying to do that. I was what was known as a "catalog artist," so they put up with me because things would sell slowly but surely.

What has been the most satisfying aspect of your career?

The fact that I can continue. I think a lot of people don't get that chance to keep being an artist. I feel really, really lucky that I didn't have to jump ship and do something else, so here I am at sixty and I still get to do a lot of projects. I feel really grateful about that, you know, because I think this is not necessarily a country where artists are particularly valued unless you're the hot artist of the month and making a gazillion dollars. That's a different story, if you're in the marketplace in a heavy way, which I'm not. That part of it I'm really happy about, and I think that also I'm really interested in ways for art to link to the overall culture. The NASA job was a case in point. I was the first but I was also the last artist-in-residence at NASA, because there was a guy who pulled the plug. He was really outraged that twenty thousand dollars was being spent for over two years for this job, you know, forget the thirty kajillion spent for other things. Anyways, I'm trying to reinstate that, not really for myself, but because I think that it would be great to have artists all over government. An artist in the White House, an artist in the Supreme Court, and an artist in Congress. Why not? We have this lame Poet Laureate position, but it's a really interesting point of view that artists have, and it's different from the general 'bottom line is money' point of view of American culture, so I think it could be a really interesting thing to have more artists participate like that.

Cosey Fanni Tutti, born Christine Newby on November 4, 1951 in Hull, England, is best known for her performance art with COUM Transmissions, and as a founding member of the influential avant garde band Throbbing Gristle. The Dada-inspired, extremist art group COUM Transmissions' final 1976 performance began the group's evolution into the confrontational, experimental Throbbing Gristle. Their sound went beyond music into a deconstructionism resulting in electronic noise art.

COUM Transmissions was a performance art group (1969-1976) with core members Cosey Fanni Tutti, Peter Christopherson, and Genesis P-Orridge, along with various guest participants. Genesis describes COUM's work as being derived entirely from the dream state. Throbbing Gristle was Cosey, Genesis P-Orridge (Tutti's partner at the time), Chris Carter (her present partner of thirty years), and Peter "Sleazy" Christopherson. They were the originators of industrial music, a phrase coined by Monte Cazazza, who founded Industrial Records. Throbbing Gristle was the first band to use pre-recorded samples, which were heavily distorted. Throbbing Gristle created noise that pushed the boundaries of sound as non-music. Their recordings include *The Second Annual Report* (1977), *DOA: The Third and Final Report* (1978), *20 Jazz Funk Greats* (1979), *Heathen Earth* (1980), and *Journey Through a Body* (1982), as well as compilations, soundtracks, and live albums. *The First Annual Report*, recorded in 1975, was not released until 2001.

During her years with COUM and Throbbing Gristle, Tutti worked as an internationally-acclaimed multimedia artist in photography, film, video, performance art, and sound exploration. Her prolific work has been exhibited at many museums and galleries, and she was chosen to represent Britain at the 9th Paris Biennale in 1975 and the Arte Inglese Oggi in 1976. Between live performances, actions, and art exhibits, Tutti lectures on her works at art schools, museums, and universities. Since Throbbing Gristle disbanded in 1981, Cosey and Chris Carter started their own project, Chris and Cosey and CTI, and launched their own record label, Conspiracy International, which became Carter Tutti in 2003. Chris and Cosey also released works with *Library of Sound (L.O.S.), Electronic Ambient Remixes (E.A.R.)* and *Collectiv*. Throbbing Gristle recently reunited, released a seven-DVD set (2007), and continue to perform live.

What was your first meeting with Genesis like?

Some friends of mine had organized an Acid Test [LSD party] at the local university with a kind of "Happening" and all kinds of odd stuff going on. I was tripping and bumped into Genesis there. He hadn't been in Hull very long and I introduced him to the people I knew who were the "alternative crowd," for want of a better term.

When did you decide to start working as partners in music?

1969.

Would your work have been the same if you hadn't met him?

We were catalysts for one another from the beginning. I haven't managed to tap into the parallel universe yet—but I doubt either of us would have steered the same route. As for myself, I was always sure that I would live an unorthodox lifestyle. I remember having a conversation with my father along those lines when he dismissively referred to looking forward to the day I was married and some other man could take responsibility for me. I was fourteen years old and outraged on many levels about his attitude. I told him that I was never getting married and would not be living like anything he could envisage. So I guess I determined my own path before I met Genesis. In fact, when I first moved into the same hippie building with Gen, I rented my own room and it was he who moved in with me. Before I met him I was involved with local musicians and artists, and my unorthodox behavior was the reason I was thrown out of home.

Would you describe your work as a performance artist, and its purpose?

I've always viewed my work as an intuitive, shared experience. Its full purpose is usually revealed after the event, but fundamentally, I address issues which I find trouble or intrigue me in some way. It's very "self" driven, but in being so, I think that I address many issues that affect a lot of people, both men and women.

Of all your video and film performances, which meant the most to you?

They all have their own unique dynamics and intensities. Because they are so personal, I regard them as part of my journey to become the person I am... as I continue to grow.

How much of your work was influenced by others?

I've never taken another artist's work as my subject matter. The only time COUM referred to past works was with Marcel Duchamp's *Next Work,* in which we used his idea as musical instruments on which we based a whole improvised musical score. My approach to art isn't based on an academic analysis of what has gone before—thereby trying to move things on. I didn't go to art college, so I regard myself as lucky in that I am free of all indoctrination of past art and its meaning, correct techniques, and so on. I have since studied academically and gained a first class degree in Humanities, which has been immensely useful at this stage in my life. I regard art as open to all as a means of self-expression by whatever means necessary. Not everyone makes Fine Art, even those taught at art school. And indeed, some untrained artists make fantastic Fine Art. It's about the spirit and feeling, not the technique. You can be a master painter and produce soulless works, or you can be self-taught and produce heart-ripping works of art. The same goes for any medium.

Do you find that in this medium there are underlying themes?

The "self" is my underlying theme. By addressing the "self," I hope to touch other people. It's all about sensibility and communication—but not a performance, and that's the resonance I hope to tap into... I don't like the term "performance art" because it suggests theater rather than art. All my actions have been just that: my actions in a given situation. I have never been performing as anyone else. Prescriptive time-based arts tends to negate the power of art actions, because I see it as surrendering to that whole culture of selecting what you want to see/hear instead of experiencing something you have never come across before. It's too predictive, not enough intuition or self-involvement from those who share the moment.

How much of your work is deliberate, compared to improvisational?

None, other than the practicalities such as travel arrangements and certain objects I use in my actions.

What are the most memorable shows you've done with Throbbing Gristle?

They are all memorable for very different reasons. The night Gen overdosed at The Crypt was pretty memorable. Funny to think we hired the church crypt and now it's a regular music venue. Kezar Pavilion, USA—utterly frenzied and magical. Butler's Wharf was a great Christmas gig in an old bond warehouse beside the Thames. The atmosphere that night in its location with the sound and people present was wonderful and subversive.

What are lesser-known works you had done as COUM Transmissions?

There were small day-to-day actions that involved Gen or myself, individually or together... and with other people who would call by our house. We had people from all walks of life come to visit us and join in whatever way they felt they wanted to. This included skinheads, Hell's Angels, accountants, professors, etc. COUM was all-inclusive and I think that's the lesser-known but profound side of our work together. It was non-elitist and almost anti–Fine Art in that we worked as outsiders within the art world. Being at the Biennale and other big art exhibitions and festivals with established artists was, retrospectively, a huge achievement, considering our methods and approach. I am always driven by the work and not by where it may exhibit or who would buy it. The focus is always the work—whatever happens post the action is secondary.

What were the ideas behind the "Prostitution" exhibit at the Institute of Contemporary Arts Gallery? Did you get the anticipated response?

"Prostitution" began as a COUM retrospective because we had formed Throbbing Gristle by then and decided to focus on that. Plus Chris did not want to be in COUM, and as he was the engine of TG, it was decided that COUM would be laid to rest and TG would take up the mantle. The exhibition included many relics, artifacts, and documentation from COUM actions, including the pornographic magazine action works I had been doing. It was these and my used Tampax that created uproar and questions in the House of Commons. I didn't anticipate this reaction at all. I thought it would be a quiet retrospective at which I could say farewell to COUM and greet the next project, TG.

The show was also about how people perceive us given what information they have of you at a given time... hence the art action documentation of me and the porn magazines giving a different notion of who I was. This was then highlighted by the press giving their idea of me in the newspapers, TV, etc. They unwittingly added to the exhibition. As the press clippings came in, we put them on the walls of the gallery as part of the "Prostitution" exhibition. We regarded the press as prostitutes of a worse kind when they behaved so hysterically.

What is your view on sexuality? Has it changed?

No, my view hasn't changed at all. I still have the view that sexuality is objectively indefinable because there are so many factors that determine our individual sexual desires and needs. Inherent sexual diversity has always fascinated me. There's no formula that will guarantee sexual satisfaction or fulfillment for everybody. This is one of the reasons I went into the sex industry—for the art actions—and subsequently went into striptease work. The front line was the best place to access all the material I needed, and also to indulge personally in an unselfconscious way. I didn't partake in the activities as "an artist," but rather as myself in the same situation as the other girls with whom I worked. For that reason, I got so much out of the experience. I've always found working with non-artists just as inspiring—and that's not said in a derogatory way at all—because the company of my workmates was always great fun and refreshing. Artists reflect society, warts and all, and I feel it's wrong for an artist to isolate themselves from the source material of their work. I like to get my hands in there and feel it myself. Life is rich and I don't want to deny myself any of it.

Who provided the most influence in your early days of experimentation?

My mother. Although my father disowned me and forbade her to speak with me, she always found a way around it and contacted me. More than that, she never once tried to get me to change my way of life. She accepted me for myself—admired and encouraged my creativity. She was an exceptional woman. I guess if I inherited any creative talent it was from her side of the family, as she was a singer, dancer, and very creative dressmaker. The secondary influence was being disowned by my father, because it gave me total freedom to go out into the world with no sense of responsibility to him. That was liberating.

What was it like working with Monte Cazazza?

Monte is a unique and incredible person. Working with him was equally so with doses of frustration and much laughter. I have about five people I regard as being fundamental in my life and he is one of them.

When Throbbing Gristle started, had music seemingly ceased to evolve?

No, that's exactly why we did TG. Because we knew music was about so much more than the mainstream music around at the time.

With Noize music, was its function to disable/dissect sound to prove that nothing was left, and you had orchestrated its eviscerated remains?

In some ways, yes, but mainly because the noises we generated were a direct expression of how we felt about those times, and they physically represented those feelings, too. We wanted music to be physical as well as audible. It wasn't about a one dimensional experience. It had to be all encompassing, overwhelming... so that people could not just dismiss it as a night out at the disco.

Is the point of Noize music is to obliterate the conscious and create primal responses from the masses? Is primal contact important?

Sound/music has had that purpose since the beginning of time. You only have to think back to hunting: men feared the cries of animals, and animals were confused by horns used for the sole purpose of man to hunt. Sound is fundamental to humankind. The pitch of a baby's cry is such that it cannot be ignored. Using sound and response is a basic human survival technique. The danger now is that with so much sound pumped at us, our primal response system is overloaded and we cannot filter the sound signals in a beneficial way. I truly believe that's why we are in the sad state we are in now that has led many people to feeling insensitive, confused, and unsatisfied. Too much of the negative all at once suffocates the possibility of positives.

How much of your early works can be credited to external influences such as environmental, chemical, or psychological?

I guess having taken LSD, mescaline, cannabis, and opium did change my view of things in terms of how the world can be seen from within and without. But that was a very brief period in my life. I only indulged for one year. I think there is a fundamental difference between taking drugs in the '60s and now. There was a tendency in the '60s for people to take drugs to 'expand their minds' (and thereby their lives), whereas now people take them to close their minds to the world around them. It's more about long term escapism now, and it is incredibly sad. But I am ever optimistic that things will swing around. People I meet now have that edgy restlessness that just oozes new art and music on the cusp of a shift.

What and whose ideals were incorporated into Throbbing Gristle?

Personally, I don't remember being that calculated. Our improvisations and Chris's inventions kept us clear of anything prior. But I guess we all subscribed to 'anything is possible' and that the possibilities are endless.

What was the deciding factor for your split with Genesis to work exclusively with Chris Carter on the Chris & Cosey projects?

True love.

How many collaborations have you done and with whom?

All those we have collaborated with are like-minded people that share a certain rapport. Too many to think of all but here's some: Robert Wyatt, Eurythmics, COIL, Monte Cazazza, Boyd Rice, Lustmord, John Lacey, COH, John Duncan...

Are you more concerned with empowering the audience through audio transcendence than sadistically assaulting them with a type of sonic lobotomy?

Yes, this is true in many ways. This is in part because TG had opened the channels, so to speak, and there's only so many times you can hit someone before they close down, so our strategy as Chris & Cosey, now Carter Tutti, is to embrace all that others can bring to us and as much as we can bring to them. Our music works as a conduit in that respect.

When you were performing with COUM Transmissions, did you intend to shock or disgust the viewers?

We didn't set out to shock necessarily because we were working with ideas on subjects that fascinated us, and we had no hang-ups about nudity, menstruation, etc. Those things we did find difficult in any way became the next subject matter.

What do you believe is the true nature of humanity? Have your ideals changed through the progression of your career?

I can only answer this one in my own opinion, which is to be true to oneself and thereby true to others around you. I have always lived my life this way.

What made you decide to do solo work and how would you best describe its meaning and content?

Because what I have to say about my 'self' can only be said by me in the way that only I could do it. There are certain events in my life that only I am privy to, so it is down to me to express those in whatever medium presents itself.

How much of the esoteric relates to your music and your personal life?

I don't discuss this side of my life in public. Precious is as precious does.

How would one interpret the last statement?

'Precious is as precious does' means that to retain something precious to you, you have to act accordingly. I regard my magickal and spiritual beliefs as precious, and their integrity is dependent on my actions regarding them. In other words, if I use them in the public domain to promote myself in some way or discuss them, then the potency and my journey is compromised. This very private aspect of life is between self and belief.

With your artwork, you've worked with many mediums: acrylic, digital, encaustic, collage. Which medium is the best suited for your expression?

It's all about mood and subject. There's not one medium that is better than another. But the physical action has featured as my dominant medium, and I think that's because I am a very physical (rather than cerebral) person.

How much of your work was purely a personal exaltation of the senses and self?

All of my work is. Communication is key. All any of us have to relate to one another is our *selves*—how we perceive the world around, assimilate, and share it.

What are your thoughts on the recent work of Pandrogeny that Genesis has undertaken?

I have no interest in it. Physical modification is a complex subject, and I'm sure there are many issues involved other than those related to art. I focus on the self in a very different, internal way. I regard my body and all that it has become, over time, as sacred. I would never change it or its path. I don't feel a need to escape it. I embrace it.

What were some of the technical strategies and creative processes that gave Throbbing Gristle its signature 'industrial' sound?

This is a question that could fill a book in itself. As Sleazy recently said at the ICA installation: "Chris is the one who provides that 'industrial' sound as he creates the foundation sounds for the rest of us to add sounds to." As a whole, we all know what *is* TG and what is not, but Chris is master of the essential initial flashpoint. Our creative process is very intuitive. Obviously, in this incarnation equipment has changed: Chris, Sleazy and myself use laptops and keyboards, so there is a process of selection and tweaking of sound sources prior to improvising. I still play cornet and guitar, and other than the programming of my guitar effects pedal, I play totally improvised. Once we have jammed together, the recordings are then given the Chris Carter/Industrial magic mixing and mastering.

It seems like you've been influenced by John Cage's "chance creation" philosophy, Situationists, Esoterrorism, and Dadists. Do you agree?

The intent was to break down preconceived notions of what music is and bring an acceptance of sound as the basis for creative audio works.

But also an embracing of the physical, psychological, and emotional power of sound, not only in songs, but in the everyday. That's why we used the sounds of our environment, because they induce a particular mood. As for changing society, I would never make such a grand claim of intent. But changes in society are incremental, and seemingly small cultural activities have an accumulative effect. With TG and our own Carter Tutti work, I'd like to think that we created works that reflect the truth of the human environment in a way that was honest but positive, albeit brutal at times. You must have dark and light... actually we're just about to begin work on a John Cage remix project.

Your work remained in a genre outside of its counterparts, whereas punk became a predictable presence. What did you think of this alter-movement?

We formed industrial and TG before punk existed. Punk was a manufactured movement, a marketing strategy, which TG witnessed first hand. It's rock and roll, nothing new or radical. What it has become since is more interesting than its beginnings.

How did you maintain the experimental and seditious without falling into the traps of others' definitions?

We defined ourselves from the very beginning, and when assimilation dared to show its face, we terminated TG.

During this time in history, was it difficult creating this type of art and music as one of its few females? Did you feel limited by your gender?

I have never even thought of my gender as being an issue. I've just gone out there and done what I want. I wasn't aware that I was one of a few women working in this way. I was just doing it because of an inner drive to explore, and an insatiable appetite for new experiences. I operate as a person in this world. If I have ever sensed a gender issue, I have confronted it with logic, not via gender, because I regard differentiating and discriminating on grounds of gender illogical. I'm aware that saying this is odd considering that I worked in the sex industry, but I feel comfortable within myself. Probably because, as a child, I was encouraged to regard myself as equal to others—so what I bring to others (in art, music, or sex work), I bring with honest intent and respectful willingness to share in the experience.

What has the TG reunion been like? Has your fan base changed?

The present TG is not a tour or reunion at all, but a regrouping for specific events or recordings. It has been both intensely exhilarating and excruciatingly exhausting, which is what I expected. The fan base has expanded somewhat, but I'd say that it was always eclectic and continues to be so.

Why is there difficulty getting shows in the US?

There is no tour, as I've said before, and that's probably what has been the problem with playing in the US, not a lack of offers. When bands do tours, the accumulative income offsets the expenses for individual venues—they effectively share the costs. TG doesn't work to this format, but also, we all live in different parts of the world and have other individual projects so it's very difficult to get together for a sustained period of time that doesn't clash with anyone's other work. There are also other internal issues, which have been interminably tiresome.

Regarding your current health problems, how do you see overcoming them? Do you incorporate this into your work at all?

I have an existing heart condition for over ten years now. It is at present inoperable, but is controlled by medication and careful lifestyle choices. I have to avoid both stress and fatigue, so TG has been a particular challenge. I don't make it an issue; I prefer to deal with it quietly. It's only brought to people's notice when necessary. I don't let it rule my life—I just acknowledge my limitations. I haven't incorporated it into my work in a blatant way, although Chris and I did a track called "Tachycardia."

LYDIA LUNCH

Lydia Lunch, born Lydia Koch on June 2, 1959, in Rochester, New York, has been a musician, spoken word, performance, and multimedia artist, as well as a writer and actress, since 1975. Lydia created Widowspeak Records in 1984 and released her first spoken word recording, *The Uncensored Lydia Lunch*, that same year. Since that time, numerous spoken word recordings have been released, and many books of her work have been published. Her literary collaborators include Exene Cervenka, Nick Cave, Emilio Cubeiro, Henry Rollins, and Herbert Selby Jr.

Her musical career began when she formed her first band, Teenage Jesus and the Jerks, with James Chance in New York's Lower East Side (1976-79). She had a brief period in Beirut Slump (1977-78), and then began performing as 8-Eyed Spy, and also 13.13, with members of the Weirdos (1980-82). Her work with these bands is exemplary of the "no wave" sound, and her work was included in the seminal no wave album *No New York* (1978) produced by Brian Eno. She embarked on a solo career with *Queen of Siam* (1979), recorded with the Billy Ver Plank Orchestra. She formed a short-lived group with Nick Cave, Marc Almond, and JG Thirlwell, called The Immaculate Consumptives, in 1983. Her many musical collaborators include Sonic Youth, Michael Gira, Einstürzende Neubauten, and Nick Cave.

Lydia started working in film with the group Colab in 1978. She starred in numerous films, including Vivienne Dick's *Guerillere Talks* (1978). She wrote the screenplay, contributed music, and appeared in Richard Kern's *Right Side of My Brain* (1984) and *Fingered* (1986), among other films. She was featured in the NYC rock documentary *Kill Your Idols* (2004).

Lydia's visual art has been displayed in many galleries, and her photographs are in the Paris Museum of Erotic Art's permanent collection. In addition to photography, she also sculpts and creates 'found art boxes,' which contain elements of voodoo, death, and decay.

Lydia has taught classes at the San Francisco Art Institute and the Belgium Institute of the Living Voice. She continues to release new work—including literary collections *Will Work for Drugs* (2009) and *Amnesia* (2009)—and performs often throughout the US and Europe.

Growing up in and around the gutters of others' creations, you have an air of "a sophisticated suffering"...

I've got one foot in the gutter at all times, but attempt to keep my head above the bilge and my nose clean. Growing up in the ghetto, the only way out is up. Literature saved me, helped me comprehend that once you understand that even if the cards that are dealt may be stacked against you, you need to find a way to reshuffle the deck, find a new game, and raise your own stakes. The inner city riots of 1967 that hit my hometown instilled in me an urge to protest, complain, and ultimately do something about my lot in life. This knowledge hit me before I was ten years old.

What type of education did you have?

Catholic school until sixth grade, a sworn enemy of the nuns who would attempt to punish my rude behavior and foul manners but had no recourse because my mother worked in the rectory. Horrible inner city school for seventh and eighth grades, where smearing shit on the walls of the stairwells over the weekend was considered a reasonable prank. Sub-par suburban high school for ninth and tenth grade, where—in a refusal to read the 'classics' like Steinbeck's *Grapes of Wrath*; I had already read *Last Exit to Brooklyn* and the collected Henry Miller—I assigned myself creative writing exercises. Dropped out at age fifteen. Ran away to New York City.

What takes priority in your art?

The poetry of a brutarian language depicting a cruel reality, which is universal in its horrific nature.

People describe you as a feminist. Do you see yourself in that way?

Too generic a term, "feminist." I deal with the perversion of the human condition and its unfortunate implication on both men and women whose addictive behaviors exacerbate the situation.

Do you ever feel too exposed in regards to your art?

No. The more you reveal, the less people might actually comprehend.

Do you ever see your writing and music as a weapon?

Yes, but in a sense it is only a weapon against my own insanity and anger, since the real enemies will never lend an ear to my words or music.

How did you launch Widowspeak Productions?

Since I am used to doing so much work, being extremely organized, and ridiculously practical, it was a no-brainer. You decide on a title, you incorporate it, and hopefully you find a trustworthy label like Atavistic to do the dog labor of distribution.

Have you completely broken off from any type of management?

I've rarely ever had management. The benefit of having it, however, is they do attempt to find you more opportunities. Although I don't feel I could actually do much more than I already do, and most of what they might dig up I wouldn't be interested in anyway. I have booking agents and a business advisor.

Why did you move to Europe?

Pure politics. This country has become such a pathetic farce of what it once represented that I can no longer participate in its outrageous duplicity of purporting to be one thing—freedom and liberty for all, etc.—and in reality being, at this point, closer to a fascist war-whoring regime of arrogant bullshit artists. I can do more work in Europe, more tours, installations, exhibitions, more spoken word shows.

How does your American audience differ from European?

I can't sum up an audience as if they were one collective mind. They are not. It is a collective of individuals. Anyone who makes the commitment of attending one of my shows is already an outsider.

Who has influenced you most in your career?

Hubert Selby Jr. He was stubborn, practical, and didn't give a shit. He wrote four of the most heartbreaking books of American literature. He was a hero who depicted the brutality of the human struggle with a blunt poetry and keen ear to realism.

Have any collaborative projects developed from romantic encounters?

No. I conceive an idea, decide on the collaborator, find the money to do it, document it, and get the project out. This question assumes I lead with my cunt and then formulate a project from it. It is the exact opposite. If sex or romance follows the project, it is only because I am working with someone who understands my vision and is not, at least temporarily, afraid of my power.

You've lived in New York, San Francisco, New Orleans... Which city was the most creative environment?

And Los Angeles, Pittsburgh, London, and Barcelona. Wherever I am at the time. Mobility is most important. I need new environments, I need to move to collaborate. I need to move to experience new energies and different points of views, ways of life.

Is there a period of work you're most satisfied with?

The entire body taken as a whole.

You portray yourself fluctuating between hapless victim and almost sociopathic, calculating predator. Is your work a sensual dichotomy?

And so much more! It's easy to just focus on the extremes, but the extremes are partially projectionary in an attempt to summarize the many moods we all embody.

What do you find most fascinating about the human condition?

The capacity to recover from wounds we continue to perpetuate against ourselves.

Of that, what permeates your work?

The ability to not only survive, but thrive under my own obsessions.

Would you consider yourself a masochist or manipulator?

An extremist. You seek an almost insurmountable pinnacle of passion, and if that means falling over and over again into the abyss, or throwing someone else in as necessary sacrifice to their own evolvement, then so be it.

What is your favorite piece of literature?

Demon Flower by Jo Imog. *The Gates of Janus* by Ian Brady.

Is there anyone you'd like to work with and haven't yet?

Shirin Neshat.

Have you had the same demons and inner dialogues since your early years?

You need to befriend your demons, give them a proper playground to run afoul in, so they cannot dominate your whole life, and ultimately respect their desires.

Do you feel most comfortable working within a group or alone?

Both. I only choose collaborators who I feel can truly contribute something to the project.

Do you have preferences for working environments?

I work with what I have at hand. Very DIY. I name-check places like the Antechamber because it was the home studio of the Anubian Lights, not some big recording studio.

You've made videos that some people consider pornographic. Do you consider yourself a sexual sensationalist?

The goal of pornography, straight and simple, is twofold: money and relief. Pornography is a tool to be used in an intimate setting, where orgasm is the ultimate point. My films have nothing to do with either of those motives. I deal with my sexual obsessions in an attempt to shine light on our darker urges. I am more insulted by the ongoing use of women to sell products than by the worst elements of misogynist pornography which, unless you seek out, you will not be assaulted with, unlike bikini-clad women selling sports utility vehicles, which are played ad nauseam on daily television. We need more pornography, more alternative pornography that address different aspects of sexuality. And no, I have never considered myself a sensationalist.

Do you feel that any criticism about your work being egocentric is due to the fact you're a woman? Or would you feel more heralded than condemned?

Bukowski, Genet, etc. were never criticized for being egocentric. But I do not consider it an insult.

What aspect of your art is most rewarding in regards to your personal life?

The freedom it allows.

Do you feel your work has progressed over the years?

Of course. I began performing twenty-eight years ago. If it hadn't progressed, it would have meant the whole experience was useless because I wouldn't have learned anything.

Are you a sentimental person? What mementos do you indulge in?

Sentimental, no. Passionate, intense, emotional, yes. I move too much to be precious about material objects. I admire a person, especially a woman, who can base a large portion of their career on an autobiographical level.

How much of your work is true to your own life?

All of the interpersonal material, 98% of the political.

What do you feel is the single most valuable trait a woman can possess?

Self-sufficiency.

Do you see yourself as a romantic fatalist?

Indeed. Passion, like beauty, must be convulsive, or not at all.

You speak out against exploitation and the marketing of oneself, yet your image plays a big role in the presentation and aesthetics of your work.

Look at any photo of myself I use, and notice it appears to threaten or taunt, and not play coy. I use my image to confront the "standard" of beauty, the sublimation of female sexuality, etc., and present a strong female image. I think the trappings of so-called beauty are a joke. I feel my physical entity is a wonderful lie that nature has played on the rest of the world. If I looked as I often felt, or behaved, I would appear as a Medusa death-head, which in rapid succession spins into an apparition of a cherubic angel, mad pit bull, angry lumberjack, and Biggie Smalls all rolled into one. (Laughs)

Your work reflects a cabaret/noir feel. What appeals about this genre?

Its intoxicating perversity.

Is there a particular project you look back on with the most fondness?

My decision to run away at sixteen and get on with my work.

You work in many media. Do you create them simultaneously?

I always have one musical project, one spoken word piece, and an installation running around my frontal lobe at once. Schizophrenia, when applied properly, can get a helluva lot of work done.

Do you see yourself permanently residing in Europe?

I don't see myself living anywhere permanently. I'm in Barcelona now, I don't know for how long. I can do more work in a variety of media, so Europe makes more sense politically, personally, and artistically.

Is a person a product of their environment, or are people born with innate character traits that aid in the survival process?

Both. But no matter what one was born into, until you can fully examine, analyze, and understand what drives you, you are not fully in control of what happens to you. We have to learn to stop being reactive and start being proactive; otherwise, we just follow what we are programmed to react against in a series of unending patterns which are so incredibly similar that they feel fated, which they are not. We become magnets for disaster, because that is what solicits the intense emotional roller coaster that becomes second nature. Problem is, we need to get back to our original nature.

Have you ever found your work as an escape, like a trance possession?

Live, of course, I practice trance induction.

After photo exhibits, installations, spoken word, books, video production, continued musical endeavors, what is left for you artistically?

All of the same, and more. At least another twenty-eight years of creation. It is what I was born to do.

Adele Bertei was born in 1956 in Germany, grew up in Cleveland, Ohio, and currently lives in Los Angeles. Throughout her career, Bertei has worked as producer, musician, actor, and spoken word artist, starting in 1976 as singer and keyboardist in Peter and the Wolves with legendary Cleveland musician Peter Laughner (of Pere Ubu and Rocket from the Tombs). Bertei left Cleveland to make New York her home after Laughner passed away in 1977 at the age of twenty-four. She became part of the no wave downtown music scene as a member of the Contortions.

During this time, Bertei became Brian Eno's personal assistant, resulting in the infamous *No New York* album compilation in 1978, which he produced. After the Contortions, Bertei formed an all-girl punk band, the Bloods. With Thomas Dolby as producer, Adele had a dance-music hit with "Build Me a Bridge" (1983), which is often cited as one of the first house records. Another hit followed with the synth-pop "When It's Over" (1985), with Scritti Politti's Green Garside on backup vocals. Bertei also was featured on Jellybean Benitez's dance-pop hit "Just a Mirage" (1988). Bertei's first solo album, *Little Lives*, was released in 1988. She has also been a backup vocalist for Culture Club, Tears for Fears, Sophie B. Hawkins, Matthew Sweet, and Sandra Bernhard, among others. In 2003, Bertei performed in a reunion with the Contortions at the All Tomorrow's Parties music festival.

Films she has worked on (as an actor or on the score) include *The Offenders* (1980), *Vortex* (1982), *Born in Flames* (1983), and *Desperately Seeking Susan* (1985). In the 1990s, Bertei moved into the realms of director, editor, and writer. With the cable network, Showtime, she directed and wrote for the *Women: Stories of Passion* series. Bertei also directed a feature for Cinemax, *Secrets of a Chambermaid*. She is now working in music again, and recorded the album *Phantascope* (2005) with Anubian Lights, creating music that is described as seductive and mysterious soundscapes. She is currently working on another solo album, and her first novel.

What was your first musical project?

I was born into a maelstrom of addiction and insanity, quite literally, and I found music to be my salvation—the one pure thing that no one could ever take away. For a kid who is so emotionally shutdown, music can be the perfect vessel to both contain and express all those unnameable and painful emotions. Not only did singing feel good, I discovered it also felt much better to be applauded than to be pitied. So I began singing with my grandmother, who played wicked honky-tonk piano and taught me to sing harmonies. The family continued to disintegrate, and I spent most of my adolescence in reformatories in Cleveland, Ohio, where I graduated to gospel, blues, and R&B. Kids who run away habitually get classified as incorrigibles—and in my case, I ran from every foster home they placed me in—and incarceration is generally the state's only solution.

At the time, Cleveland was totally segregated, and I grew up in an Italian/Irish atmosphere of racial hatred. I would never have been exposed to black culture if it hadn't been for the state taking custody of me. Anyway, I was emancipated at seventeen and started singing with drag queens as a drag king, doing Joel Grey *Cabaret* impersonations. But the first true band formation sprung from my jumping up on stage to guest with a local Cleveland blues band. It was the first time I really belted out a song with a real band. I was terrified... I sang "Summertime," doing my best [Janis] Joplin imitation.

Peter Laughner, of Pere Ubu fame, was in the audience and I caught his ear. On the spot, he asked me to start a band with him. Peter opened up a whole world of music to me that I hadn't been aware of—white leftie folk music like Pete Seeger, Dylan and Baez, Richard and Mimi Fariña. Bands like Roxy Music, the Velvet Underground, the [New York] Dolls... Jazz, Charles Mingus, Miles [Davis], Sun Ra. It was pure magic. Our relationship was all about this sibling Bonnie and Clyde-type legend that we were concocting for ourselves. Our band was called Peter and the Wolves. Peter was wholeheartedly invested in decadence; he wore his shadow like a cloak of protection until it ultimately deceived and did him in. We had always planned to move to New York together, and I left Cleveland alone to follow our dream shortly after he passed.

The Contortions were called the most important No Wave band. As the Contortions' keyboard player, would you agree?

I don't know if I'd agree we were the most important, but we were certainly the most diabolical! There were so many truly transgressive bands around at the time, but musically, the Contortions were in the forefront of what people are now calling 'skronk' which basically means noise as music. James Chance's approach to putting the band together was based on style, a razor-sharp sense of rhythm, and the appropriate fascinations.

In my case, at the time, these were Vladimir Mayakovsky, Buster Keaton, Fela Kuti, and Anna Magnani. I remember hanging out with Lydia Lunch in her Lower East Side loft, and in those days you stole electricity by running extension cords from the shops below; she had a whole band rehearsal space going on power by boosted electricity. One night, James Chance, Pat Place, and James Nares were making an incredible row at her loft and I was floored—hypnotized by the sound. I asked James if I could sit in on drums and started banging away some polyrhythm to what they were playing. He told me that I had "natural rhythm" and set me loose on an AceTone organ. I had come to New York to sing... but the music I heard that night coming out of the original Contortions was something so startlingly new and visceral in every aspect, I just had to be part of it.

I've often likened the No Wave movement to being like a pack or a tribe of wild children. All of the cultural rot, angst, and catharsis of the period expressed through our instruments with our nervous systems as the vehicle—be those instruments musical, filmic, painterly, poetic, or whatever. So much has been said about the No Wave. I saw it as an amazingly liberating period of revolutionary attitudes toward art specific to New York City at that moment in time. The tribe flowed in from everywhere—USA, as well as Paris, Berlin, Italy, England—which added to the hybrid nature of the mix. People collaborated very unselfishly... trading equipment and talents.

It was also a time that was psychologically and sexually freeing. There weren't any locked-down distinctions between straight, gay, transgender, drag, or convoluted sexual identity politics per se. Sexuality was very fluid, which left your head free for the work. There were occasionally still issues from the men concerning women... you know, the usual fear-based crap. But we women were not about to adhere to any ludicrous roles or censorship. Being involved with this period of art in NYC has completely influenced and impacted my approach to life in its every aspect. Although No Wave is often described as very dark and all about rage and vitriol, it was deeply transcendentalist and primal at its core in terms of its emphasis on deconstruction and catharsis, and anarchistic in terms of its absolute refusal to regard any known boundaries as sacred.

Do you have any significant memories from the Contortions experience?

I remember playing with the Contortions at a gallery in New York called Art Space with several other bands from the No Wave at the time: DNA, Teenage Jesus, Theoretical Girls, Mars, etc. This particular gig felt like the beginning of a movement in its combination of players and personalities for both performers and spectators. James, who was prone to violent, provocative antics toward the audience, flailed out into a sea of bodies sitting on the floor Romper Room-style, and rumors flew after the gig that he had kicked [*Village Voice* music critic] Robert Christgau's pregnant wife in the stomach! Of course, this was a hyperbole, based on the combustible nature of the night's music, and James's crazed, physically threatening antics. He may have kicked her slightly in mid-flail, but he would never have hauled off and deliberately kicked a pregnant woman or I would have quit on the spot. I did end up quitting the band over his behavior—not that mine was much better at the time. But this is the stuff that legends are made of. Extreme provocation in art and politics, historically—in reaction to stasis and corruption—was very influential to the No Wave in that some players in the scene somewhat naïvely glorified the Badder-Meinhoff gang, its ensuing RAF, and the Brigate Rossi [extreme anti-industrialist/anti-capitalist European terrorist groups]. Actually, the back cover of *No New York*, the Brian Eno-produced recording of the No Wave, was based on a 'Wanted' poster of Badder-Meinhoff mugshots.

Were there other driving factors or significant parallel expressions?

Driving factors were the times: the beginning of consumer culture and a deathly flat landscape in terms of music, film, literature, and art in general. We were coming out of an incredibly fertile time in American film, the '70s, but truly there wasn't much going on otherwise. There had been a backlash of boring crap after the Warhol scene and the glam scene. Deep American funk like James Brown, Dyke and the Blazers, the Meters, Brazilian and African music were all influences for many of the No Wave bands as well. Everyone was sick of the white-bread ethic. The combination of breaking down and mixing such seemingly disparate influences as concrete musique, international music, funk, jazz, and rock and roll was explosive and completely new.

Systems of creativity like Burroughs and Brion Gyson's cut-ups, or Ginsberg's poetic exercises, Antonin Artaud's Theatre of Cruelty, or Eno's *Oblique Strategies* were all influences, as well as feminists like Monique

Wittig. The Surrealists, the Situationists, were also influential. I was actually in a feminist art salon with several women in the late '70s and we called ourselves Les Guérillères, based on Wittig's book. Members included Nan Goldin, filmmakers Vivienne Dick and Sara Driver, Lydia Lunch, photographer Beate Nilsen. We'd meet informally on Vivienne's rooftop and discuss issues of art, politics, sexuality. We'd read one another's writing, show a film or recent work.

Also we were seeing the emergence of important and welcome feminist voices in art at that time, which I consider parallel expressions to the music. Artists like Barbara Kruger and Jenny Holzer were subversively deconstructing ideas of advertising, culture, and women's roles in much the same way the No Wave musicians were deconstructing notions of how music should sound and be played, or what entertainment should be. Filmmakers like Jim Jarmusch, Amos Poe, Lizzie Borden, Vivienne Dick, John Lurie, James Nares, and Sara Driver were doing the same with film. And John and James were also musicians and painters, just as Jean-Michel Basquiat was also a musician. We encouraged one another to take it all on.

Which musical genre was most satisfying?

The period of the Contortions and immediately afterward when I was working in film, writing poetry, and doing solo work with taped backing tracks and a guitar was probably the most creatively freeing for me. I was doing a mix of Brechtian cabaret, skronk, and twisted dark folk/punk, which, if I gaze into a crystal ball, could be returning in my imminent future. Each style of musical expression does fulfill different desires, and I have many. I'm creatively insatiable. There's a part of me that is totally happy to do dance music, something extremely fulfilling about standing in a DJ booth and watching a crowd of thousands shaking their ass to your music, I cannot tell a lie! With my newest venture, the Anubian Lights, I feel we're able to bridge many genres of music to create a style that is also ass-wiggling, yet with elements of thoughtful provocation as well, for anyone who ventures to listen carefully beyond the groove.

Of all this work, how have your vocal stylings changed with each project?

Singing is very pure expression; it comes from your body and is immediate emotion. It hits the air and you can't expurgate, there's no going back. When I'm singing in my own purely personal voice, my own words, this is what I feel: very risky and vulnerable. I'm fortunate that I'm an extremely versatile singer and can embrace many styles, so I also enjoy the aspect of giving and working with my voice as an instrument in the service of someone else's song or story, if the fit is right.

You were the frontwoman in one of the first all-girl bands of the punk era, the Bloods. What were its foundations and how do you see this work?

The Bloods were truly wild and, unfortunately. very self-destructive. We fancied ourselves the female Stones and worked harder to live up to the idea of an image than we did on the music! Initially, I formed the band in reaction to so many misogynistic boys telling me that girls couldn't rock, like David Thomas from Pere Ubu, who was such a woman-hater at the time. Thankfully, he's softened a lot in his old age. I really needed to feel the company of women musically. It provided freedom not to be judged in the way that only men can judge women: that insidious, undermining thing they do even when it's not blatantly apparent. I don't care if it comes from fear, it's still so tiresome.

Kathy Rey, the guitar player, and I got together and started writing songs, very punk rock funky stuff. We took out a *Village Voice* ad and found Annie Toone on keyboards, our bassist Brenda, who is a kick-ass funk player, and our drummer Kathleen. Within a few months we were playing gigs at CBGBs and the Mudd Club. I was an out-of-control addict and alcoholic at the time, which is what our image was all about. When I listen back to our music, yes there were highlights, moments that shone, but also a lot of very sloppy playing due to arrogance, drugs, and laconic attitudes. Because there weren't many all-girl American bands at the time, we toured Europe very successfully in the early '80s, and nearly got run out of Amsterdam for corrupting its young women! But the most exciting moment for the Bloods was playing the Venus Weltklang Festival in Berlin with other all-girl bands or bands with prominent female members, like Malaria, the Slits, Delta Five, and the Au Pairs. At the time, there were literally hundreds of bands with women musicians, and this was also a crucial element of the whole movement at the time. Women were finally saying 'Fuck it and fuck you' and picking up instruments to make sure their voices would finally be heard. Listen to bands like the Slits and Malaria back to back, and the innovation and spirit is mind-blowing, incredibly inspired.

Throughout the '80s and '90s, you sang backup vocals with numerous musicians. Any fond memories?

I guess I'll just say that my fondest musical memories are singing with such incredible voices as Oleta Adams, Jocelyn Brown, Biti Strauchn, Valerie Simpson, and now Nona Hendryx. My friend, Jake LaBotz, recently brought me to a small Baptist Abyssinian church in Compton, and I sang with the choir. I felt so high and realized in that moment just how tired I get of white society! And this is something I discovered upon moving here: LA is about (much to my consternation) segregation. I know me putting down white folks makes me sound like a "wigger" but I don't care, seriously. There's something about the warmth and unpretentiousness of black women's voices that is like warm, rich earth, like a cradle. And once you get a taste of your voice blending within its grasp, you just wanna rock inside it forever. The depth there cannot be matched or surpassed by any musical experience I've ever had.

You've worked with musical talents like Thomas Dolby and Brian Eno. How did your affiliations with these musicians come about?

I met Brian through Steve Mass, who owned the Mudd Club in its heyday. This was during the height of the Contortions' most extreme notoriety. Brian had expressed to Steve that he needed a personal assistant, so Steve introduced us and Brian hired me. I ran errands for him, bought him French voile socks and porn mags of women with bald heads and enormous breasts. Honestly! What I loved about Brian was his spontaneity. He'd make music constantly, play a percussive melody on household objects, and he was the first person I'd met who made his own carrot-ginger soup and did yoga, which seemed incredibly exotic at the time. He had heard about the downtown bands and asked me to introduce him to people like Arto Lindsay of DNA and James Chance, so I took him around to the gigs. The term, No Wave, originated from the record he produced of us, titled *No New York*, which came about when the four bands involved had a meeting to discuss the project at Brian's flat on West 4th Street.

I really liked Thomas Dolby's first LP and asked him to produce my first single when I was signed as a solo act on Geffen in 1982. Unfortunately, my A&R man at Geffen took the tapes and had a New York DJ remix them without discussing it with Thomas. He wouldn't work with the label again, which meant my album would not be produced. Instead, Thomas brought me over to Pete Townsend's studio, Eel Pie in England, to work on his LP, *The Flat Earth*. We performed the duet "Hyperactive" for that record. Thomas's record blew up and I drank myself into oblivion as my own record disintegrated. It didn't help that I was stuck with a lousy producer, alone in a depressing bed-sit in London, with a green A&R man helming my drunken little boat. A recipe for disaster as well as typical major label bull.

As a poet and writer, you worked with William Burroughs, Allen Ginsberg, and Kathy Acker. What was that like and did you tour with them?

I never toured with those writers, but did have the honor of performing with them on different occasions in New York. Writing poetry and fiction has always been my greatest challenge. I used to fantasize about committing the perfect crime that would put me away for the requisite year or two I'd need to complete a novel, my Jean Genet fantasy. The solitude and the time, I seem to never have enough of either. But I have finally embarked on my first novel and hope to finish within the year.

Kathy Acker was my mentor and friend for many years when I first arrived in New York. She had an apartment on East 5th Street and kept finches and canaries, and her bed was bordered by walls of books, like a literary citadel. I loved being in her company. Kathy was so prolific and subversive, as well as inspiring. But I like to think that my wildness and lack of propriety inspired her as well. I was quite the waif at the time, always hungry for food and books, never eating enough of either, so Kathy would fill me up on Trocchi and lentils. She always encouraged me to write, based on the little scraps I would show her. I was terribly saddened that we lost Kathy at such an early age.

My writing at the time was very much inspired by Paul and Jane Bowles in its quiet moments, and Pasolini and Mayakovsky at its most aggressive. Much of it was agit-prop poetry, angry yet idealistic manifestos. I opened for both William Burroughs and Allen Ginsberg at different benefits at the Mudd Club and CBGBs, and all I can remember from both brain-addled performances was the arrogance of feeling that I was just as good or better than both these old geezers! Internally, I saw them both as mentors, studied their work, and was very inspired by it. Once, when I was in William's company, he mistook me for a boy, which in those days was easy to do since I had the Buster Keaton complex; my head was practically shaved, I wore flea-bitten suits and pimp-walked like Iceberg Slim. We started talking about prison and writing, me spinning my fantasies. I was incredibly drunk and made some off-color comment about his late wife that caused him to smirk and walk away, and of course I thought I had insulted him. He soon returned with a glass that had a naked Vargas girl on it, which he handed to me. The gig was up. He said: "You wouldn't make it in Sing Sing, kid. You'd eventually have to stand up to pee. Just keep writing and enjoy your freedom." To which I drunkenly replied, "Thanks, Bill, but I *do* know how to stand up and pee!"

And Ginsberg, who I only met briefly... well, I'll have state my favorite quote of his: "Democracy! Bah! When I hear that word, I reach for my feather boa!"

Are your writings or recordings of these performances available? What writing projects are you working on now?

The only documents of my early writings that still exist are a story I wrote to get into Paul Bowles' writing workshop in Tangiers in 1978, and a few short stories and poems I've hung onto. Paul accepted me, but I couldn't scrounge up the money to go. At the time, I remember it being a fortune. There's a Super-8 film clip that Beth B. still has of me reading a piece I called the "Ragazzi Manifesto" at Club 57 in 1978 or '79, but that's it, as far as I know. I'd like to gather these pieces and publish a chapbook one day.

The novel I'm presently working on is a fictionalized memoir, which begins three generations back in time and focuses on how these generational histories inform the main character. The novel ends when the character leaves for New York and the second book begins with her arrival there. I'm approaching this as a trio of books, in the same fashion that Satyajit Rey did his *Apu* trilogy of films.

You starred in the underground film Born in Flames, *among others of equal notoriety. How was it working with the infamous director Lizzie Borden?*

Lizzie was extremely collaborative, which was in keeping with the spirit of that time in NYC. She was influenced by the cinema verité approach of New Wave filmmakers like [Jean-Luc] Godard. Many of the key actors in *Born in Flames* wrote the story, scenes, and dialogue as we went along, so in this sense, it was a true feminist alliance. I remember coming up with the idea of mobile units for the radio stations, and subversive on-air DJs, and I believe Becky Johnston and Kathryn Bigelow were responsible for a lot of the featured newspaper plotlines and trajectories. It was guerrilla filmmaking all the way. Get an idea for a scene that would bridge to another scene, grab a camera, and go for it. Lizzie was the catalyst and facilitator. Her approach was that the film appear as a documentary, and this ideology continued into the editorial process. Lizzie also edited the film, and I can tell you, knowing what all was shot, that the story in the film truly came together on the Steenbeck, as is the case in documentaries. This approach infused the film with much power and immediacy. I was surprised and happy to discover recently that the film is still being included in the curriculums of many feminist film theory courses, and is also finally available to buy and rent.

What was it like working with Scott and Beth B?

Once again, very collaborative. We all wrote together as we went along, there was no such thing as a pre-written script. These films were not about the auteur spirit, but were more like collectives. Usually Beth would have an idea for a story, or an actor would have an idea, and then the actors would work with Beth and Scott on the scenes together: the dialogue, the production design, etc. The exciting thing about working with them to produce *The Offenders* kind of sums up the whole spirit of the No Wave art scene. We'd shoot, say, two scenes, and we'd score it with live instrumentation. We'd book a date at Max's Kansas City, and let's say the Contortions would play. Before the band went on, a screen would get set up to show the two scenes we had shot the week before. Many artists and personalities from the downtown scene were in the films, and between the bands and the films, we'd always pack the house. We'd then split the door money with Scott and Beth, which would in turn finance the next two scenes of the film, providing another band for another Max's date, and repeat the process until the whole film was paid for and shot.

What goes into writing musical scores for films like Vortex?

When people understand how to integrate the two mediums, music and film inform one another brilliantly and sublimely. The greatest and most profound films are like a symphony with movements and very precise rhythms that lie beneath, supporting and giving breath to the visuals... and it's very tricky, working music with film. I love doing it, and enjoy scoring live to picture. But I also understand the importance of silence in film as well as the silences within a piece of music. This is a particular sore spot with me—when musicians or filmmakers so obviously do not understand the concept of quiet and can't stop themselves from filling up every nook and cranny. Crazy. People are so afraid of stillness these days... as if to pause and reflect for a mere moment equals death or something. Filmmaking encompasses such a breathtaking scope of storytelling and of talents, and I hope that I'll be fortunate enough to continue to create in both mediums of music and film throughout my life.

Will you talk about your experience with Women: Stories of Passion?

Women: Stories of Passion was a series of half-hour narrative erotic films, produced by *Playboy* for Showtime [cable TV network]. Initially it was the brainchild of the best producer I've worked with to date, Elisa Rothstein—who imagined a series like *The Red Shoe Diaries* from a woman's point of view. I'll never forget the first meeting we had at the *Playboy* office in Beverly Hills. Elisa brought about sixteen women together that she wanted to participate in the series, both directors and writers, to pitch stories. We sat around discussing our erotic fantasies and how we'd approach doing softcore [porn]... how different and enlightening it would be to see the erotic from a woman's point of view. Of course, Elisa had the best intentions to keep it very female, with promises of support from *Playboy*, but when we actually started digging in, production censorship reared (or, in this case, hid) its ugly head. No full frontal nudity on the men, and only certain types of male ass-shots, but full frontal on the women was expected, if not demanded. Now, if this was supposed to be erotica about women and *for* women, what were these guys expecting— that the show's audience would be entirely lesbian? Straight women want to see cock, guys!

But the reality was, these *Playboy* producers expected and targeted the usual male audience—knowing that as soon as some punter on his couch scrolling through the stations saw a nice tit-shot, the audience would indeed quickly become male as opposed to female. And if this punter is watching with his best buddy, lo and behold, he can't actually be witness to his buddy watching a man's penis, or vice-versa, on television, because, well, is he enjoying watching that man's penis? This was homosexual panic run amok, and porn—even at its softest—is still a man's world when it comes to television, despite Elisa's efforts. Witness how the creators of *The L Word*, an erotica series about lesbians, had to insert a male voyeur into their storyline on the show, which I'll assume is a dictate, once again, of Showtime's male bureaucracy. There's always a compromise. Men are such tyrannical babies. They've been exclusionary toward women for century upon century, but give them an indication that we might want to exclude them from something, anything, for good reason, and they start stomping their feet and showing us "who's the boss," no matter what the consequence.

Many of us lost heart about the *Women* series and resigned ourselves to treat it as being paid to attend film school. But still, we did our best for Elisa to push the envelope as far as we could. I met Mary Woronov, a brilliant writer, painter, and actor during the making of that series. She also directed for the series, and acted in a film that I subsequently shot for *Playboy* called *Secrets of a Chambermaid*, a softcore comedy.

Are you planning any new film work in the future?

I'm not ruling it out. But I've never been good at negotiating the world of producing in terms of funding—the art of convincing someone to give me millions of dollars to make a film—even though I'm certainly capable of handling large budgets. It will have to be a story I feel completely passionate about, with a producer or producers who would have my back and firmly believe in my vision. It's just too much work to attempt to take a film on any other way. For my last directing job, I spent seven months on a lousy soap opera in Miami with absolutely horrible producers. I took the job with the hope that I'd learn how to direct network television. You may have guessed that I enjoy acquiring new skills. The only skills I acquired on that job were those of restraint—trying to restrain myself from committing genocide! With the exception of a few great actors and fewer stellar crew members out of a cast and crew of over two hundred people, it was a complete and utter nightmare of incompetence and exploitation. I had to act like a complete bitch which after seven months of hell wasn't much of a stretch so that I could get fired and collect some severance. I will never go through that again. In film or television, it's all about how good your producers are, and in this case, I was working with power-crazed mojito-addled idiots. But Miami is stunning! Especially Little Havana. Love those *cafecitos*.

Would you talk about Anubian Lights?

I hadn't been doing music as a storyteller or singer outside of scoring my own films for a long hiatus, at least twelve years. Lydia Lunch and I have remained friends throughout the years and she was living in LA, working with the two guys in the Anubian Lights on some tracks for an upcoming Lydia record. She asked me to do some backing vocals and write with her—so I met Len and Tommy and heard their music. I was really surprised at the scope of their work and the cinematic ambience of it, which really excited me. They had been working together for many years and felt they had hit a wall, and it was time to add a singer to take the music to the next level. We had a mutual admiration thing going, and when they asked me to write and record with them, I had to think seriously about whether or not I could handle re-involving in that world. It was never a question of the music, but rather the world of the music *business*. The good thing is that the whole infrastructure of the music business has changed dramatically since I was actively making records, and independent companies are doing such great work in terms of supporting their artists so that things have changed. It's a good time to be re-involving.

Len, Tommy, and I work closely together, musically and lyrically, on the tracks. And it's very much a group project, hence a system of checks and measures, as well as a channeling of all of our influences and personal visions. It's challenging, being part of a group, but also can be great fun and less focused on your individual ego, which is also liberating. I think every band is a bit of a dysfunctional family—we have our struggles and our illuminated moments, and we'll all ride it out until it's no longer enjoyable or creatively provocative. So for now, I'm committed to seeing the band through to wherever it may take us, and... I am also really enjoying the performance aspect of it. Our music is very eclectic; you'll find many genres on our CD *Phantascope*, which certain critics find to be over-stimulating. They actually think our music is too diverse; it makes them have to *think* too much, poor things. I refuse to apologize for not making a record where every song sounds the same with slight variations, or for not toeing any ideological lines. I will always defend the renaissance approach to art—which is to wear as many hats and to celebrate all forms of expression that excite you. Go for it all. Take the risks, fight the good fight, never be afraid to be a loner, for that is precisely where you will find community. Risk is the fountain of youth and the fire of transformation. It's all about alchemy—learning how to transform the basest shit into the purest of gold, and these days, we are sorely in need of master magicians.

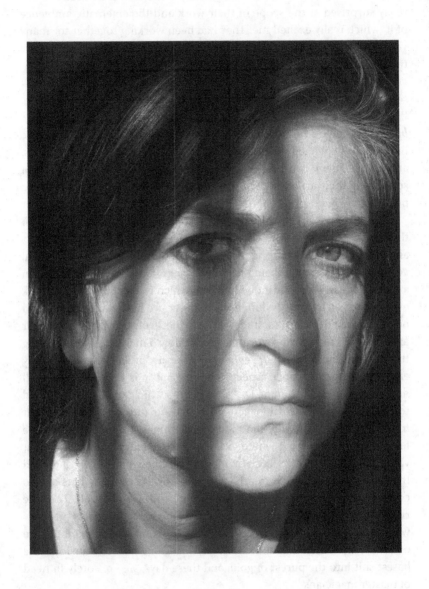

Ana da Silva was born in 1948 in Madeira, Portugal, and formed the Raincoats with Gina Birch in 1977. The band became all female by 1978, with new members Palmolive (Paloma Romera, from the Slits) on drums and Vicky Aspinall on violin and guitar. Their unique sound, attributable to the violin and vocal harmonizing, differentiated them as they combined folk, experimental, and punk. The band released their first single in April 1979 with Rough Trade Records: "Fairytale in the Supermarket," "In Love," and "Adventures Close to Home."

Their first album, *The Raincoats*, was released in November 1979. Palmolive left the band and was replaced by Ingrid Weiss. The Raincoats' second album, *Odyshape* (1981) included guest musicians Robert Wyatt, Charles Hayward, and Richard Dudanski. In 1982 they released a live album, *The Kitchen Tapes*, recorded at New York's The Kitchen art space. Subsequently they recorded *Animal Rhapsody* (1983) and *Moving* (1984). The Raincoats disbanded in 1984.

In 1993/94, the band's three studio albums were re-released, and Nirvana's Kurt Cobain wrote the liner notes for the first album. He then asked the band to open for Nirvana on a major UK tour in April 1994. Ana da Silva and Gina Birch reformed the Raincoats with Anne Wood and Steve Shelley from Sonic Youth on drums, and played some shows together. They were intending to join the Nirvana tour, but Cobain passed away a week before it was scheduled to begin.

The Raincoats released two new recordings in 1995: *Extended Play*, a four-song EP, and *Looking in the Shadows*, which included guest vocals by the Buzzcocks' Pete Shelley. Gina Birch and Ana da Silva have performed at various festivals and shows since like Ladyfest in Leeds ('07), the Nuits Sonores Festival in Lyon ('07). Ana da Silva has embarked on a solo career of electronica and experimental music using digital instruments with her first solo album *Lighthouse* ('05). Ana da Silva's new work can be found on the 3-disk set *Girl Monster Volume 1* ('06), a massive compilation series of alternative women musicians from the punk era and beyond.

What initially drew you to become a musician and specifically a guitarist?

All my life I enjoyed listening to music, a lot. As a child I heard Elvis and the Everly Brothers on my older cousins' 45s, and from then on I developed a passion for music. I also sang in a choir and had some piano lessons, which gave me a basis that is still helpful to my music making today. In my late teenage years I came to England for two months where I heard the Beatles, saw the Rolling Stones and a few others, bought a few magazines, 45s, and albums (to take home and show my friends), and I purchased a really precious piece of clothing—a black polo-neck sweater. A few years later I went to Germany and learned a few guitar chords from an American girl. Eventually my sister bought me an acoustic guitar and I played Bob Dylan songs, just like everybody else. This was an awakening time, as I realized then that so much could be said and expressed through music, and that it was such a powerful, rich, and easily available medium. It is poetry, movement, structure, and personal experience turned into a shared one. It's immediate, or it can take you into a complex journey. It's fun, introspective, and so varied—not only because of what's in there as far as lyrics and composition go—but because of the variety of instruments that exist and the advancement of technology that brings new ways and sounds to the pot.

What were you doing in your life before you founded the Raincoats?

I finished my studies in Lisbon, Portugal, and came to live in London—a place where people expressed themselves in a less restricted way than in most other places. It still is. I decided to come here and study art. I completed a one-year foundation prior to getting a BA in Fine Art at Middlesex University. Coming to London and going to this particular college changed my life completely.

How did the Raincoats initially form?

I met Gina Birch at art school in 1976. There was a female model and another student who played electric guitars during the lunch breaks. I was drawn to that and bought a Fender copy at the Portobello Market, and later a small amp. This made me really happy. The other important thing was that at the college there were two boys that knew the Sex Pistols' roadie and who introduced us to punk. One of them asked me to cut his hair badly, which I did, and enjoyed doing so. Gina and I started to go to lots of gigs. Everybody was saying you didn't need to know how to play well to do something interesting and strong.

Early 1977, we were sitting in a pub and decided to start a band. The initial decision was purely for fun. Nothing came of it at first. Meanwhile, I had gone home for the summer and started writing songs: "The Void," "Black and White," and one or two more. Gina bought a bass and started to learn while I was away. If rock music had not become more simple and direct, we probably would have never found out that we could actually write songs and use our need to create in this way. When I got back, she told me she had been practising. I already knew a drummer, Nick Turner, and my flatmate, Ross Crighton, also played guitar. So we got together just for the fun of it and started working on lyrics that Ross had written, and by the end it felt amazing to have a song that sounded so complete. It really is an amazing, rewarding feeling. We started to work on my songs also. I started singing them just because there was nobody else who wanted to sing. Eventually Gina also started writing lyrics.

In November 1977, Richard Dudanski made us an offer to open for his band, and we did our very first and hugely nerve-wracking gig. I think we all wanted to evaporate. We played about five songs. One of them was a medley of "Hey, Hey, We're the Raincoats." Ross wrote a verse describing each one of us, and yes, it was an adaptation of the Monkees' song, an instrumental in E, then going into "Real Good Time Together" by Lou Reed, but we did it because the Patti Smith Group had done it live. The gig went down quite well, as our friends were generous with their comments. We got the taste for it.

I remember feeling quite strongly that the ideal situation would be that people of both sexes should work together and strive for similar things. We went through some changes of personnel. Richard Dudanski joined us for a bit until Palmolive left the Slits and he suggested that she should work with us. Palmolive did join us, which made Gina and I really happy. We couldn't believe our luck. We loved the way she played and the joy she gave out. Until watching her, I had never understood drums or noticed them. They were just there, in the background. So this was really an important step for us because she had been in an all-female band, the Slits, and she was keen on continuing that with us, too.

So she put an ad in a bookshop for a female keyboard or violin player and Vicky Aspinall answered. This was the first time we were an all-female band. With this line up we developed the songs we already had, and worked on new ones, and eventually recorded the first EP and first album. At this time, Shirley O'Loughlin started working with us on the managerial side of things. So from this point on, there were five of us working together.

The Raincoats were labeled as punk folk music. Was this accurate?

We never really sat down to make big decisions, and that included what sort of music we were going to play. Things always tended to evolve organically. So musically and lyrically, each one of us was expressing herself in a particular way, depending on our character, tastes, background, etc. It was the differences or the mix of these four people that created the music we played. But of course, we lived in a particular time, and punk heavily informed this early body of work, therefore it sounded immediate and loud.

In 1979 we had just come back from touring England after releasing our first single, and went into the studio to record our first album, *The Raincoats*. The recording was very much like a live performance, with hardly any overdubs. Gina and I met at art college and maybe this, together with the punk ethic, made us feel that anything was possible. We didn't want to follow any rules of how to structure our music or how to present it. We were always exploring and risking, an approach that made our songs sound different to each other, and each album very different from the one before it. Our second album, *Odyshape*, was a lot more spacious, and we used lots of acoustic instruments and noises, but no acoustic guitars, and some people thought it was a bit folky, others found it experimental. This shows we didn't really fit, or want to fit, in a particular style or genre. Things evolved because of quite simple things. For instance, when we went to play on the east coast of the USA we bought a kalimba, a thumb piano, a shruti box, and a balophone. They are as far from punk as you can get, but we didn't think in those terms, and because we liked their sound, we used them mixed up with more edgy sounds on "Only Loved at Night," "Shouting Out Loud," followed by "And Then It's OK," respectively. We just always tried what came to our heads.

What inspired and influenced the band's sound and lyrics?

It's always really hard to know what influences you. Some things you know, others are second-hand or hidden. Obviously everyone is a fruit of their time and history, and it is within this framework that you move, choose paths, and seek inspiration, and hopefully have something to give—something that, in turn, will make someone else's heart beat faster. When we were working on the singles "Fairytale in the Supermarket," "In Love," and "Adventures Close to Home," Mayo Thompson, who was going to produce it, came to rehearsal and helped us turn the violin into a more Velvet Underground sound. This was a band we really loved. I would still have their first album as one of my all-time favorite five. That's the closest we got to striving for a particular sound, but it was a really important step because the violin became such a strong element in our sound—piercing, dangerous, as opposed to pleasant and decorative. It's what you do with something that matters, and one should not be judged by what instrument they play but by what they do with it. As far as lyrics go, I can only speak for myself. The person I had paid more attention to lyrically was Bob Dylan. I loved so many of his lines. I like the idea of poetry. Lyrics have a slightly different purpose, though, but it's good if they also look good on paper. So, like with music, I tried to go as far as I could with them. Some people think that lyrics don't matter, but for me they have to have a purpose, an ambition, just like the music.

As a founding member, how much of the content and music were yours?

On the first album my influence was stronger than on the others. I wrote the lyrics and basic musical ideas for "The Void," "Black and White," "No Side to Fall In," "You're a Million," and "Fairytale in the Supermarket." I also helped Gina with the basic music for "In Love" and "No Looking." We already had all of these songs before Vicky and Palmolive joined. So they basically wrote their parts. We only worked from scratch on the arrangements for Palmolive's "Adventures Close to Home," Vicky's "Off Duty Trip," and "Lola," the Kinks song. But having said this, I have to add that things weren't static, and we always changed things and bounced ideas off each other. Each part had a varying degree of input from other members of the band. We arranged, decided, and strived together for the good of the songs, so that they would do what they had to do in the way that we wanted them to do.

For the other albums, Gina and I roughly wrote the same amount, with Vicky contributing at times. My lyrics were inspired by thoughts I had, but they weren't necessarily about me. Only I know when they were autobiographical, because it's irrelevant for anybody else to know. They might sound personal, but they're meant to be out there for the listener to enter the song. That's when it truly lives.

Since the Raincoats were one of the first feminist bands to come out of punk, how much of the music was meant to have a feminist message?

For me, the Raincoats was about art. Art is related to life. They walk hand in hand. We are women and speak as women. Our hearts, minds, and hormones are female. Our voice is female, and because we are proud women, we speak our minds as women. We strive for change or improvement in the many areas of life, and we try to value what is of value. We started being seen as a feminist band when we were all females and had a song about a soldier who, despite having raped a woman, had been protected by the powers that be and walked off a free man ["Off Duty Trip"]. I resented some people reading us exclusively as a feminist band. We were definitely that among many other things... and anyone who wants to live in a richer and more interesting world has to strive for equal opportunities for people of any gender. Prejudice creates a negativity that spreads like a virus.

The Raincoats were respected for not playing into gender stereotypes by refusing to dress in a provocative manner. Was this intentional?

The way we dressed and presented our artwork was an expression of who we were. We didn't talk a lot about clothes, at least not in a band sort of way—didn't coordinate or even dress up. Each one of us had our own personal style, and we did care about how we looked—but not as a member of a band... just everyday style. And we took that to the stage. It was a charity shop, second-hand style, and therefore in opposition to fashion house trends. This is what we could afford, and it was definitely a fun and creative way of dressing. Nobody that we worked with, including our record company Rough Trade, expected us to be any different. I don't feel we 'refused' to look like sexual stereotypes, because it was never an issue. We circulated in an environment that didn't relate to that sort of thing, and none of us pushed in that direction... so we didn't even discuss it amongst ourselves.

What type of aesthetic did the band mean to present?

We just wanted to push boundaries, look out the windows, hear the music outside, fly the sky. We wanted to tell our fairytales... sing our love songs.

Did you ever feel your work was dismissed because you were female?

We were one of Rough Trade's bestselling acts so we always had people who enjoyed what we did. Maybe for some it wasn't clear enough or played well enough to be appreciated, but you can't please everybody. Had we been men, maybe the reaction would have been similar, or maybe we would have been considered geniuses... probably the first, because it was all too quirky for easy assimilation. Some people manage to challenge and be widely accepted, but their challenge is at least partly limited— although if it's spread widely, it'll have a strong effect.

What reactions did the Raincoats get from critics?

As far as the press goes, you try not to get dispirited by bad reviews, and lots of times their negative comments are based on really silly premises: a bad review ends up being a good one. If it's intelligent criticism, you can choose to take it on board or not—be it a negative or positive one. People are paid to listen to something carefully and comment on it, so they also have a responsibility to be conscientious in what they do and should think carefully before they write a critique. They are supposed to be guiding the buying public to choose amongst the enormous amount of work available... so that profession shouldn't be taken lightly, as it can be of great influence. The only time I was offended by any journalists was if they targeted a group of people and made ageist or sexist comments that were purely based on the fact that we were either too old for their taste (hope they'll grow up, that's all I can say) or that we didn't fit in their scope of women. I was not offended personally, but instead as a human being, for the group of people in question. I think that on the whole, writers gave us good reviews and made our records Singles (or Albums) of the Week in their paper or magazine.

Did you have one particular type of fan base?

As far as fans are concerned, our music appeals to both sexes, which is good because we were writing for anybody who wanted to listen. Of course, our female fans got something out of us that was different to what they got out of male bands. They could relate to us more directly, identify maybe. I think some males felt that too, though. We get a bit more perspective on this subject now because of the comments, messages, and friend requests we get from MySpace.com. It makes us feel more connected with the people that listen to our music, and I feel very grateful that they voice and share their feelings about it with us. This has brought us a lot of joyous moments. It makes us feel, in turn, more accompanied and connected.

What was your exposure like regarding the types of venues you played?

We played mainly in clubs, but also colleges, big venues, festivals, radio, and television. I must add that I love playing live.

Did you wish for commercial recognition at any point?

We always wanted recognition, but the commercial side of things wasn't the most important one. It's always good to be able to make a living doing what is important to you, but that was certainly never the motivation and the reason to do it. I would like us to keep selling those records, mainly because I think our body of work is still relevant and good enough to do so. I'd like to think it's timeless, and that people will get something out of it well into the future. I really hope so.

Was the band ever used as a platform for social or political agendas?

Occasionally that was the case. We got put with other female music acts under the umbrella of 'Women in Rock.' When you try and reach out in as wide a way as possible, being labeled as some type got to be a bit frustrating. It was all done in good faith, but it got to feel rather limiting.

What type of audience were you hoping to attract?

It was always good when a discerning audience liked us. We played for men and women alike and hoped they would all take home something good from their point of view. One of the most gratifying things would be if they found us inspirational. It makes me feel really happy when I come across something that is inspirational. By the looks of it, we achieved this to a certain degree.

What should the band be most remembered for?

I would like people to remember us for our musical exploration—for having stuck to our guns and pushed barriers, for having been there. If they remember us with a smile, it's even better.

What did you consider most gratifying about the band?

By being so close to the other members, it enriched my views about lots of issues, too numerous to mention. We learned a lot from each other because of being very different characters and having come from different backgrounds. This journey we went through together was, however difficult at times, very important to our development as creative individuals. In my eyes the band was definitely successful, and still is.

Are you satisfied with what the early Raincoats produced? Any regrets?

I am very satisfied with our early work, especially the first and second albums. There might be the odd little annoying thing here or there, but there's no point in wasting time regretting things and wanting to change the past. Some people don't like to listen to what they've done, but I still find things in those records that I enjoy, so I still listen to them now and then.

What was the collaborative process like for the early and later Raincoats?

The collaborative process was similar in both instances, but this time it was just Gina and I writing and being responsible for how the songs were in the end... although we left room for collaboration from other members who worked with us for *Looking in the Shadows*. This time our violin player was Anne Wood, who still plays with us if we do a gig.

What are some of the fondest memories you have with the band?

We did have some fun times together. There was plenty of good humor flying around to make it pleasurable. I also liked working with the others and hearing a song come alive. One of the best moments was when our first single came out. This was a definite exhilarating moment. Also, when the first album came out, it really felt like we were totally there with the other people we respected and with the best label we could wish for. Also, when playing live I feel so... alive.

Were you ahead of your time or is there greater appreciation now?

Although our music had been appreciated, everything was a bit quiet after we disbanded in 1984. The records stopped being available for awhile. We were doing other things. In the early '90s though, we started thinking we should re-release them on CD. Meanwhile, we realized that some people were mentioning us as an influence, and it seemed even more appropriate to do so. I'm not completely sure why they liked us. Some people do think we were and still are ahead of our time, especially with *Odyshape*. I wouldn't really know because of my close relationship with it. I think we are still popular due in great part to the fact that a lot of people got to know about us through Kurt Cobain. He was a fan and talked about the band on the liner notes to *Incesticide*. We also asked him to write something for the liner notes of the re-issue of our first album, which he did. That meant so much to us.

Was your live sound different from your recorded music?

It was quite different because we were always changing things and also because we changed drummers a lot. And when we played again in the '90s, Anne would play Vicky's parts with her own interpretation.

How did you feel about Kurt Cobain's acknowledgment of your work?

I met a friend near my home and she told me about the *Incesticide* liner notes. I thought she was exaggerating. So when I read them.. I felt so, so happy. I didn't know who Kurt and Courtney were when they came to find me, and Kurt asked for a copy of our first album because his copy was worn out. In the meantime, I had become acquainted with his music and loved *Nevermind*. I love his voice too. If I respect someone else's work, it obviously means a lot to me if they like mine.

We were re-releasing our albums in the UK, but because he voiced his love for our music so many times, Geffen, Nirvana's label, approached us to re-release them in the US, and some time after to record a new album, which came to be *Looking in the Shadows*.

After the Raincoats, what other projects have you worked on and why?

The most important collaboration I did was with Gaby Agis. She is a British dancer and choreographer. I did music for some of her work, including a commissioned film by Channel 4 and two theatre pieces. I found this very interesting because it was a different project compared to what I was used to, and a different way of working. It was a two-way collaboration. She would tell me her ideas for the choreography, then I would do music, and then we'd fine tune. It was great to see her working with dancers to my music. The dancing took it to another level.

Why did you decide to start working solo in a different musical genre?

[The Raincoats] stopped working together but I didn't want to stop writing songs... so I kept working on lyrics and musical ideas. I came across a small electronic instrument, a Yamaha QY70. Mostly it's used for developing ideas because of its size and portability. It is a sequencer with lots of different sounds. It has a tiny keyboard and it can be used with batteries. Its simplicity appealed to me. So I bought one, dug into it, read the manual, and started composing. I worked in such detail that, in the end, I came to the conclusion that I actually liked what I was doing as it was, and didn't see any point in transferring what I had to another instrument. The backing tracks of *The Lighthouse* are exclusively done with the QY70. I recorded them and the vocals onto a Roland digital 8-track recorder and mixed these together. Working in this way was a long and technically (sometimes) boring process, but when I overcame those difficulties, it was very rewarding. I didn't set out to do anything in particular, as far as a style or concept. I just wanted to write songs and see what would happen.

I started to listen more to electronic-based music and found that I had a lot of pleasure in just listening to some of the sounds—especially some synthesizer sounds. They can be so strong and pure, even when noisy... it's so great to fiddle with them until you get what you want. They give you so much freedom and variety. All this started having an impact on what I was doing.

How did working solo compare to your collaborative work?

Frequently I wished that I had someone with me who would sort out some of the technical problems—or rather, my own lack of knowledge. Sometimes I missed the collaboration side of it, but mostly, I just got on with it and enjoyed the fact that everything was as I wanted it to be. Obviously having had the rich learning experience of working with other people helped me in my solo journey. I wouldn't say that one is better than the other. It's just that sometimes one is better at a particular time in your life.

PAULINE BLACK THE SELECTER

Pauline Black, born October 23, 1953, in Coggeshall, England, is best known as the singer of 2-tone ska revival band The Selecter, which was formed in 1979. Based on Jamaican ska, reggae, and rock steady music of the '50s and '60s, the 2-tone movement emerged in the late '70s out of Coventry, England. The phrase '2 Tone' was coined by Jerry Dammers of the Specials and became the name for his record label, 2 Tone Records, in 1979.

Pauline has worked as a musician, writer, singer, activist, TV and radio host, and actress. With the Selecter, she earned acclaim from originators like Prince Buster and peers like the Specials and the Jam. The Selecter released several singles which became instant hits on the British charts, including "On My Radio," "3 Minute Hero," and "Missing Words" in 1979. In 1980, their first album, *Too Much Pressure*, was released, followed by *Celebrate the Bullet* in 1981. The Selecter is featured in the documentary, *Dance Craze* (1981), which also included Madness, the Specials, the English Beat, Bad Manners, and the Body Snatchers. Pauline went solo in the early '80s, releasing two singles in 1982 and 1983.

After success with her band, she pursued acting and won a Best Actress award for portraying Billie Holiday in *All Or Nothing At All* (1990), and won again in 1993 for her performance in *From the Mississippi Delta*.

Pauline has also worked with the Blue Jazz Trio, performing songs of Nina Simone and Billie Holiday. She also worked with the Ska Divas, and 3 Men and Black. 3 Men and Black started with a tour in 2001, and consisted of Pauline with members of the Jam, Stiff Little Fingers, Bad Manners, and the Stranglers performing acoustic versions of ska hits. In 1991 Pauline reformed the Selecter, releasing live and new recordings, including *Out on the Street* (1992), *The Happy Album* (1994), *Pucker!* (1995), *Cruel Britannia* (1998), *Perfect World* (1999), and *Reel to Real* (2003). Pauline and Nick Welsh started a side project as the Selecter Acoustic, recording two albums: *Unplugged for the Rude Boy Generation* (2002) and *Requiem for a Black Soul* (2004). Over a three-year period, from 1999 to 2001, she released the *Trojan Song Book* in three volumes. Pauline still performs frequently, and works in radio and television, doing shows like *Off the Page*.

Did you grow up in Coventry?

No, I grew up in a place called Rumford, which is in Essex and is one of the counties that surrounds London, so the center of London was about twenty-five miles away from where I lived. It was one of those places where you don't actually go into London very often, so it's just a suburb, really. My environment was kind of strange because of my parents. My birth mother was English and my birth father was Nigerian, and I was given up for adoption when I was a month old. So I was adopted by white people who were in their late forties and had already had four sons. I grew up very much in an environment where I was the only black kid in the school. I tended to listen to white folks' music until I was about ten or eleven. The whole early '60s Civil Rights movement in America sort of woke me up, and the kind of music that was beginning to come out of the States at that time. Then I got into soul and Motown and reggae.

What were you listening to specifically?

It would have been early '60s pop music, the Beatles, the Rolling Stones. Then my taste began to refine itself a bit when the whole Civil Rights thing was going on, the whole soul thing, the whole 'black is beautiful' thing was beginning to happen. I began listening to the Supremes, anything that was coming out of the soul stable: Aretha Franklin, Marvin Gaye, Otis Redding, all those kind of folk.

How accessible was it in the area you lived in?

Very inaccessible. When I started listening to these people, it was just on the radio. Fortunately, the radio began playing quite a lot of that stuff. We had a couple of reasonably forward-thinking TV programs, one called *Ready Steady Go* which had a lot of the black artists over at that time, and was the first program really to do that. With Marvin Gaye and the Supremes, people like that. Also Desmond Dekker, the early Blue Beat, reggae/ska artists that came over they would feature. That was really my in road to listening to black music.

So you were exposed to this American music before you had gotten into the first wave of ska? Ska originally started in the '60s?

Ska started late '50s, early '60s, you're absolutely right. I went to a school that was kind of split down the middle, like by the time you got to the sixth form (I don't know what grade you'd call that, that would have been when you were about fifteen or sixteen years old). There was a group of kids who came from an area about six miles away, and mainly a lot of them were into the skinhead thing because that was going on at the time, and the rest of them were hippies, so I sort of straddled both of these movements. (Laughs) I heard a lot of the stuff that the kids were playing who were dressed as skinheads, and liked a lot of it, that would have been early ska like Desmond Dekker, "Long Shot Kick de Bucket" [by the Pioneers], "Madness" [by Prince Buster], and "Ten Commandments" by Prince Buster. All those kind of things, but they weren't my records as such, I was listening to other people's records. I was quite taken by the sound of it. The whole mod thing was going on as well, and I just rather liked the whole way the skinheads looked, the way they dressed and stuff. I didn't know about certain kinds of ideas they might have that might be right wing or not in keeping with mine at the time. I didn't recognize that with any of the people I went to school with.

When you were going to this all-white school, were you self-conscious at all or did race not concern you? Did you just rise above it?

Oh god, it concerned me, absolutely. But it was a question of just rising above it. As far as I can remember, apart from some playground taunting, there were no real racist attitudes around as such. I was just another kid. And probably because my parents were white, do you know what I mean? People knew my circumstances. I think that if my parents were black, it might have been different.

When you got to college you studied biochemistry and radiology?

Yes, I studied biochemistry, but I didn't finish my degree because I decided I really didn't like it, and then I trained to be a radiographer. That's what I was doing when I joined the Selecter. I had to make a straight choice between: did I carry on with my job or did I join a band? Well, that was a no-brainer... I joined the band. (Laughs) When I first got into the Selecter I was about twenty-six years old.

When you were a teenager, did you have plans to be a musician?

No, not really. I learned to play the piano when I was about six, and gave it up when I was sixteen. Then I taught myself to play the guitar, and I used to go down to the local folk club and thought I was Joan Armatrading for a bit. It was an artistic outlet; music was just something that was in my life, and I wrote a few songs but I certainly had no inclinations particularly to go beyond playing locally in clubs. Then I got talking to a musician who said, "Hey, you ought to come write some songs with me," which I did. Then we just got into trying to form a band, and half the people who were in that band—well, three of the people—would then go on to be in the Selecter. While we were rehearsing, Lynval Golding from the Specials stopped by our rehearsal, and I didn't really know who he was at the time. I was dimly aware that this band the Specials existed—in fact, they may have been called Coventry Automatics at the time, it was before they changed their name to the Specials. He just asked myself, the keyboard player Desmond Brown, and the drummer Charley Bembridge whether we'd like to form a band with some other musicians: would we like to go to a meeting? So we went along to the meeting, and all the people who were in the room (seven of us) ended up being in the Selecter.

Were any shows you saw before the Selecter inspirational?

In terms of music, I hadn't been to that many live shows. When I was a student, I used to go along and see various bands if they were on, but it was never anything that I particularly wanted to do. When the Selecter formed, I was just kind of thrown in at the deep end because the Selecter actually started life as an instrumental tract, which was on the B-side of the Specials' single "Gangsters". Then the person who wrote that, Neol Davies, the guitarist in the Selecter, formed a band from various people who were musicians around town. I kind of got in, really, (1) because I could sing, and (2) because I had written some songs and they ended up being on the first album. It just kind of came together in a very quick way; we were just thrown into supporting the Specials. One particular gig, which was really the first gig that we did (in Leeds, north of Coventry here, in Yorkshire), when we turned up, I remember Elvis Costello being there because he was going to produce the Specials. He was just kind of wandering around, and I was in absolute awe of him. He had records on the charts. I really didn't know how bands worked, I didn't even really know what a PA was at the time. So I just got on stage, and somehow I suppose I must have convinced some people, and it just all kind of started from there. That's how green and how much of a novice I was right at the beginning. It wasn't a burning ambition of mine to be in a band.

What was the scene like? Which clubs did the ska musicians perform in?

There are clubs these days, aren't there, that sort of support a particular kind of music. It really wasn't like that back then. There were a few venues dotted around Coventry. The actual sound of 2-tone came out of Coventry, and why that is I have absolutely no idea. I think it was probably because there was a very healthy mix of black and white people in Coventry that rubbed along together well and got along. All the kids had gone to school with each other, so you just kind of gravitated from school and ended up in each other's bands. A lot of white kids, sort of more forward-thinking ones, I suppose, had been exposed to reggae and ska music that the black kids' parents had listened to. So it was an actual progression to kind of mix that up with the whole kind of punk thing that was going on at the time. And of course you gotta remember that the Clash was around just prior to 2-tone happening, and they kind of began that experience. I guess we were all, in some ways, influenced by the Clash and that whole punk scene.

What sort of venues did the Selecter play when you started out?

We would play small clubs that probably held 200, 250 people, and very quickly from that we began doing bigger venues, say, 500 capacity venues. Then we went out on the 2-tone tour, which was the Selecter, the Specials, and Madness (which had originated in London), but we were all kind of doing the same thing at the same time, a bit of a zeitgeist moment, I suppose. We were all traveling on the same bus and we began doing bigger venues called "top ranks." They were cinema venues that had been turned into places that had live music, and they were anything from 1500 to 2000 capacity.

This would have been 1979, late 1979. When we were on the 2-tone tour, we had our first hit with "On My Radio," which went Top 10. I think when we were on this 2-tone tour with the Specials and Madness, all three bands were simultaneously in the Top Ten, so that kind of put the whole 2-tone thing on the map. Within a two-year period we had about five hits, not all Top Ten. Then our second album, *Celebrate the Bullet*, was a bit untimely really, because when that went out John Lennon and Ronald Reagan had just been shot. So no one wanted to play the single "Celebrate the Bullet" on the radio. So that kind of killed that one dead.

Did you expect to have that kind of immediate success?

Oh god, no. It wasn't a question of wanting, really, it's just that we were out there and it just kind of happened. When we were on that 2-tone tour we were playing big places, packing them out and gigging an awful lot, but the ticket price at the time was like three pounds, which would be about $1.50 for you. (Laughs) We cut off our nose to spite our face, really, because we were trying to hang on to our principles in that way, so that the kids who came to see us should be able to get in for a cheap ticket price. We deliberately kept ticket prices low so that fans could get in to see us. When you compare that with ticket prices now, and then they play for three-quarters of an hour or something silly like that, it seems crazy. I just thought it was just really good fun at the time.

Did you write most of the music for the Selecter?

No, I didn't. I wrote some of it, but the main song writer was Neol Davies, the guitarist. Some was collaborative. We tended to bring a song in and then the process happened from there. The song called "Black and Blue" was about my formative years growing up and how I felt, which was quite an angry little song from a black young woman's prospective at the time. That was on the first album. Then there was the song called "They Make Me Mad," this one completely summed me up at the time. Which was very much my political leanings, left wing and quite anti-establishment, and that was on the *Too Much Pressure* album.

Were you politically active before the Selecter? Was the band a platform?

I never used the band as a platform, but I had been politically involved before that, for some number of years, so it was a natural progression really. That was the way I wrote, that was the style I wrote in, and I couldn't see any point in adding to the pot a whole heap of love songs like women are supposed to do, or they did do at that time, and I felt there was enough in the world and it didn't need me to out do it. It's all a load of bunkum anyway. (Laughs)

Did you experience sexism or racism? Why did you dress masculine?

No, that was a load of rubbish. There was a Rude Boy style obviously, and our stage act was very, very active. So the fashion at the time was ski pants, and I really liked ski pants and they did that job, you could run around the stage quite well and be quite athletic in these things, which you obviously couldn't do in a skirt. I was never ever interested in that obvious sexual image that there was at the time through, say, Debbie Harry in Blondie. I mean, she did it so much better than I would have done! I mean, that was kind of me, I wouldn't say I was tomboyish at all. I know that some people have written that I started dressing as a man— that couldn't be farther from the truth. It was just a way of dressing, and the hat very much became my trademark, and I look good in a hat. It was never like a pork-pie hat, it was always a nice sort of gray Trilby style. I just thought it was cool.

When the Selecter first came together and we knew that we were going to appear on a TV music show, I was still working at the time as a local hospital radiographer here in Coventry and I was really afraid that the people were going to recognize me or my name would get out, so I had my name changed by Deed Poll [legal name change in the UK]. We were all sitting round one day and everyone was saying "What shall we think up for Pauline's surname?" And someone just said, "Well, okay, Pauline... Pauline... Pauline's black." Pauline Black came out of that. I had been adopted by a white family, all of whom were... I wouldn't say they were racist... but they didn't really embrace black people coming to this country, although they had adopted me, as illogical as that may seem. They would never ever acknowledge the fact that I was black, and I was always really pissed off about that. Well, they gotta know now. Growing up, the only exposure I saw of blacks when I was young was on TV, where the only roles blacks portrayed were maids and servants. On American TV, the news showed blacks being hounded out of the universities and dogs being set on them. And if you're the only black kid in the school, all the other kids in the school are seeing this news footage, too. I became very entrenched in my ideas, quite militant in my own head. I was young still, and couldn't actually do anything about it. I remember being absolutely incensed, and feeling *this is not right.* And the same thing was going on in South Africa at the time, and all the events that led up to Nelson Mandela being let out of prison. I grew up when there was apartheid really being carried on in the southern states of America and South Africa, and feeling very incensed that there was something not right with a world that could allow that to happen. We all sit here now and we're allowing a whole generation of people to die of AIDS in Africa, when drug companies have the wherewithal to be able to provide at least some kind of palliative measures, and it doesn't get done. I will fight that to my death, or at least make people aware that is what's happening, and not necessarily in a comfortable way, like "Let's all have a great pop concert where we'll invite all these people along who just want to sell records!"

Who were fans of the Selecter? Did you have any expectations?

Well, I didn't have any expectations; I didn't particularly know exactly who was going to be interested in this music. In the beginning it was pretty much a cross-section of people, predominately white kids I guess. In those days there'd be far few black kids around. I think the thing that made a bit of a problem is the fact that the early skinhead stuff that was around in the '60s did get a bit of a right wing following from people in the National Front here. I'm not sure what you'd call it there—I'm sure the KKK would eat them for breakfast. They got a bit of a reputation for beating up people of a certain ethnic persuasion, and things like this. That element kind of resurfaced at the time that we were about, because it was associated with that kind of music, so you would get a certain proportion of skinheads who would come to the gigs—mainly in London really, more than anywhere else—and they would *Sieg Heil* at the stage. The rest of the audience would really not be into this, and were just there because they were enjoying what was happening at the shows. And you would have to stop the show and wait for these people to either shut up or be cleared out. So sometimes it was a bit of a struggle to get through a show, if that kind of element turned up. That was by no means at every gig, but occasionally they would turn up and they would deliberately cause trouble. This would have been about 1979, 1980.

And they just kind of disappeared after a while? Did it just die out?

Well, everything just sort of turned into being New Romantic, so they just kind of had their day and then disappeared. I mean, there's a resurgence at the moment of all things skinhead-wise in youth culture that I'm beginning to notice, but I think that fascist element is now being got under control, because there's lots of little organizations all around the world called SHARP, Skinheads Against Racial Prejudice, so they're more conscious now.

It's too bad some of the original working class proletariat skins are racist.

Some of them are. Just the history of the whole look is from the working class. That's where I come out of, that's the kind of kids I went to school with. My parents were working class, that's how I grew up. So I could see where they were coming from, and never really had a problem about that. When you're young they're like tribal markings, you differentiate yourself, stuff you want to align yourself with. When I was growing up there were mods and skinheads. I wasn't going to choose sides as such, because these were different cultures I could embrace, so I went off on my own trip, really, decided I would find out as much as I could about the Civil Rights movement, about Malcolm X, Martin Luther King, Angela Davis. Because I had no one else to talk to, I had no black friends, there were no black people in the school that I went to, a grammar school in Rumford. It was a little bit like manufacturing your own life, certainly until I went to the university. The SHARPs is not what I'm doing at the moment, but my history is that.

Any amazing moments or sentimental memories from the Selecter?

The most sentimental memories I have are on the 2-tone tour. During *Too Much Pressure* we erroneously came together: occasionally at gigs there would be violence, particularly if there were fascist skinheads. We would all pile into each other in the middle of it when there was a beat breakdown to show people violence to other people was not a thing that should be condoned. But I think maybe some people got the wrong idea, and thought that we were actually thinking it was a good idea. We just wanted to exhibit that this is what happens when things get out of control. It was all a fake thing on our part, it was always accompanied by strobe lighting and things, but I'm not really sure the message got through. We all piled into each other as though violence was actually taking place, but there was seven people doing this on stage and I was the only woman. So I was game as good as I got, but it was all mock fighting in our way, and that's why the whole thing is too much pressure.

One of the fondest memories was on the 2-tone tour when it was my birthday, and all the bands were singing "Happy Birthday," and our single was in the Top Ten at the time, "On My Radio." That was just so perfect. The Selecter was the only band I'd ever been in and suddenly it was just all happening, I'd only been in this band about two months and it took off just like that.

How far into the Selecter were you when you started doing major tours?

I think it was about six months in when we found ourselves in America. We were totally unprepared for anything like that, because it was just a completely different way of looking at music. We had gone out as the Specials, Madness, and Selecter on the 2-tone tour, and we were only charging three pounds for a gig for people to get in. In America it was all about how much product you had 'shifted,' and record people always coming down to the gigs for a meet-and-greet and a shake and all the rest of it. If you were nice to them, then they'd go out and really push your records in the shops. It just all seemed like pounds, shillings, and pence to us, (or, well, dollars, cents, and nickels to you). Do you know what I mean? It was just a completely different way of looking at the music business. I mean, it was an actual *business* way of looking at music, and we really hadn't come up against that until then. Maybe we should have done that, then we could have been a bit more savvy dealing with record companies. It was pretty strange.

Do you remember where you played, what cities?

Yeah, we started out in Seattle, came down the coast to Portland, Oregon. Then we came all the way down to San Francisco, then into Los Angeles, carried on down to San Diego. Then we went cross country over to New York, then we came back, flew back from New York to Los Angeles, and did about seven nights, two shows a night. Which was a new thing for us. At the Whisky a Go Go in Los Angeles they managed to paint the floor in black and white, which was really wonderful. We had the floor painted black and white as well in some club in Boston, so it was like the whole world going black and white at that time. It was a very strange tour; when we were mainly in the north it was fine, but our forays into the south, I mean New Orleans, we really didn't like that very much. It was still a little strange down there. I mean, we were a predominately black band and we had one white member, Neol Davies the guitarist. At the time, we had a blonde, white female tour manager, and when we were in the south, if we went into a truck stop or a restaurant, we could just stop the whole place dead for about fifteen minutes and nobody would come and serve us. But this was 1979! We knew that things would be a little more tricky down there, but we were a little unprepared for that. Do you remember that series *Dallas*? That hideous series was huge in Britain. A music journalist who wrote for a paper called *Sounds* flew out from Britain with a photographer to do a photo shoot with us, a piece on the Selecter, when we were playing Dallas. They decided to take us out to a Dallas ranch called Southfork Range to do a photo shoot. Of course we were all excited, and just thought it was funny and reckless, so we all piled out there. There we were, all on that lovely little white praline fence that they had. We had a bus driver named Romaine, we had one of those really whizzy tour buses, in fact it was Dolly Parton's tour bus. (Laughs) The thought of him taking out Dolly Parton, and there he was suddenly with us, which I think was bit of a shock for him. But business is business, as it were. While we were all sat—bear in mind this is six black folks sitting on their nice white wooden fence with our nice white guitarist—and this flatbed truck drew up with a little posse of what I can only think was the local racists, all armed with baseball bats. They all had a quiet word with our tour bus driver, who came over to us and said, "We better get out of here because they're not very happy about this," and that's exactly what we did. (Laughs) And this was in 1980! It was strange, a bit of a frisson for the whole thing.

You were successful with the band, but didn't you leave to do other work?

Well, yes, I left the Selecter. By that time, we'd gone through a line-up change. I wasn't over-enamored with the people that had come into the band. You know, it's all those things one cites: "musical differences," but I mean that was twenty-seven years ago. We were really silly probably that we didn't stay together. I left, then I had a solo deal with Chrysalis for awhile and I put out a couple singles. I also worked with Lynval Golding and Neville Staple out of the Specials, because they had left the Specials by that time and formed Fun Boy Three with Terry Hall. We recorded a single called "Pirates on the Airwaves," which is Pauline Black and Sunday Best. I was just doing things like that. Then I got into acting and I did a lot. Presenting, as well: I had a show called *Black on Black*, which ran for two series. I just tried my hand at anything, really.

What was Black on Black *exactly?*

It was like an art magazine program. It was just supposed to deal with black issues. If you can believe back at that time, there were no programs on the TV in Britain that catered to black folks at all or Indian/Pakistani people, so they formed two programs—they were sister programs—one was called *Black on Black* and the other was called *Asian Eye*. That would have been in 1984, because I came over to cover the Democratic Convention [in San Francisco]. Jesse Jackson looked as though he might be running for the nomination for the Democrats. So I got to follow Jessie Jackson around and got an interview with him at Atlanta airport. I met Coretta Scott King and interviewed her, which was actually in San Francisco, in the Transamerica building downtown. I spent about a week in SF, following those people around, interviewing Coretta Scott King, Mayor Marion Barry, and Jesse Jackson.

Do you have any particular memories of that trip?

Oh yeah, they were all brilliant. Though I remember being in Atlanta and Andrew Jackson, who was the mayor at the time, sort of took one look at me and said, "Oh my god, my daughter ought to take you to Neiman Marcus!" I think he just thought I looked a mess because I didn't have a weave in my hair and I didn't have the right makeup. He couldn't believe that anybody looking like me could be presenting a TV show. I thought I looked great! (Laughs) Well, it was just fun. It was like meeting all your childhood heroes from the Civil Rights movement. I had a whale of a time. Going to the church where Martin Luther King used to preach and meeting Reverend Ralph Abernathy, meeting all these kind of folk.

You returned to music and had other projects like the Ska Divas?

That was Rhoda Dakar from the Bodysnatchers, Jennie Bellestar of the Bellestars, and myself. Well, it was very short-lived, we did about three gigs with each other. I considered it slightly cabaret, and I really wasn't into that. I feel as though whatever I do, I need to feel that I'm actually saying something, rather than just singing greatest hits. This Ska Diva thing was very much geared towards that and I didn't really feel as though it was going to move too much away from that. Also, I'm a fairly solitary person, really. I mean, I know what I'm about. Sometimes I don't really understand what other people are about. It's probably better if I do my own shtick.

Would you talk about the Skavoovie tour and how that worked out?

When we first did Skavoovie, we went out to Japan, we were there with the Skatalites and Prince Buster, which was absolutely excellent. The Selecter also re-recorded "Madness" with Prince Buster, which was really great. He did gigs with us, and we did a gig with him in Florida in his hometown. Then we did Skavoovie in America in 1993. We went into Canada, too. That was with the Skatalites, when Rolando Alphonso and Tommy McCook were still alive. Also on that tour was the Special Beat, which was various members of the Specials and the English Beat, which was Ranking Roger and Neville Staple. I can't remember who else was there from the Beat. So that was the package, and we took it in turns to go on first or last. It was always really good fun, I think the most enjoyable thing certainly for the members of the Selecter was sharing a tour bus with the Skatalites. It was like all your greatest heroes come to life, hearing all their little arguments, their late night conversations, and what they watched on the video. It was just magical.

How was the Selecter's first audience here, as compared to England?

This would be about 1980. It was great; it was absolutely great. As long as you were in the major cities, it was comparable to anything in England. But as soon as you got into the Midwest, as it were, it was pretty strange. You were playing very small places, they had absolutely no idea who you were, and you probably went on after a wet t-shirt competition, with loads of guys standing around in big old cowboy hats. It was very strange.

What's ska originator Prince Buster like?

The thing with Prince Buster is he's a consummate businessman, and when you go to his house you get invited into his office and he's got a book (I know a lot of those business-types in the '80s were really into it) Sun Tzu's *The Art of War*. Which I think is quite strange on his bookshelf. (Laughs) I think he operates his business in that way. I think he spotted the whole energy of everything that surrounded the whole 2-tone movement. It's like all those bands wished to pay him the debt because we are indebted to him forever, writing songs like "Madness" or "Ten Commandments" or any of those, and starting the whole thing in the first place. He would come to our gigs and we would go to his gigs and play with him. So it was a good kind of way, everyone can learn from what has gone before, and likewise those who've gone before can also kind of see the new in what's going on at the time. It was a little bit like that.

Did he ever comment on your work?

No, not at all to me. But most of the time, whenever he saw me, he'd always ask me to make him a cup of tea with lemon and all that sort of stuff. (Laughs) My only note about that is, he never asked any of the men. Oh, it's kind of *old habits die hard, that's the old school way of being.* I think that women on the ska scene have been considered a bit of an anomaly.

It's okay if you're in an all-girl band because at least you're all together, that's just a little anomaly that's happening over there, it all gets tolerated, and the cuter you are, the better. But if you're actually *in* a band, it has to be looked at in a slightly different way. I feel that probably none of the musicians that I was ever around quite knew how to either understand what I would like to do or did, or quite what I was trying to say.

When playing with men, are you an equal yet held to a higher standard?

Yeah, I think it's a little like that. The other thing as well is that I certainly wasn't the only female fronting a band at the time; you've got Chrissie Hynde, and the Slits. I think that men did see all-female bands at the time—like the Bodysnatchers, the Bellestars, or the Go Go's—as novelty acts in that respect, but the Slits were something else, it was very hard for people to actually stick them as being a novelty act. Like Poly Styrene of X-ray Spex, she was around before I was. She got respect from the punk scene, she wrote her own thing, she had her own way of being. So she got respect, but it may have been grudging respect because, let's face it, the music business, particularly back at that time, was very much a male kind of province, so it was always going to be a bit of an uphill task. But that's life, isn't it?

What did the ska and reggae originators think about whites like the Clash playing their sound?

I thought it was good. All the best music comes from hybrids, it always comes from a particular type of people. I mean, the Clash were obviously white and into punk, but then they started listening to reggae. Really that came about because Bob Marley was over here and some of the reggae bands were in England and they were showing off their music doing shows. So the more conscious elements of the punk movement thought that reggae had a social and a political message to it, much the same as what their music was. They started experimenting with those kinds of forms and those drum patterns and those rhythmic patterns. Out of that of course comes new music, a new kind of hybrid music, and that was the Clash. I feel that all of 2-tone wouldn't have happened if the Clash hadn't been around and started off that embryonic process. I'm not privy to what Bob Marley and the Wailers themselves actually thought, but I think that was a really good time in music, that there was some sort of cross-fertilization process going on. There was still a vestige of politics in the minds of people who were making music. You still had something to be *against*. I tend to feel that has been rooted out of music a lot these days. There's always been an independent kind of music; there's always been an indie movement, an alternative music. The mainstream music has always been fairly conservative. We've never really been part of that mainstream, even though we were selling quite large numbers of records during that time. You wouldn't have actually called us mainstream; every now and again it's just that some of the alternative lot finds their way into the charts. Everyone goes, "God, how did that happen?"

Has your work had any lasting impact on society?

I think the most fundamental thing really is the whole organization, these little groups of Skinheads Against Racial Prejudice (SHARPs), from all over the world, from Venezuela all the way through Costa Rica, to Malaysia over to Japan, they are all there. They actually make a point of saying *we like this music, but we don't like any of the fascist connotations of it, and we may be skinheads but we just aren't into that kind of thing.* Now that is the most fundamental change, and if anything that has to do with 2-tone has brought that about in young people, their ideas and the fact that they just say that racism is just not on the agenda anymore, then 2-tone has done at least a bit of a job. Because the worst thing really that we face in life at the moment, to a large extent, is this whole idea of being able to oppress another nation, either because of the color of their skin or that they may have a different religion to us, whatever reason it may be. It's the young people we need to educate, so if young people are educating themselves in that way and we've done anything to make that [happen], then that's great.

Do you have one particular moment that makes you proud?

Well, I think one of the best things was after the Selecter had reformed, I remember doing a gig, and often you get people who come backstage, and often they might be skinheads. I remember one particular guy who came back and he had a lot of tattoos, and I'm always fascinated by tattoos. I just asked to see them, they were on his arms and things, [and] then I saw he had some on his back. So I said, can I see the ones on your back? He said "Oh, no, I can't show you those; I've got a swastika there." He was actually ashamed, but he obviously couldn't afford to do anything about it. He just turned around and said "Look, I was really young, I was really stupid. I'm absolutely ashamed of it and I'd get rid of it if I could." Now, for somebody to actually make that admission, I just think, well, he's grown up and he's thought about it. As young people you do make mistakes, but if he's still coming to our gigs then that's something positive.

You were involved in a union-related cause?

Oh, that was the Unison thing. That was a festival we did last year and they happened to be there. I think about the value of workers belonging to a union and not being split up. As people are these days, short-term contracts, they don't have any kind of feeling of unity between themselves. It's just, what you're given is what you get, and that just leads to all the rights that people have actually fought about over the years and shed blood over. Some people have died to actually form labor unions that have just steadily been eroded, particularly with this whole globalization thing that's going on now. That was just speaking out about that, that's pretty much the way I feel. If people do have the opportunity to join a union, then they should. Unions, I hasten to add, may be slightly different [in the US] than they are in England, so I'm not going to go there. There's another organization I've worked with called Love Music, Hate Racism, and that has lots of little cells or groups of people, not just here but in America as well, and I will always support and do gigs for them.

Did the press approach you with an agenda?

When I say people came with an agenda, I mean what they saw was an angry young black woman on stage who was going on about things, about the riots that had gone on, we're talking about 1980. There were riots in Miami and I was likening the riots in America to some of the riots going on here, we had some quite bad riots here in some of the ghetto areas in Liverpool and in Bristol. And obviously, if you stick your head above the parapet and write songs about that, which I did in a song called "Bristol and Miami," people are going to ask . Maybe I should have been a little more circumspect in what I said to people who wrote for newspapers or the music press, because sometimes people really twist your words and just say things that make you into some weird kind of militant that may be not quite what you were meaning.

How did the Trojan Song Books *project come about? Was it your idea?*

No, they came to us. It was Frank Lea, the managing director of Trojan Records, who came to us initially and said would we like to do some of the back catalog of Trojan Records. And of course we said yes, that was where a lot of our heroes were. So we did the first record, and that lead to three albums. For a lot of people, they really enjoyed us doing that, and it gave us an opportunity to do all kinds of songs which ordinarily we wouldn't have done. It was a lot of work, but it was a lot of very enjoyable and interesting work.

Tell me about the award for your performance as Billie Holiday in All or Nothing At All.

The stage play was written by Caryl Phillips; he's actually a novelist. A director, Nicolas Kent, who works at Tricycle Theatre here in London, collaborated with me. I won the Time Out Award, London for that role. Currently I've put the Selecter on hold for a while because I'm taking out a show called *The Very Best of Billie Holiday and Nina Simone.* We've started doing shows, and it's going very well. I've Pick with us, who was the drummer with Dire Straights, on drums, and a young keyboardist called Dominic Pipkin who played with Morcheeba. It's really good; they make up a trio who back me. It's split down the middle, a twenty-song set, half Nina Simone and half Billie Holiday. Also I inform people about Nina Simone and Billie Holiday's lives. At the time and the era they were in, the Civil Rights movement with Nina Simone and what preceded the Civil Rights movement with Billie Holiday, and maybe which led to her early demise with the drugs and the drink, just the general problems she had throughout her career were very much aligned to racism, so I'm trying to point those things out to people, but through song. That's the history of what this is, and it's like Billie Holiday really passed the bat on to Nina Simone, who to a large extent then passed the bat on to my generation.

Anything you'd like to say that we haven't mentioned?

It constantly amazes me that after all this time, which is going on over thirty years now, 2-tone actually still means so much to people, and the ideas behind it. That is very, very exciting. And it's like 2-tone is held in people's minds even more so than all the individual bands that held up that whole idea. As long as that idea carries on in people's minds, then they'll remember the music, which is really being against any ism: sexism, racism, whatever people think up to divide people.

Patricia Morrison, born 1962 in Los Angeles, started playing music in the mid-'70s when she was sixteen years old. She played bass and sang in many of Los Angeles' primary punk bands: the Bags in 1976, Femme Fatale, and Legal Weapon in 1981. During her time in the Bags, she caught the eye of Kim Fowley, which almost led to her playing bass for the Runaways, though she turned down the offer.

After the punk bands, Patricia gained notoriety by joining the Gun Club in 1982. The Gun Club, founded in 1980 by Jeffrey Lee Pierce and Kid Congo Powers, created a distinctive sound that was a mix of punk and blues, and released many live and sturdio albums, including *Las Vegas Story* (1984). Members of the Gun Club have been involved with other musical projects, including the Cramps, Bad Seeds, Jesus and Mary Chain, 45 Grave, and the Cult. Due to the Gun Club's popularity in the UK, the members moved there. Patricia subsequently left the Gun Club and, with Kid Congo and Murray Mitchell of Siouxsie and the Banshees, founded Fur Bible in 1985, releasing one EP. Patricia performed with the Ledge's Legendary Stardust Cowboy on his European tour in 1985.

In 1985, Andrew Eldritch asked Patricia for help during a turbulent time in his life with the Sisters of Mercy, which Andrew had temporarily reincarnated as the Sisters in the mid-'80s to resolve copyright issues after previous members had left, releasing one album, *The Gift*, in 1986. Patricia and Andrew reformed the Sisters of Mercy, and within two years, and released *Floodland* (1988), which included the hits "This Corrosion," "Lucretia My Reflection," and "Dominion." Patricia never performed live with the band, and she left in the early '90s to pursue a solo project, releasing the album *Reflect on This* (1994).

In 1996, Patricia was asked to step in for Paul Gray, who was recovering from an injury, to play with the punk rock group, the Damned. Soon after, she became a full-time member of the Damned. Patricia toured with the Damned regularly, and plays on the album *Grave Disorder* (2001). Patricia and Dave Vanian, lead singer of the Damned, were married in 1996. When Patricia gave birth in 2004 to their daughter, Emily, she decided to leave the band and devote herself to parenting.

What got you interested in becoming a musician? How did that develop?

I wanted to play guitar when I was around ten years old, but my mom was a single mom and worked, so I had no one to take me to lessons and I forgot about it. I always loved music and would buy albums whenever I could. Sometimes I bought them just by the cover. Roxy Music was one I found by the great covers they had. I always seemed to like the music that was a little bit out of the mainstream. I loved all the wonderful '60s songs that were played on KHJ, the big station in LA at the time: the Zombies, Turtles, the Monkees, Doors, and on and on. I bought my first single in... I think it was 1967. *Sugar, Sugar* by the Archies.

When did you first start playing? Did you sing first and then learn bass?

I didn't start playing till I was seventeen, I think. Two girlfriends and I decided we wanted to start a band. Alice wanted to be the front person and Margo could actually play a bit of guitar, so I turned to the bass. My first bass was from Save-On drugstore and cost $35. The intonation was out, so you had to tune it slightly out to be able to play it. I was an Irish step dancer, and we sang songs when we performed, between the dances, so I did sing, but I don't think that really counts! (Laughs) I was in church choirs as well, so I sang before playing an instrument, but not when I started playing bass. Never got the hang of singing and playing at the same time. I would forget to do one or the other.

How did you learn to play the bass?

We just decided to do it and we had some male friends in local bands who were horrified. A couple of them were kind enough to help us a bit, but it was more amusement than anything else. And looking back, a couple might have been hoping they'd 'get lucky.' When I started playing, there were no girls in bands except for singers and keyboard players. It was outrageous to think girls could have a rock band! There was a band called Fanny, who I saw in *Creem* magazine, and there was... her name escapes me... the woman who played on many a Motown track and who defined a lot of that sound, but all in all, women were scarce on the ground in the rock world. They were groupies who inspired and boosted morale for the guys rather than played instruments. There was Carole King and other wonderful female songwriters, but not really in the rock world that I was aware of at the time. I learned to play by copying the bass lines from

David Bowie, Queen, and Aerosmith. "Train Kept A-Rollin'" was the first song I learned. An old blues song. And bizarrely, from a Jeff Beck record I picked up secondhand.

Would you talk more about your first band?

Alice (who became Alice Bag) and Margo Reyes, who played in LA bands in the 1980s—we went to three different schools but had heard about each other as we were all very into Bowie and the glitter bands. I later found out many of the other punks had been into it as well. It was just the three of us. We heard Kim Fowley was looking for musicians for an all-girl band and we went to the audition. He rang me later and said he wanted me in the band but not the others. I got really irate and told him I wasn't going to leave them for him and his band. He was pretty slimy anyway, and although I regret many a decision I made regarding my music career, that was not one of them. He went on to invent the Runaways from that audition. We named ourselves Masque-Era, and Margo had business cards printed for us. So in our minds we had a band and were on our way to fame and fortune! She had just put 'Mick' for the drummer, as it sounded cool and British. We then had a couple of songs Margo had written. She had the most musical talent out of the three of us. We hooked up with a girl drummer who we had met at the Fowley auditions, and we did some rehearsals with her but it didn't work out. After going through quite a few drummers—including a Playboy bunny, who was wonderful but went off to Japan in her Bunny duties—we split up. I decided an all-girl band, just for the sake of it, didn't appeal to me any longer.

At the time, were you already immersed in the punk scene?

When punk started up in LA, Alice and I were at the legendary 'first punk' Weirdos/Germs gig at the Orpheum Theatre on Sunset Boulevard and started talking again after our failed venture into having a band consisting of all girls. We decided to try it again. Margo wasn't into the punk stuff, so it was just the two of us this time. We answered an ad in the *Recycler* from a drummer who was "into the Ramones and Mahavishu Orchestra." We knew he was the drummer for us. Joe Nanni joined Wall of Voodoo after being in the Bags. He said he knew of a guitarist who was willing to wear a bag over his head and was an accomplished musician. That was Geza X. That band was rounded off with a childhood friend of mine, Janet Koontz, on second guitar. The Bags were born and we played at the Masque and then the Whisky a Go Go on their afternoon punk gigs. The punk label scared a lot of people back then, so the Whisky tried it on for size at afternoon gigs instead of normal night ones. Our big gimmick was to wear bags on our heads so no one would know who we were. Well, they melted off in the heat at the first gig, and that was the end of that big idea. Also, we were shocked to see a photo of the Damned with bags on their heads for their single, "Neat Neat Neat." It was such a ridiculous idea and someone else was doing it too—how on earth was that possible? So we lost the bags and just wore our thrift store finery.

What was the punk scene like in LA compared to the UK?

In LA punks were colorful. Brightly-dyed hair and odd thrift store clothing. There were some kids who copied the English style, but it was a broad scene. There were arty bands, electronic bands, and a lot of real one-of-a-kinds. People have forgotten that punk was not one single sound.

England was a different world, and after hearing what it was really like from David, it couldn't have been further from the life we had in LA. The English punk scene was born out of real desperation and a sense of 'no future.' It wasn't an empty slogan. New York punk was black leather jackets and jeans and 'cool' you only found in NY: Ramones and the CBGBs bands. I loved them and Blondie. Debbie Harry was considered punk and I thought that was great, as she was not only talented but gorgeous, too. The San Francisco scene was very arty with the Mutants, Crime, and the Nuns.

What were you listening to then? Who were your peers, musically?

Just before punk, I was into Bowie, Queen, Sparks, Aerosmith, New York Dolls, Iggy and '60s music. When I heard the Ramones it changed my world. And then the Damned's first album was a big influence in Los Angeles. I remember when the Sex Pistols record came out we thought it sounded like a rock band, not much more. The content was confrontational but the music wasn't. The Damned and Ramones bit you. Lots of melody, but such energy as well.

Which instrument do you enjoy playing most?

I think of myself as a bass player. After doing it for thirty years, that would be my title, I think.

What was it like performing with the Gun Club?

I loved playing in the Gun Club. Loved the songs. We didn't consider it anything other than a blues-influenced pop group. They called us 'swamp rock' first. Then death rock, then goth. People would come on our van and expect to hear all this depressing, pretentious dark stuff, but would be more likely to get Led Zeppelin, the Beach Boys, or Culture Club.

Did the fans and critics see you as death rock or goth?

Our audience was pretty much into the music, and the interviews were always about the influences of the past on the music. Jeffrey was very well-read on seminal American musicians. That is what made the band successful... and destroyed it: Jeffrey Lee Pearce. It wasn't a band that copied trends, it created them.

How did the Gun Club work for you as a musician?

I am very proud of my recordings with the Gun Club. We worked very hard for years touring, and it was a wonderful experience, which I look back on with nothing but great memories. I learned to really play the bass while in that band. Experimentation was a good thing, and that made the music very edgy. You never knew what the gig would be like. I loved that. I would be bored still being in a group that plays every note exactly the same, like the recording, every night. That is why I also love playing with the Damned. It keeps you on your toes!

Do you have any particular sentimental memories from the Gun Club?

There are so many, but mostly just doing gigs where we went for it each and every night and you never knew what would happen. Sometimes there were riots. Once in Denmark I remember we hit one note and the audience went crazy. The sound system was knocked over and I looked down to find a guy licking my boot. And on the other side, some gigs we barely made it out alive, like the Billy Idol gig.

I remember playing Baton Rouge on Halloween and feeling very lonely and homesick. I'd not been in the band long, and the boys were picking on me. I didn't know how to fight back yet. I was sitting outside the van feeling sorry for myself when an outrageous blond girl dressed up as Mae West came up to me and we hit it off. I ended up that evening dancing the night away with people dressed up as Confederate soldiers, Frankenstein, etc., and having the time of my life. The stage bit was great but the best was before and after! It was always great fun to have people come over to the house or hotel before gigs and get ready, have drinks, etc. I have the best memories of my beautiful girlfriends getting all gussied up. Thinking back, all the bands I've been involved in had the 'anything might happen and usually does' factor. I've never been in a band where you play every song exactly the same every night. We did one tour that lasted nine months. I did it with one bag of clothes. Started in the deep South in summer and ended in Scandinavia in winter. One medium-sized bag. Beat that! It really was all about the music. And Bacardi.

Why did many early punks evolve into the '80s death rock scene?

I've no idea. I think it sort of split, and punk went very male and hard. Violence crept in. I went to a Black Flag gig and remember we had to hide under a car as a huge fight broke out. That sort of stuff didn't appeal to me, so I moved on. If you didn't want to go that way, you went a bit more foppish. People maybe wanted a bit more mystery and romance, as you say. Grew up a bit, added a lot more minor chords, and goth was born with varying results.

When your image changed from punk to death rock, what inspired you?

My friends and I always thought we looked Hollywood Glamorous. We bought big amazing dresses and ballgowns when we could find them, or '60s cocktail outfits with heels. My first finds came from my mother's closet. Boots and shoes from Frederick's of Hollywood. Fantastic old stock that had been sitting there for decades. If you look at old photos of me, besides being a bit better groomed later and with a better haircut, I'm pretty much the same. I always liked the same style. I never saw a change, went from thrift store buys to vintage shops as I could afford. In the Sisters I made my own clothes a lot, as there were very few shops for that style at the time, nor did I have the money. Hard to believe, eh? Today you find punk and goth shops in malls. Can't see that helping imagination and creativity. People always think of me in black, but there was a large part of the Sisters of Mercy where we both wore white.

There seems to be a huge difference between today's goth scene and the death rock of the '80s. Do you see differences between then and now?

I never knew it as death rock. I think I heard the term 'gothic' first. The friends I had just liked dressing in a dark, glamorous way. A bit threatening to those who liked Stevie Nicks' style and Farrah Fawcett hair. Also, being in Los Angeles, it was the opposite of what was considered beauty. And there was all that sun! Every day. All day. We did it all with a great sense of humor and joy for living. We were not depressed nor felt 'poor me,' and all the slogans you can now buy in the mall on the t-shirts you see on slouching kids with grumpy faces we would have worn with irony. We walked tall with a 'don't you dare mess with me!' look. There was no victim-feel to it, which I notice now. We had a riot! To me, it all turned around and bit itself on the ass with its sour attitude. Even while in the Damned I would see girls glare at me as I smiled at them. What's with that? Too cool, eh? Meanwhile, old ladies loved the look. They would say "It's great to see girls dressing up!" I loved that attitude.

Why are punk and goth now part of mainstream consumer marketing?

Everything that is a scene or a trend usually goes that way. Once Madonna does your style, it's over. The goth bands now seem very, very big rock band and corporate. I am jealous; they are all very, very rich. I do like AFI. They worked for their position in the world of goth; they didn't just appear in black clothes, fully formed.

How many bands were you in over your career?

The short-lived Masque Era. Then the Bags, Legal Weapon, Gun Club (with a short stint in Castration Squad), Fur Bible with Kid Congo, two guest tours with The Legendary Stardust Cowboy, the Sisters of Mercy, my own band, and the Damned. I think that's it. Looking back, I tended to be in bands for five years or so, but before I stopped to have my daughter I had been in the Damned for ten years.

Of them, which ones do you look back on with the most satisfaction?

Definitely the Gun Club and the Damned. I am so happy *Grave Disorder*, the album I did with the Damned, got such great reviews. I can take that one happily to my grave. The Gun Club was a very hard-working band and we toured for years, sometimes for nine months or even a year at a time. It was a different world. I'm very pleased I was part of the music scene as it was then. I saw the world that still had a foot in the past.

How was working with Andrew Eldritch in the Sisters of Mercy?

If I had to do it again, I wouldn't. I think anyone who has worked with that outfit would say the same. When I was fired I was told, "Patricia, your timing is shit and you are of no further use to me." I was famous at the time and had nowhere to live and no money. But I had very good friends, so I moved on with their help. Bands these days get lawyers before they write a song. I can understand that. Being ripped off is no fun.

Is this true that Andrew Eldritch and you were romantically involved?

My time in the Sisters was an extremely non-romantic time! But if you want Byronesque wistfulness, well, it was full of that. It was like being in exile and holding your breath for years, waiting for someone to come save you. No one came! I remember spending a Valentine's Day in Toronto doing a press trip. All the questions were about what Andrew had given me for Valentine's, and no matter how much we both said we were not together, it was not what they wanted to hear. We were not together and I was very lonely, which I guess is very gothic-novel in its own way.

Many of the popular songs from Floodland *were played in dance clubs. Did it differ in the UK as opposed to America?*

We both thought that was wonderful. The US audience was a lot wider. The UK audience had already been defined by the previous releases. A lot of them didn't want to share their band. The old "they've sold out" chant came out. Anything could have happened in the US, and nearly did, but the record company admitted they "let it get away" with "This Corrosion," and although on a trip to LA I heard "This Corrosion" on the radio every fifteen minutes, when I returned to the UK they told us it couldn't get airplay. I was jumping up and down and yelling during this meeting, as I knew they were liars. It was later admitted that they had missed the boat and wanted "Lucretia" to be the second single and would run with it. Andrew refused, as he had written "Dominion" and wanted that to be the single. And that, as they say, was the end of that.

How did working with the Legendary Stardust Cowboy come about?

I think Willem, our Dutch promoter, hooked us up with Ledge. The shows were bizarre. We had papier-mâché gophers, prairie dogs, and cactus on our amps, and Ledge was in full Western gear, with a trumpet to top it off. He had had a minor hit with "Paralyzed," which he did in the '60s on *Laugh In*. We did that and "Fly Me to the Moon," I recall. I have a video of it, and I'm pretty sure it's out there somewhere. We played the Clarendon in London and several others in the UK, but mostly we toured the Netherlands. Ledge was very popular there.

Do you realize today that you're an icon of a truly unique movement?

Yes, ha ha. Back in the day, there were a lot girls into the scene [that] looked like me or Siouxsie. I always get women coming up to me and saying I am why they started playing or wanted to be in a band. I always try to encourage them.

How did you meet Dave Vanian?

We met in San Francisco. It was love at first sight. No, more than that. We had fallen in love through pictures we had seen of each other, but thought that was impossible. It wasn't. My good friend Chichi, who I met when she was managing the Dead Kennedys, asked me to come up to San Francisco and we went to see the Damned at the Old Waldorf. When David and I met, we knew we were in trouble. I actually tried to sneak out, but the door I tried was locked. I was rattling it when David found me. I was in the Gun Club and we didn't meet again till I toured the UK a year or two later. Nothing had changed, but it took twelve years before we could be together.

What is life like married to one of the great punk musicians?

Not what people would expect, I think! We both love to garden, which confuses the Damned to no end. It is strange for him to go on tour and I stay home. Till I had Emily, we pretty much toured with the Damned a lot of the year, so we were never apart. Music is a big part of our lives, and I think Emily has inherited the love for it that we have. At her last birthday party she wanted "Wild Thing" playing for the pass-the-parcel game. As far as the rest, I cook, I do the laundry, I'm married!

Pretty much the same as other married couples I know. We just both wish we had been together earlier. Time is flying by and no vampire in sight to give us eternal life. Yet.

Will you talk about how you were married?

Certainly. Unfortunately my mother was ill at the time, so we flew from being on tour to LA to see her, and then off to Las Vegas for a few days. An Elvis dressed in a black jumpsuit married us, and there was no one else there but us. We then drove a pink Cadillac to see Tom Jones. When Elvis asked us how long we'd known each other and we answered "twelve years," he started singing, "It's Now or Never." The most Vegas wedding experience, but amazingly, it was very romantic. I remember walking through the casino and a woman coming up to me saying she had been married twenty-five years ago on that same day in Las Vegas, and she wished us as wonderful a marriage as she still had. Our good friend Chichi got us a suite at the Flamingo, Bugsy Segal's original, so that made it perfect.

What is performing with the Damned like for you?

At first I was just excited I was in one of my all-time favorite bands, and playing those wonderful songs. I didn't come down off cloud nine for a year or so. And for once in my life, the singer had a good behind to look at. Being behind the singers at most of the gigs, you notice things like that. I love listening to Captain play guitar. He is very underrated and David's voice is beautiful. Not something you get with many punk bands.

What is the most memorable part of your career?

There are many memorable bits. Usually mundane things, just the camaraderie of doing a good gig and being happy you are with those four or five musicians. Or being somewhere you never would have gotten to except by being in a band, and seeing something special or even having a good meal. First getting on a stage was something I will never forget, being so nervous but wanting to do it again and again.

Why are there so few women performers from that era who really made it?

Because we didn't turn into a sellable product. I have seen women artists that were very, very good, but they didn't look like they were supposed to, so got nowhere. Men can look like crap and do great. Not women, until lately. I've seen some very interesting body types and styles out there! Talent doesn't have to be in a Barbie Doll package.

Any specific memories from your career that you'd like to share?

The *Grave Disorder* album I did with the Damned. The Damned did a festival with Arthur Lee and Love, and the Electric Prunes, and it was what I would call a perfect gig. And the very first gig I did with the Bags at the Masque in LA. Just having the nerve to get up there and do it.

Any specific memories of contemporary bands you've worked with?

I have done gigs with all manner of bands supporting, or me supporting them. Back in the '80s, the Gun Club played with Billy Idol, who was a huge fan of the band. Jeffrey thought it was going to be great. The rest of us knew it would be a disaster. I actually taped it: 30,000 people yelling for our blood. The skinny tie brigade was very riled up by us. Not their cup of tea... scary but memorable. The Gun Club played with U2 in France on Easter Day. After the Sisters, when I was at a very bad low, I met Pop Will Eat Itself, who were wonderful friends and had me on *Top of the Pops* with them. I was thrilled when I got an email from Clint Mansell, who had been in that band, telling me he was up for a Golden Globe for a soundtrack he did.

How is settling down and raising a child?

If I'd had more success I might feel differently, but I look at the past as a great time where people paid me to go places that I'd never have seen without being in a band. I scraped along, supporting myself by playing music for nearly thirty years, which in my world is a pretty decent accomplishment, in hindsight. Having Emily has by far been the greatest adventure, and I love every moment of it. I feel I've had more than one life. The punk days were a very special time, and then moving to London and the gothic scene there, followed by meeting David and having Emily. I've been blessed.

NINA HAGEN

Nina Hagen, born Catharina Hagen on March 11, 1955, is a singer, songwriter, activist, producer, and actress from Berlin, Germany. Nina's vocal stylings cross many genres, including opera, punk, pop, reggae, disco, avant garde, metal, funk, and punk rock. As an activist for eco-awareness and animal/human rights, she's been called the Matron Saint of Mother Bearth, and has performed at many charity events promoting spiritual understanding, world peace, freedom, and unity.

As a one-woman revolution and 'multidimensional intergalactic muse,' she spreads her gospel of sexuality, cosmic awareness, compassion, joy, and love through the world with her work. The daughter of Eva Marie Hagen, an opera singer, and Hans Hagen, she was raised during her formative years by her stepfather, Wolf Biermann, an anti-establishment protester and singer/songwriter. She left school at sixteen and starting performing in bands including Automobil and Fritzens Dampferband. Her family left Germany in 1976, and Nina spent the next year in England's punk scene—befriending bands like the Slits and the Sex Pistols. In 1977, Nina formed the Nina Hagen Band back in Germany. Their first album, released in 1978, contained covers of "V Glotzer," the Tubes' "White Punks on Dope," and "Gott Im Himmel." *Ubehagen* was released in 1978, and both albums went gold in Germany.

As a solo artist, she released *NunSexMonkRock* (1982) and toured with the No Problem Orchestra. She then released *Angstlos* (1983), released in English as *Fearless* (1984). *In Ekstase* came out in 1985, (in English: *In Ekstasy)*, which included "Universal Radio," and covers of "Spirit in the Sky," and "My Way." Over the next twenty years, she released an additional twelve albums, including *Om Namah Shivay*, an album of thirteen traditional Hindu songs, which Nina did for charity in 1999. She also released many singles and live albums, as well as collaborative recordings with Lene Lovich, Marc Almond, and KMFDM, among other musicians.

A documentary by Peter Sempel, *Nina Hagen: Punk and Glory*, was released in 2003. Nina Hagen's memoir, *That's Why the Lady is a Punk* (2003) has been released in Germany.

What was baby Nina like?

I was the baby of Eva Maria and Hans Hagen. Mom is seventy now, Papa died eleven years ago. My mom finally escaped, and lived through the fascist era and the wartimes during her childhood. Her father died in the war. She grew up with Mother Agnes, Sister Ingrid, and Brother Günther, who got run over by a train when he was only a little boy. He was my mom's best friend. Both legs had to be amputated. Eva became a *maschinenschlosser* and aspired to become an actress.

Papa Hans was twelve years older than Eva, and his childhood/teens where during the onset of fascism in Germany. He was the son of a German mother and a Jewish father, had five other sisters and brothers. Hans was an anti-fascist, and working also in the underground resistance. He got captured by the Nazis and put in jail, with extremely bad treatment, even abuse; *folter*. Grandfather Hermann and Grandmother Hedwig died in Sachsenhausen Concentration Camp. All his brothers and sisters made it to safety. Hans and Eva met in the Presse Café in East Berlin in May 1954. They got engaged right away, because I was hovering above them since quite a while, and I was extremely excited by the possibility of becoming Nina Hagen! Then, I was born to be me, even before I discovered the sound of the typewriter my dad Hans was working on all the time. He was a film scriptwriter. He was busy writing a very successful film, a comedy about the people in Germany right after the war: the anti-fascists, socialists, and communists. The Russian Zone became the GDR, German Democratic Republic, and the rest of the zones became the BRD, Bundesrepublik Deutschland, also called Westdeutschland. So Mom and Dad were in the East German communist part. Very interesting for baby Nina!!

There also always was Tante Trudchen. She is as dear as my mother and father to me! God knows where she found my dad, she was his and mom's housekeeper and my nanny. Gertraud Reichel was her name. I spent most of the time with her and her people, then I was a lot at Mom's girlfriends' families in the countryside, and had friends all over. But Hans and Eva got divorced. I was only three. *Schnief.* No more father, he got kicked out. I once, around 1974, recorded a song about this divorce—thing called, *ähm*, "Mama es ist Papa," or something like that.

Anyways, I became the best East Berlin City Roller the world has ever seen! I rollerskated to visit my dad every day! I escaped and ran away, into the little church on the corner. I had a great childhood: Mom's TV and theater rehearsals, singing, guitar playing. One day, when I was nine,

Mom introduced her new man: Wolf Biermann, East Germany's public enemy number one. He was and is a fabulous singer and songwriter philosopher. He became my fabulous teenage-time stepdad, and a great one! Still, I was faithful to my dad. Because of my dad I learned to trust and be friends with other women. There I have learned true sisterhood! When women trust, love, and respect each other, each has her place at the lion's heart, and they know how to share. It's important to learn to be honest and outspoken about what you want to happen in your life or not!

Then I was twenty-six: Cosma is born, twenty-seven, twenty-eight, twenty-nine, thirty, thirty-one, thirty-two, thirty-three, thirty-four: Otis is born. Soon we go to India again and again and again. At forty-seven I met my love, Lucas Alexander. My life at forty-eight, I become his wife. I'll be forty-nine soon.

When did you first start singing?

I am alto, but in my youth I was mezzo and soprano also, I am still everything. I just try to give each song what he wants, it's with love and happiness and ecstasy! I always recorded music from the radio and sang along. Also my mom had many records. I was an autodidact, so to speak, sang along to Tina Turner, Janis, Aretha, Mahalia, Lotte L, Hildegard Knef, Marlene Dietrich, Judy Garland, Trudy, the Stones, Otis Redding, James Brown, the Beatles, Bob Dylan, Joan Baez. I became a sponge, I even imitated different voices, like the one of [French singer] Mireille Mathieu. One day my mom entered the room and said, "Oh god, Nina, you do have an ugly voice, please don't become a singer, ever." But I was in my teens and I hated her guts at that time, she was so off the roof. I guess every girl has that happening at one point with mommy dearest. I did go to an entertainment-school when I was eighteen, for one year. Became a professional singer, also had classical singing lessons.

Of all your performances, which ones were most memorable?

I am so happy and focused on what I am doing now, I mean my life everyday, that it becomes like a task to try to hammer something memorable into myself. So many great new projects are in the works that going down memory lane feels lame. I remember everything. When I was pregnant with sweet baby Cosma, one day I started feeling the morning sickness, it became noon, afternoon, evening, twenty-four hours a day, sickness. I was never so skinny like in the first three months. While in that phase I was on stage a lot. It is my passion to sing. So I went into a children's toyshop and bought a nurse-station, with syringes and all that medical jazz. I took it on stage, it calmed my "vomitness" to be able to actually give myself a fix of anti-vomit cocktail with a plastic syringe and rubber around my upper arm. Still I had to run off and vomit once during a song. Pregnant women become motherships, it's a whole bio-chemical neuro-energetic transient express experience! I stopped feeling sick right before I saw a UFO in Malibu, when I was four months into the pregnancy. I let it be. Hail Mary.

Are you still seeking God?

You are God, we are God, I am God. Having a human experience once again, why do you think Christ let Himself be nailed to the cross? Because that's what we do with ourselves and each other, every freaking single day! Not recognizing God, not recognizing each other.

What is XIXAX?

The three question marks. The 3 Xs mean question marks, but also sexuality. "XIXAX" I call the place where one is born, it's another name for "somewhere on planet earth." It brings along the three Xs and the two vowels, I and A. Three questions: 1. Who am I? 2. Where am I? 3. Why am I? I stands for you and I, the self, the individual, and A stands for all. So we all have the same questions. What is my source (who am I), where do I come from (where am I), where do I go to (why am I).

With your kaleidoscopic, psychedelic, explosive image that seems to constantly change from day to day, what goes into this creative process?

It's so simple, you won't believe it. I look the way I look because I look the way I look. It took what it took, but then I ended up with that look.

You have such a childlike playfulness, and seem deeply happy. Have you always been this way or is this something you've worked at over the years?

I have found God, but I am still human. I am not at all so cool minded at all times as you want to think, I promise you. But I am like the frog under the water waiting for the ice to melt. Partially amphibic.

Is a sense of humor, which you possess, one of the truest paths to nirvana?

When you experience it then you'll know that I am experienced. Jimi Hendrix once asked me that question, "Hey little girl, over there behind the Berlin Wall, are you experienced?" And I found *it*, the day I found God, when I had to die. I was nineteen, in East Berlin, during my first LSD trip. I had the ultra, on-the-spot religious experience! I have met God, talked to him all night. I can feel him ever since, always, at happy and sad times. Let it be. *Om namah Shivay.*

How many 'teachers' do you currently work with? Solely with Muniraji?

Muniraji is a very special friend and teacher. Always. But also my husband, my daughter, my son, everything!

How many religions did you practice before finding Hinduism?

Who told you that? I cling to no isms!! I believe in following the religion of your heart, and my religion has no name, it has only love, beautiful music, words, teachings, great work, and friendship and happiness and embracements. My religion is called Embrace-ism today!

For those who may not be familiar with Shiva Nights, *will you describe it?*

I do this show a lot, always have, always will. Sometimes by myself, sometimes with MotiMa and Ganga or our friends from Ibiza, who do Namaste Parties. It's one of the very best devotional music in the universe. Of course, I also love gospel, but traditional music from the Himalayas, from Mother India, is very high. Also reggae is sky high. Such amazingly beautiful rhythms and melodies, lyrics and instruments.

What prompted you to do the film Om Gottes Willen?

My inner-visionary teleprompter! It tries to document Babaji's great message from the Himalayas, which is also my message: fighting for humanity, for human rights, environment rights, living in love truth and simplicity, happy and free, creating a world where lion and goat may drink from the same well, the same source.

Your film Punk and Glory *played here in San Francisco a few years ago. What was that process like, having your documentary made?*

It was okay. He is a funny fellow, that independent filmmaker colleague, Peter Sempel, who wanted to make a film with and about me so bad!

Will you talk about your book That's Why the Lady is a Punk?

The book is just a book. It looks into my life a bit with photos, stories, all sorts of stuff I move on. You must understand, that one cannot nail my life into a book.

During your career, is there anyone you feel blessed to have worked with?

I treasure every joint venture I took! Working with Apocalyptica was amazing. Let's see what will happen.

What would you most like to be remembered for?

You must always remember not to forget me. Me and my life is just another amazing human experience on Planet Earth, AKA Planet Bearth, birth, breath, life, and death. We will all see each other's true faces, later on, anyways.

Back in the punk days, were you a vocal trainer to younger female punks?

I wasn't a vocal trainer. I was a slightly enormously experienced and talented singer myself, and I just gave Ari-up from the Slits some girlfriend tips of how not to become too hoarse, how to train the voice in different ways.

Will you talk about your experience having children?

The wish and longing to be Mother, and have a baby. So much that I stopped my doll's pram every other moment, strolling my favorite children—the dolls—through the street. We also played father, mother, child a lot. I slept with my dolls in one bed. I talked to them, held up a school class for them, I had a chalkboard. I also criticized them for having bad or wrong answers in class. That longing for a wonderchild to materialize with my help was strong, growing stronger. Both my children are my wonderchildren! I have become a really, really happy being with them and because of them! I urge everyone to follow their hearts in becoming a mother and father! Becoming a mother means everything. Only if by chance a child won't materialize, then so be it. Good luck with and in receiving the wonderchildren!

Do you have any particular moments with Otis or Cosma Shiva that made you most proud?

It's a big list. So big, that it doesn't fit into infinity anymore! Just see them one fine day for yourself. Then you might understand this humble but very proud mama!

What are your future plans with your career?

I have no plans, just the things I'm constantly working on and being creatively busy with. I only do the work. I plan to work.

Do you have a personal mantra or maxim you live by?

Om namah shivay.

And lastly, what would utopia or heaven on earth be like for you?

True at last! And you?

Jarboe, born in New Orleans, is a singer, composer, and performance artist who began performing in Swans in 1986. Formed in 1982, Swans was known for their heavy, slow, brutally dark music and extremely loud performances. After 1986, the core members were Jarboe and Michael Gira. Jarboe is a singer who expresses herself in great vulnerability. Her vocal stylings fluctuate in extremes from an almost evangelical celebration of prayer to mournful sounds of sorrow and vitriolic rage.

Jarboe provided vocals on Swans' albums *Holy Money* (1986), *Children of God* (1987), *Burning World* (1989), *White Light from the Mouth of Infinity* (1991), *Love of Life* (1992), *Great Annihilator* (1995), *Soundtracks for the Blind* (1996), and *Swans are Dead* (1998), a collection of live recordings. Jarboe and Michael's side project, World of Skin, released work from 1987 to 1988. Michael left the band to form the collaboration Angels of Light, and Jarboe began focusing on her solo career.

Jarboe's first solo recording was *Thirteen Masks* (1991), followed by *Beautiful People Ltd.* (1993), *Sacrificial Cake* (1995), *Anhedoniac* (1998), *Disburden Disciple* (2000), *Dissected* (2000), *Process* (2004), and *A Mystery of Faith*, a compilation of unreleased Swans and World of Skin material. *Anhedoniac* (1998) was dedicated to Jarboe's breakup with Michael Gira. Some of her later work has been collaborating and touring with the band Neurosis, resulting in the album *Neurosis and Jarboe* (2003).

Her recordings total more than eighty albums, and she tours extensively. Her collaborators have included Chris Connelly, Blixa Bargeld, Alan Sparhawk, Iva Davies, Bill Laswell, Jim Thirwell, Lustmord, Pan Sonick, Mark Spybey, Steve Severin, Larry Seven, and Larry Southern. She has also collaborated with visual artists and filmmakers including Richard Kern, Beth B., Wim Van De Hulst, and Laura Levine.

Jarboe currently aspires to continue to build a very intimate relationship with her audience whether it's via her music, her stage presence, or the regularly updated journal on her website, TheLivingJarboe.com. Jarboe released a spoken word album entitled *The End* (2006), with music by Cedric Victor. *The End* is an awareness and fundraising project for Amnesty International.

How did your involvement in Swans come about?

I joined because Swans was music in an elemental and primal form. It was pure. I felt a powerful pull towards this form. I moved to NYC in 1984 to join Swans. The band was a spiritual journey to me. It took me deeply into and out of myself. It was transcendent. I contributed instrumental melodies, arrangements, sounds, and harmonies. I fine-honed vocal parts, vocal melodies, and often guided the parts that contributing musicians played in recordings, and also guided Michael's vocal performances. There was the muse factor as well, which was considerable. I believe my input was a vital one.

The progression was a natural one based on the skills of the various members of the band. I was coming from a place as a singer/songwriter-trained musician with an art background, so I brought those elements.

Being in Swans has informed everything I do in music. I consider Swans my school—my formal education.

How did this change over time?

As time went by, my own vocal and performance style developed to fit my internal development as a performer, and a woman. I developed a sense of command and nuance and discipline all my own.

What fueled the musical creation during Swans? Was it emotional, sexual, intellectual, spiritual?

It was and is all of those things. I use my body in my work and I am a visceral performer. At the heart of my work is a funneling of intense emotion. My newest work is a spiritual path. The recent shows involved an evolution of mantras for contemporary times. This concept will continue, as it is, where I am now—as a conduit. An example of this approach would be "Seizure" on the *Neurosis and Jarboe* album, or my *Process* CD.

What are some of your fondest memories of Michael Gira?

The answer can't be put into mere words. I don't experience work other than from a place within solid alignment. MG and I worked together intimately and it is impossible to separate the work from the relationship even today because of that tremendous power. His influence over my entire approach to music is vast, and I believe it is mutual.

What are some other collaborations that you've worked on?

I did a collaborative CD called *Blackmouth* years ago, which I now see as a type of artistic preface for the more recent and established *Neurosis and Jarboe* CD.

How do you decide which musicians are best suited for touring?

I have never stagnated in my musical explorations. I like to be stretched and challenged and excited by the musicians with whom I work.

Do you feel your American audience differs from your European one?

Yes, in some ways. In parts of Europe there are venues and audiences that welcome the frontier.

If you were a conduit to anything, what would it be?

In my work, I have channeled the longing of human beings, and the wrath of Kali.

What was your concept behind your sculptures, as with The Heart Box? *If you could keep fewer than five objects of value, what would they be?*

I have made fetish boxes since 1984. I was a visual installation artist before I joined Swans. Objects sacred to me would include photographs of my mother, and Bartholomew, my teddy bear, and my black pickup truck.

What do you consider the most significant events of your past?

Significant events of my past include: moving to NYC, joining Swans, world travel, Buddhist studies, and realizing what performance is all about for me.

What does 'realizing what performance is all about' mean to you?

It is to be a conduit. It is to be in service to others for the benefit of others.

Who or what inspired your music, both with Swans and your solo work?

Life is my inspiration: meditating, running, being awake to consciousness.

Do you ever feel "too vulnerable" with your music?

Not at all. I have always embraced vulnerability: "It's actually a strength to be willing to be vulnerable...," a line from "Under Will," from my CD *Anedoniac*.

How is vulnerability a strength for you?

To be truly strong, a performer/artist must enter into extreme vulnerability. A way of doing this is through an open heart and meditation, and through letting down personal barriers. If you embrace vulnerability, you emerge fearless from staring your fear in the face. The more open you are in your work as a performer/artist, the more strength you gather.

How do you handle your public accessibility, in terms of the online journal and discussion board?

I have never had a problem by being accessible that I could not resolve through patience and understanding and an open heart.

What is the most fulfilling way to spend your leisure time?

Leisure time is rare for me. I have dinner parties. I go to art gallery openings and carefully selected concerts.

How did growing up in the South affect who you are today as an artist?

Growing up in New Orleans and Atlanta, and traveling around the South, had a huge impact on my work. The street performers in New Orleans and the Mardi Gras costumes... and the utter eccentricity of the many characters I observed as a child, all informed what I do today.

Does your audience understand your music?

I dialogue with my audience from time to time, and I receive letters. I just finished my CD *The Conduit,* which included a collaboration with my mailing list (they contributed names and phrases that were meaningful to them). The thing about what I do is that my attitude is not one that concerns itself with what may be traditional considerations in the music business. I took Bodhisattva vows in 1992 from the Dalai Lama, with the intent to be an embodiment in my actions of compassionate nature for the benefit of all mankind for the rest of my life. I see my music and performance as channeling the emotions and suffering of the audience, and so I see myself as in service to others with my work. This is not the typical music business attitude, as you know, and it does carry over into my non-musical endeavors. There is really no separation between me and my work. So this means that I love unconditionally and do my best to be helpful when I can. It puts me at odds with some folks because they see me as being a martyr. I am not a martyr per se. I am simply doing what I believe to be "right action."

Will you be working with any new media or forums?

There's a digital download album available from TheLivingJarboe. com. After *The Conduit* CD is released, *The Men Album* CD is to be released. I am adding live drums to the song "Steve Von Till," played on *Feral,* and will make his guitars loud. I am going to give this song the full treatment, as it were. It also features Blixa Bargeld on vocals and Paz Lenchantin on bass and Nic Le Ban on guitar in duet with Blixa. After these two albums are out, along with the four albums Atavistic just released... I am in a position to go to Europe to tour.

I am doing a week-long tour of the East Coast with Amber Asylum and Unto Ashes this May. I am going to perform my set with a woman pianist and soprano named Renee Nelson.

What type of environment or atmosphere do you work best in?

Any atmosphere. Any environment. I adapt. I prefer live venues like cathedrals and art spaces and theatres. I prefer creating at home late at night.

Who are some of your contemporaries, musically?

Michael Gira, Nick Cave, Diamanda Galás, Einsterzende Neubauten, Neurosis, Meshuggah, Tricky, Lydia Lunch, Amber Asylum, Jim Thirlwell,

Tool, A Perfect Circle, Slipknot, Maria Callas, Black Metal, Nic Le Ban, Lustmord, Metallica, Janis Joplin.

What was your most profound, cathartic moment on stage or recording?

For me, every performance is *momentum profundus*. Yet it isn't cathartic for me per se. Rather than self-centeredness as a basis, it is more accurately... one of channeling.

What song has had the greatest effect at provoking the emotive in you?

I channel emotions through the songs, and every song has within it its own specific emotional basis. I move through the tapestry of the songs.

Have you ever become emotional on stage?

Always. In every moment... it is channeled and directed energy.

Have you ever felt out of control or frightened by what you created— something that you didn't truly understand?

In order to channel energy, one's ego identity leaves. One is simply a vehicle. There is nothing to understand per se, as it is outside the intellectualizations of ego.

How do you see yourself mirrored in your audience?

We mirror each other. I mirror in the nature of channeling. One experiences what one wants to see in the mirror.

How would you like to be perceived?

If I could actually direct a preference towards what others perceive of me, it would be that of simply doing work with sincere and honest intent.

If you could sum up the following words with sentences and quotations from your songs to reiterate your expression, what would they be?

In review, I could make this particular list huge. But, off the top of my head, so to speak:

Fear: "Still is the water green and thick, he'll drag you under with his stick, see flaxen gold floats there through the mist, he killed someone's daughter with his wick. An arm with grey skin bobs slowly in the pit." —*Troll Lullaby*

Terror: "We are the wild. We are the risk. Come little yum yab, come slash your wrist." —*Yum Yab*

Love: "I was smoldering.. then you breathed deep." —*Lavender*

"Oh lover I wept and you laughed like always. Just like a beast." —*Dear 666*

Beauty: "For beauty is free, beauty cannot be tamed." —*Beauty's Punishment*

Growth: "The malignancy grows with fibrous insistence as the body wastes and rots." —*Forever*

Sickness: "Come and give me what I need—insidious with cruelty—come and give me what I need—come fill your cup with a vile disease—come and give me what I need—come to your drink." —*Anhedoniac*

Spirit: "Blessed are piss and shit. Come now, anoint." —*I'm A Killer*

Divinity: "She is an expression of their nameless hunger. She is an expression of both good and evil. She's become the mother of their nameless hunger." —*The Believers*

"Disease remission. Divine intervention. I've been busy making my effigy." —*Forever*

Anima: "And every time she sang for them, they worshipped her." —*Everything For Maria (For Callas)*

Hatred: "Come in, infuse my hate" —*I'm A Killer*

Philanthropy: "Take pity please, Lord Misery, how shiny your throne as you view the stage. Oh Majesty, you flatter see, before you o' this our humble play." —*A Man Of Hate*, Act III

Intellect: "Open your mind... anything at all, but not logical." —*Not Logical*

Prosperity: "And what do I do with the gift you present to me? The one no one else would buy?" —*Sinner*

Death: "My heart stopped on the way. I felt life draining." —*I'm A Killer*

Sex: "We reap the fruit we're calling the vultures a terrible joy transmit—HER." —*Ode To V.*

TERESA TAYLOR BUTTHOLE SURFERS

Teresa Taylor AKA Teresa Nervosa, born in Arlington Texas in 1962, was the drummer of the outrageous post-punk band, Butthole Surfers. Teresa performed with the band from 1983 until 1989. The band effectively combined heavy psychedelic sound with elements of punk rock, shock, avant garde, experimental, and metal. Butthole Surfers was formed in Texas in 1981 by deviant genius pranksters Gibby Haynes and Paul Leary, and included drummers Teresa Nervosa and King Coffey, as well as several bass players over the years, including Kramer, Andrew Weiss, and Jeff Pinkus. Both Teresa and King Coffey played stand-up kits at shows.

The shows were famous for a circus-like atmosphere with slide shows, naked dancers, props, fire, bullhorns, and strobe lights. Their videos, music, and live shows were meant to overwhelm the senses, to disturb and alter the reality of those who witnessed them in an attempt to share their psychedelic mindset with the audience. The band lived like a cult, with Gibby as leader, in which everything they did was for the band, and often under the influence of LSD and alcohol. They lived on the road for two-thirds of their career.

At one of their first shows, they caught the eye of Dead Kennedys frontman and Alternative Tentacles Records founder, Jello Biafra. He released their first EP, *Brown Reason to Live* (1983). Over the next 10 years, they released 10 more albums including *Rembrandt Pussy Horse* (1986), *Locust Abortion Technician* (1987), *Hairway to Steven* (1988), and *Pioughd* (1991).

Teresa has also been in a few films, most notably Richard Linklater's cult classic *Slacker* (1991), in which she played a character selling Madonna's pap smear. She also appeared in an 8mm film short *Bar B Que* in 1988, directed by Alex Winter. *Bar B Que* was a farcical, BS acid-laden version of, supposedly, the *Texas Chainsaw Massacre*.

Teresa found out after leaving the band that she truly had suffered for her art: she developed a seizure disorder from the constant exposure to strobe lights. She later suffered from a near-fatal aneurism, from which she has fortunately recovered. In recent years, she has toured North America and Europe with the reunited Butthole Surfers.

Were you in other bands before playing with Butthole Surfers?

Well, I was in school band.

Marching band?

Yeah. All I did at first was play in school, but then I really didn't think about it making any connection to anything. It was like, because you were a girl, you didn't think of having any future in it. It wasn't like you imagined that you would be in an all-girl band. It just didn't cross your mind. As a young girl, once I got bored with it in school, I dropped it, and then it seemed to have no relevance in life.

Did you have any lessons as far as the standard drum kit?

I took lessons starting from the time I was ten years old, but they were lessons to learn rudiments on the snare. I never took any lessons to learn a kit, and I still to this day have trouble on a standard kit. I wish I could play a killer standard kit and play it well.

What were you doing after that?

I was playing in a band called Meat Joy with Gretchen Philips, who was later in a lesbian band called Two Nice Girls From Austin. Meat Joy was real 'experimental'—no one could really play.

Did you record anything?

Yeah, there's one album, and I sang one song on it real badly. I have a terrible singing voice—I can't sing. I have a song on it called "Party Time is Over." It was a spontaneous moment when I thought if I drank a lot of alcohol and sang into a microphone, maybe, just maybe, I'd turn into Patti Smith. But it really didn't happen for me. (Laughs)

Gretchen and I moved into a warehouse in downtown Austin. It was occupied by a band called the Buffalo Gals—a trio. They were great, just great. Gretchen and I really liked them. They lived in this warehouse downtown. We moved in, and for a period of time, Gretchen and I were in the Buffalo Gals. I stood in and played different percussion instruments. In this really great warehouse, I paid $40 a month rent, and Hüsker Dü played in the living room, which at the time was a big deal, totally packed our little warehouse. We had killer punk rock shows there.

How did you meet Paul Leary and Gibby Haynes?

All the Buffalo Gals and Meat Joy members worked at a cool restaurant. Paul and Gibby got jobs there when they moved to town, dishwashing at Pecan Street Café. Later we called it Peecorn Street Café. They had this loft above the kitchen where you could climb up this little ladder and smoke weed. All the employees smoked weed up there and it just constantly reeked.

Paul and Gibby were in college in San Antonio. They had started the Butthole Surfers, the two of them, before King [Coffey] had joined. Some other members went out to the West Coast with them, and that's where they met Jello Biafra and got the deal with Alternative Tentacles. They came back to San Antonio but wanted to move to Austin, which was a cooler music town. They came to Austin and asked if they could practice at our warehouse. So it just worked out.

At that time they were looking for a drummer—they got King. It was kinda cool because I already thought they were huge rock stars since they had met Jello Biafra. I figured if you met Jello Biafra, you really made it. I was about twenty years old, and Gibby and Paul were about six years older than me. They were coming out of college and I was just a few years out of high school. So we were goofing around at the warehouse. I remember Gibby was hanging out, playing one of the Buffalo Gals' guitars. I sat down to Jamie's [the Buffalo Gals drummer, Jamie Spidle] drum kit, and started playing a little bit, doing stupid little rolls. Gibby was playing guitar, and I didn't think anything of it—things like that happened all the time in those days.

Spontaneous stuff?

Yeah. Well, really, it was my dream come true. My ship came in when all of a sudden, out of the blue, Gibby said, "Do you want to play second drums with us and go to California?" I was like, "Hell yeah" in a second, in a heartbeat. I had gotten really into punk rock, but I hadn't gotten into the idea of playing. I said that I would go to California. I had nothing going on, that was what I wanted to do, but I had one hang-up. I had been busted for a small amount of marijuana when I was just barely eighteen, and I was on probation. I would have graduated high school but I dropped out. It would have been about '81 or '82.

What was your first show with the Butthole Surfers like?

I'll tell you exactly how it went down. It all happened real suddenly. They're very serious guys in some ways, as far as the way they treated the band at the time. I felt like I had to step up my game, and it was necessary. Chris Gates of the Big Boys in Austin (with Biscuit) let us stay at their house. They had a garage in the back where we drank Schaefer beer and just jammed while Chris was on tour. We practiced really hard, day after day. They taught me every song. It was like a *Rocky* movie of getting me into shape. Right now we would have a montage of me playing the drums and figuring out a way of setting up our drum kit. King was already standing up by himself, but it was not as full without a kick drum. That's when we first realized that King and I kind of look alike, and we started to tell everyone we were brother and sister. We're not really brother and sister. That was the lore for a long time. We got it all together and we booked a show at Club Foot in Austin and that was my big debut, I guess, with the Dicks. Immediately we got in the van and just left our whole lives behind. I didn't keep a residence. I just took off and totally blew off probation and everything. We got in a van and headed for Phoenix for my first out-of-state show.

How was the band booking shows at the time? Was there an album out?

Right in the beginning, there was this guy named Bob O'Neil who had this studio in San Antonio called Boss Studios. Now this guy, I don't mind saying, he was like a buffoon of a guy. He had this gazillion dollar studio he didn't know what to do with, and for some reason he was allowing us to sleep on the floor all night. We had to kill time in the day while other people booked hours. Then at night we could record and sleep on the floor, so we basically lived there and recorded the *Brown Reason to Live* EP and the *Rembrandt Pussyhorse* LP. And we were taking tons of LSD and we were just melting into that studio. See, there was a lot of dual genius going on: Gibby was really good with finances—he was a Certified Public Accountant with a business degree and all of that. He could book shows really well, he could get money really well, and organize and finance really well. Paul could just take over in a studio, like it came naturally to him. So we had all this high dollar equipment this guy wasn't really using, we took tons of LSD and just burned vinyl like crazy. Then it was time to promote our vinyl. The first record was on Alternative Tentacles, that's when we hit the road. Those *Rembrandt Pussyhorse* recordings would come out later on Touch and Go.

First it was just *Brown Reason to Live*, and that was on Alternative Tentacles. We went to California. We had these tapes put to the side from the San Antonio sessions, but we only had one record out. We went to San Francisco and we lived in the beer vats, which was where they had once made beer in these giant brewery things [*the beer vats were at the abandoned Hamm's Brewery, 1550 Bryant St., SF - ed.*]. It seemed like some industrial post-nuclear set. The doorways of the rooms were like portals, I don't know how to describe them, like on a submarine. In Texas I had never dreamed of such a thing.

Wasn't it claustrophobic in there?

There were a lot of things about the Butthole Surfers that were claustrophobic, and you just learned to live with it. That time we traveled in a packed van with a dog—five people and a dog. But later we would travel in a Chevy Nova, and me and King would lay down in the trunk. So the beer vats seemed like a relief from that, to keep it in perspective. The beer vats were inhabited by punk rock squatters and we totally just dug that whole scene. There were lots of musicians in bands there, people had their equipment set up. People offered us their little area to set up our equipment and practice. Everywhere we went, we always practiced a lot. In those days, there were periods of time where we would stay in a town and we'd be practicing, and Gibby would be booking a show for the next place to go. And trying to stay afloat in the meantime.

It was a real exciting time, my dream come true. We went straight to Jello Biafra's house and stayed there for a couple of nights. We played all these clubs in the early '80s: the Mabuhay, the Stone, the On Broadway, a few others. We took a lot of acid... man, did we have some good times. I think at the Strand Theatre, Gibby and I had windowpane acid—clear LSD. We were in the women's bathroom, which was very ornate. Right as I took my hit of LSD, he dropped his on the floor. I thought, "Oh no, we have to find it, 'cause I don't want to be the only one tripping." So we had to crawl around on the floor and find this hit of clear LSD. It was like looking for a contact lens, and people were coming in and out. And Gibby's like 6'6". So we're in there, crawling around, looking for a hit of LSD. But he finally found it and took it. We tripped and watched Andy Warhol's *Trash*.

We come out and the whole city is all color, we're thinking *we don't know anyone here*, completely new experience. Here we are in San Francisco and a block down the street we run into Gary Floyd from the Dicks. We ended up spending the entire evening going around the whole city. We did the whole trip of going to Haight Ashbury and soaking up the idea that a lot of people had gone through a lot of psychedelic experiences in that particular area. There was sort of a feeling of trying to carry that on. Later I sort of felt guilty that we had been proponents of it, so many people had lost their minds on cocaine, methamphetamine, or heroin. But I have to admit, there were elements of the LSD phase before any of those other drugs entered the picture where we did a lot of laughing and we really had a good time.

Did you guys ever encounter bad trips? Was that ever part of the music?

We drank a whole lot of alcohol. Everybody had their moments of breaking down, so I can't really say that anybody had more of an inclination than anybody else. I just want to say, I was as guilty as anyone else of having moments where you just totally lost your shit. Where you had too much alcohol and too much LSD and wigged out a little bit. (Laughs) But no one more than any other.

We were still trying to maintain as far as Gibby booking shows and Paul recording us in the studio. We were trying constantly to practice, play, record, book shows, and travel on. We went to LA, and that was all good. That first round in LA, we stayed with Carrie Faber from Goldenvoice Productions. We then wound our way around to Detroit, and that's when we met Corey Rusk from Touch and Go. Really great guy, nice guy. He wanted to put out the record. Back in those days, everything the Butthole Surfers ever did was just on a handshake. I never signed anything. Well, after I left the band, the Butthole Surfers signed with Capitol. Up until that point, nothing was ever signed with anybody about anything. Not even the members of the band unto one another. Nothing was in writing.

How much were you roughing it? Was money just not a concern at all?

It was a constant stressor, a constant concern. We didn't know how we would make it from one town to the next. But there was sort of like this drive that was weirder than being in a rock band, it was like being in a carnival that just had to move on. By somehow performing some stupid act, if we could get out there and do our little show, like you would in a carnival, and get our payments, we could move on to the next town, then figure out how to do something again. But it was very hand to mouth. I don't know how we were doing it. Gibby was booking shows, people at the shows would ask us if we needed a place to stay and we would go to their house. There seemed to be these pockets of punk rocker communities in every city across the country at that time. If you just went to a town and asked where the punk rock club was, you could go in and book your show, network.

Was there a time when things were too much?

I had to go to the hospital in Canada for food poisoning. A club in Toronto gave us this delicious meal of uncooked chicken. Then we went right on stage. The minute I went on stage I started hurling, and hurling uncontrollably. Every now and then I would stand up and I would play the drums for a little bit, then I would go back down and throw up, then stand back up, play the drums, then throw up. This went on and on. Then it was time to go to the hospital. The bill at the time was $30. Go socialist health care!

There were all kinds of things. One time Gibby got cut when we were in Vancouver. We were excited because Emilio Estevez was in the crowd (laughs) and we were backstage taking mushrooms. We offered Emilio Estevez mushrooms and he said no thanks, but the buddy that he was with wanted some. We were also drinking. You know, the alcohol can really be a factor. We went on stage, the strobe lights started flashing, the smoke machines started going, the movies started going, and everything was very chaotic. We started to go into the very first song, and the next thing you know Gibby's arm started bleeding. So he went to the hospital to get a couple of stitches. Pinkus and Paul were fighting real heavily that particular night, just real alcohol-fueled. I got real irritated and threw my drums out into the crowd. We never saw Emilio Estevez again. (Laughs)

Is it true that Gibby used to take out guns and shoot at the crowd?

Yeah, we used to do stuff like that all the time, we had all kinds of stunts we did. We knew this girl named Michiko Sakai, her father had been a WWII fighting ace, very famous man. She was real important in the early Butthole Surfer's history. We did this song called "Cowboy Bob," and she's screaming on it. So the first time we went to New York City she came with us, with a toy machine gun. She jumped on stage and started shooting at the crowd. So we had this petite Japanese girl with a machine gun on stage during that one particular song, it was her cue to do that. But we had trouble at the Austin airport with the plastic machine gun—even way back then. We had done California and Detroit, so we came home and started getting the tapes together for Touch and Go Records. Then we did that first show in New York. New York was very important. That was really exciting too, because everything was like different plateaus of thinking that I was cool. Like the plateau of meeting Jello Biafra and definitely playing New York City. We played Danceteria, after that we played it many times. It was totally fun.

Did you have any casualties in the audience, where somebody just completely flipped and you had to stop playing?

We didn't stop playing, but we did hear about someone having a seizure that wasn't me. (Laughs) People would come up to us though and say things like, "How dare you show something so disturbing!" These were *fans*. One incident I remember was a dear old friend of ours, she thought we took a turn for the worst with the car wreck movies. We used real highway traffic fatality educational films. We got these films through a catalogue. It was weird: we would drive to a guy's house in California and he had a garage full of 16mm educational films. Gibby had ordered them over the telephone. Another time, we were at this house in Austin called 1401, (we have a song called "1401" based on the address of that house), and we saw the industrial farm traumatic penis injury film. I was up in this loft we built, suspended over the living room. We turned on the projector and it was really bad. I could stand it being a woman ... I was like, "What?" The other guys were like, *"Oh my god! Oh my god!"*

Were there any opening bands at that time?

We played a lot of shows opening for Sonic Youth. We were labelmates on Blast First. The problem playing with Sonic Youth was that we were so loud and often had a lot of food coloring, beer spilling, things happening, and chaos, smoke machines, strobe lights, dancers, films, and all of that going on that they usually didn't want to follow us. We always left a big mess and the crowd was all gross. It was confusing because they were always the bigger band that sold more records, but there were actually times when Sonic Youth opened for the Butthole Surfers because they didn't want to deal with that. It was always a strange thing.

Did you play a lot of European shows?

Oh yeah, lots. France was the only place we didn't play. We had taken New York by storm, it was kind of going through a dull phase, there was nothing going on, this was still early '80s. On our first trip to London, we took acid as soon as we hit ground. Actually, Paul took acid on the plane and we all ate it in the parking lot of Heathrow airport just upon landing. I thought that we had made fools of ourselves and it was going to be terrible press. We did these interviews with *NME, Melody Maker,* and all these great music magazines I had grown up reading. I thought that all this press that we did right away—the first three days in London was all press—I thought the debauchery and our behavior was going to be really bad for us. We just loved the beer there tremendously, too, which didn't help. I thought, "Oh no, here goes our whole career in the toilet," because we had been so bad in these interviews, doing these sessions in these pubs, lots of beer intake.

As it turned out, that was the best thing we could have done. I don't know about the shows as much as the rumors that started about our behavior. But they were like, "Don't worry about it, everything is cool." I said, "I don't know, guys, I think it's all over for us." There were a lot of times where I misjudged what was going on and Paul, Gibby, and King said, "No, just be cool, everything's cool." I'd still say, "I don't know." Then, sure enough, we got all these splashed big articles. What would have been small reviews of our first shows abroad turned out to be big splashy articles claiming we just ate LSD like candy, and it started this legend. It turned to be the best thing we could have done, it was sort of just right off the bat.

There are some filmed interviews that were so hysterical...

Back in the day, Gibby had a flow, sort of a stream of consciousness. He was really good at that, just amazing. The big thing that he did all the time was come up with band names. He was so outrageous, I'm not even going to repeat any of them.

How did anyone know when to take him seriously?

Well, he could switch into businessman mode. When it was time to take care of business, he was serious.

Did you have a cult following yet?

Well, we had one follower. It sounds like something out of a Tenacious D movie, but it actually happened to us. We had this one girl who came to all of our shows. She got a used van and started following us on the road, and she would have homemade t-shirts of the band. She was really wonderful. Well, I'm afraid we kind of neglected her and didn't pay much attention to her. She jumped off her mom's building and killed herself. Then her mom, who was on a lot of medication, came down to Austin and wanted to meet the Butthole Surfers. So we were like, oh no, we had to meet her mom. I don't know what we were thinking, taking this real classy lady from New York City to this sleazy biker bar in Austin. We bought her a pitcher of beer. She said, "I just wanted to meet you guys because my daughter loved your band." She said, "Here's the last picture of us taken together." She passed it around the table and it was a picture of her daughter in this homemade Butthole shirt and a dog collar. Her and her mom together. We were like ... bummer.

You know, there were times that I remember when things were real shiny and new and everything was going our way. There was a period of time where everything started to transition from being very bright and light and funny to not being funny at all, and things started to get very dark. It wasn't because anyone was on too much acid, it's just because of things that happened. And people said they saw it in the band, and our performances started getting darker and darker.

What period was this? After which album?

I really liked the album *Hairway to Steven*, but I remember us being in a lot of turmoil. It just seemed like everybody was really unhappy. It was after that album that I quit. I did take a big break in the middle.

What happened when you took the break?

For six years I didn't live anywhere. For six years I was just a Butthole Surfer. That meant we ate every meal together. Gibby controlled all the money. We just ate, slept, and thought about being in the Butthole Surfers. So when I say we were living here and there, that's how it was. For six years we were traveling. For a while, we were living in Atlanta in the club the Metro. I was sleeping on the stage, sleeping on the drum riser. I woke up and there was a rat right in front of my face. That's when I got on the telephone and said, "Mom and Dad, can you send me a plane ticket home?" I quit. That's when I decided I wanted to get a video camera. So I was just out of the band for a little while, and then Gibby called and wanted me to come back. I wanted to come back, I wanted him to ask me to come back, so that was all mutual. And when I returned, I had worked at a restaurant and saved up the money to get a video camera, and started documenting being on the road. Those are the tapes I'm just now putting onto DVD that have never been released. I think I'm going to release them now. I think I'm going to turn them over to Latino Bugger Veil Records.

What about the move to Georgia? Didn't you move to Athens?

In about '84. We were watching *Man with the Top Hat*, the movie we saw in Seattle while we were tripping and inspired. The flags in the movie flew in all different directions, they had a miniature U.N. and the flags flew to represent turmoil in the world. Based on that movie, when we were on LSD, we looked at a map and decided to move to Athens, Georgia. We tried to think of where to move to and we thought the funniest place was to move to where REM was from. Of course, the B-52s are from there, too—they're a great band—but it was all about REM. We went to Winterville, Georgia, and we rented a house for six months. We had this old workhorse tape recorder 8-track and that's where we recorded some songs. But basically the joke at the time was that people took so much note of Michael Stipe that he couldn't flush the toilet without the whole town knowing about it. People lived and breathed Michael Stipe.

Didn't you guys terrorize him?

Yeah, we moved to Athens just to terrorize him. We spray-painted on the side of a van—Athens is a tiny town, so we parked it at a real prominent spot—and it said: "Michael Stipe, despite the hype, we still want to suck your big long pipe."

So this was a joke, right? Did you think they sucked?

No, we like REM, they were okay. No, we don't hate them. I think we were jealous.

A lot of people thought they were brilliant.

No, we didn't think they were brilliant. We covered "This One Goes Out to the One I Love." It's recorded on the *Double Live* LP. At shows when we played the song, Gibby would turn my cymbal upside down and put rubbing alcohol in it and light it on fire, hit it with a stick and make flames shoot up. When he got to the part where he goes "Fire..." he would do that. So he would exaggerate other lines in it like, "Another *prop*, to occupy my time." I mean, just imagine "This one goes out to the one I love... fire, fire, fire." (Laughs)

When you were putting songs together, were they impromptu or planned?

Gibby never wrote down anything. He never sang during practice, mostly to save his voice. The band would be mostly Paul coming up with a guitar riff and everybody else coming in, making up a part. Then we'd make up a song and sometimes we wouldn't know for a long time what they'd be called. Like songs for a long time wouldn't have titles. Like the song "Cherub" was called "Dur Dur Dur" for about a year. We wrote down "Dur" on the set list at shows because we couldn't come up with the title. The first word is "cherub" so the title became "Cherub." For a long time we might practice a song without having a title or lyrics, and then go into the studio. That's when we might have been tripping and manipulating tapes and equipment, and that's when they would lay the vocals down. It would usually be a big surprise what Gibby had in mind all along for the vocals.

And with the sound effects?

Well, the stuff that's guitar and taped studio manipulation is Paul, and the stuff that's vocal, the megaphone and later echoplex deal, those things were Gibby. So the combination of the two made a lot of noise, you kinda couldn't tell what was what.

When you first started out, did you feel comfortable with all these guys?

Well, that's a multi-spectrum answer. I've been asked many times how does it feel to be a girl in a band. It's like how does it feel to be anything.

As a female, how did you relate to these guys that were, at times, sexist?

The deal with me is that I didn't have any brothers growing up. I felt empowered by having this sort of big strong gang that was kind of aggressive everywhere I went. I felt like I could go anywhere—I could go to New York, I could go to Europe—not that I couldn't get to those places as a woman, but as a young girl in my twenties, I felt like I was on top of the world because I felt really safe.

So you were an equal to them?

In different areas—in finances, in the studio, and in making major decisions for the band—no, I wasn't equal. But the problem is I was in the band, and I played the drums, and it's hard to say that I was part of the creative process. Financially, the reason we never had good success in regards to money and breaking it down was because Paul and Gibby were more the leaders of the band. But the more thought I've given that, there's nothing wrong with that. There's nothing wrong with the leaders of the band getting paid more.

There used to be no money, and it's hard to imagine that no money is a blessing, but when there was no money, there was nothing to fight over. We all had just enough to eat, and just enough to make it. But when there started to be more money, it was like, "Well, how do we divide it up?" The problem was that Gibby and Paul would say, "Well, we do more." And I would say, "Well, then pay yourselves more," and they would say, "Well, how much more?" I'd say, "Well, I don't know." I still don't know.

I will say that I had a lot of resentment for a while about money, but I no longer have any of that resentment because they sent me money recently and everything's cool. See, I never got into it for that, I really swear I wasn't ever. In fact, it was a problem when things started to get more affluent. We launched more into a phase of snorting coke, we had our own home, and a recording studio in the house we bought in Driftwood. It seems like the more stuff we got, and the more upscale we had everything, the less the creativity came. That seems to be the story for a lot of people. Then we started having resentment towards one another about the money, and where's the money going, who's got the money. I got caught up in that. To this day I regret it. Probably the biggest regret in my life is quitting the band as early as I did. I would have kept going longer if I had it to do over again. Things got a little out of hand there. Then there was the transition later from cocaine to heroin. I really don't think I would have survived that round of it. I had to get out.

What was the sexual dynamic like? Were there any awkward moments?

No, it wasn't like that in those days. It was like a carnival family on a mission.

Gibby once had sex onstage with Kathleen, the nude dancer?

Yeah, that was when I had quit and was saving up to buy my video camera. It was in Austin. What happened was I quit for a little while and this crazy girl from Atlanta named Cabbage played drums, she was sort of a stand-in. Kathleen was traveling with them. I had quit and they were here in Austin and I felt too weird to go to the show. Then I heard that Gibby had totally fucked Kathleen on stage. Nobody got busted for it. Things were usually real chaotic between the strobes and the movies. It was hard to see what was really going on. That was the time when some people actually saw penetration on stage though but I wasn't there for it. To me, Kathleen was like a performance artist. She didn't seem that sexy to me, not sexual. She seemed more like a 'movement artist'. People are surprised that we kept things pretty clean... as far as in the RV. (Laughs)

There were times when we pulled over, like on Mount Rainier, and threw away Paul's gym socks. It was all snowy and beautiful on the mountain peak. We pulled over and tossed those things, they had to go. Then there were times when we had to tell Kathleen she had to bathe. Kathleen would save things like lobster claws, tucked away in her laundry. We had to catch her. After a few days, we were like, "Damn, what is that?"

Oh, and everybody in the band got scabies from a mattress Paul got. So it got into the RV we were traveling in. We all had to take scabies medicine at the same time. We had do everything at the same time, where you do the upholstery, clothing, linens, and medicine to wipe it all out or it won't go away. It was an accident. We were touring real scuzzy then. (Laughs)

Kathleen had this approach to life that even parasites deserved a fighting chance. We had to hold her down to put the medication on her. She said, "No, no, they can live with me!" We said, "No, no, they can't, Kathleen!"

Butthole Surfers are often credited for influencing the grunge movement. Do you agree with that?

Well, I've seen that whole interview with Kurt Cobain. He said, "We were all pretty much into the Buttholes."

Didn't he meet Courtney Love at one of your shows?

I think maybe. She owes us money. (Laughs) During her brief career as rock promoter in Minneapolis, she put together this show that was a great idea. It was all these great bands from Minneapolis opening up for the Butthole Surfers in this giant theater that held way more people than the entire Minneapolis punk rock scene had. Like the whole scene had about one hundred people, and this was like a thousand-seat venue. We played. It was a great show. The next day, she was like, "But I don't have any money. I swear when I get my royalty check from *Sid and Nancy,* I'll pay you guys."

What were you listening to? Who were the band's influences?

It was a lot different. I really had a thing for girl bands or girls in bands. So I listened to a lot of Slits, Marine Girls, Raincoats, Kleenex, the Au Pairs. When I joined the band, I still tried keeping up with girl bands.

Well, I loved Frightwig and they opened for us a bunch of times. Later, I loved the Luna Chicks. They were really cool. They opened for us on my very last show, when I had a total fit and breakdown. And I felt bad about it because I felt embarrassed that not only was I freaking out and breaking down during what I would come to know later was my last show, I did it all in front of the Luna Chicks. They witnessed it all.

The Butthole Surfers' influences were... well, Paul listened to Black Sabbath. We're playing these songs where Paul is coming out with these guitar parts where he's like, "Play this on the drums..." Then we start playing these shows and it's noisy and people are like, "Children of the Grave!" And you're like, "What? No, that's *our* song ..." Now I listen to Black Sabbath and there's three different songs where I'm like, "We used to play that!" (Laughs)

We called one song "Dumb Dumb"—it was the sister song to "Dur Dur." There was "Sweat Loaf," that was "Sweet Leaf." Oh, but we called it "Children of the Corn." It would be cool if it was a Black Sabbath song, (singing) "Children of the Corn."

What was Gibby listening to?

He had this great cassette we'd listen to all the time that was all this '60s psychedelic American music. That particular tape had Creedence doing "Suzie Q," it had "I'm Your Pusherman," and "Crimson and Clover," stuff like that. I mean, he was a little bit older than the punk rock kids that were into the Dead Kennedys. He was a little bit more influenced by the '60s than the punk rock kids. I also found out that they used to say we sounded like Captain Beefheart. Since then, I've listened to Captain Beefheart and I'm like, "Man, we sounded like we were trying to be just like them."

When you finally left the band, was that related to the seizures?

We were in a recording studio and we were sitting on tall bar stools and I toppled over from my stool. Later, when they put strobe lights on me, they said that I have seizures having been around too many strobe lights.

Diamanda Galás was going to do Donna Summer's "I Feel Love" with us. We were getting ready to mix it but she was doing it all gothic, medieval, operatic, (sings melodramatically) *I feel looove, I feel loooove, I feel looove.* Then she found out that Donna Summer had said those things about gay men and AIDS, and withdrew from the whole project.

At the same time, I was friends with Sandra Bernhard, and Paul had recorded this kickass version of "Barracuda" by Heart, and he took a DAT machine out to LA, and she was able to record her vocals there. He brought them back to Austin and synched them up with what we had recorded and her vocals just *suuuucked.* They just sucked. I thought the Buttholes did good backing tracks. We ourselves had to squash the project with Sandra Bernhard. I guess Paul still has the master tapes from that, but it was just atrocious. That was about '85. We were doing lots of stuff, collaborations, we were giving people songs to be on compilation records. That was the big thing at the time, was to be on compilations, but you gave them throwaway songs.

What happened with your aneurism?

I had to have brain surgery. It was about three years after I left the band. I was told I was born with it and it could have happened at any time. It's strange to live with that.

DEANNA ASHLEY FRIGHTWIG

Deanna Ashley, born in Bakersfield, California on September 9, 1958 was a founding member of Frightwig, an all-female punk band from San Francisco. Firmly rooted in the '70s punk scene, founders Deanna Ashley and Mia Levin starting playing together in 1981. Frightwig also included Cecilia Lynch. On their first East Coast tour in 1984, Susan Miller joined the band. Rebecca Tucker joined the band when Mia left in 1986.

Frightwig often played San Francisco's venues, including the Mabuhay Gardens. In 1984, prior to releasing any album, Frightwig toured the East Coast with the Butthole Surfers. Frightwig toured throughout the US and Europe during the '80s, playing their final national tour in 1989.

Frightwig's first album, *Cat Farm Faboo*, was released in 1984. Their second album, with Eric Drew Feldman (Captain Beefheart, Snakefinger, and P.J. Harvey) on keyboards, *Faster Frightwig, Kill! Kill!* (1986), was a humorous reference to Russ Meyer's film *Faster Pussycat, Kill! Kill!* They reunited in 1990 and released the EP *Phonesexy*, produced by the McDonald brothers of Redd Kross. Their most widely known album, the compilation *Wild Women Never Die* (1995), is a cult classic. Many riot grrrl bands credit Frightwig as an influence, from L7 and Bikini Kill to Bratmobile and Babes in Toyland. Frightwig became the voice of female punk lost in a sea of testosterone, shining a ray of hope that girl power was possible, with songs like "My Crotch Does Not Say Go," "Hot Papa," and "Vagabondage."

By the early '90s, only Deanna Ashley and Rebecca Tucker remained from the early lineup. In 1994, Frightwig regrouped with Deanna, Mia and Bambi Nonymous, and toured Switzerland together. Kurt Cobain wore their shirt on Nirvana's *MTV Unplugged* in 1993. In 2002, Frightwig reunited for their twentieth anniversary tour with Mia, Deanna, and Cecilia. From 2002 to 2006 Deanna and friends performed for fun as the band Greywig, playing country music. Other Frightwig members have been in numerous musical projects, like Caroliner Rainbow, MudWimmin, and Fabulous Disaster. From 1994 to 1999, Deanna formed No AB Booking and booked punk and electronica bands nationally. Susan Miller became a professor of Women's Studies and Rebecca Tucker has become a costume designer.

Frightwig were a staple in early punk rock history: "Wild women never die, they just dye their hair!"

What were you doing with your life before starting the band Frightwig?

I was going to punk rock shows at the Mabuhay on Broadway. I started going to the Mab club in 1977 when I was eighteen years old. I spent my formative years there. I did a stint at the Holiday Inn on Van Ness, trying to play it straight. I ended up having a mental breakdown and being hospitalized. I realized in the San Francisco General psych ward, life is fucked up, and playing the game in middle-of-the-road society is crazy. I decided that I could play music and be in a band. I played the violin since I was in the first grade. So out of insanity came my passion. I followed that, went back to Fremont to my parents' house and got my shit together. I came back to San Francisco and started to sing in a couple of bands, like the Ghouls, which was a really interesting project. I started Frightwig with Mia in 1981. We couldn't play at all, I couldn't play bass and she couldn't play guitar, we just started practicing. Her boyfriend was Bruno, AKA Steve Demartis. Bruno played in Sluglords. But he would tell us how shitty we were. Our thing was to drink alcohol because it always sounded better. (Laughs) We would sit there and beat on our guitars and sing dirgy songs. But my thing then was to go to shows. I was so involved in the music scene and it was such a scene, it was so great, such a cool time.

What shows did you attend at the time?

My favorite punk band was the Nuns. I really loved Alejandro Escovedo, he was so cute and he was really nice. Jennifer wasn't very nice though; they were kind of snotty. I liked a lot of bands, like Crime, then came the whole Dead Kennedys thing and DOA. I was booking a club on Turk Street, Club 181. We booked this 1982 hardcore show and we had a lot of bands, and DOA came down from Canada. The big thing was to have it All Ages. 181 was a bar, so we had to sneak the teenagers in. We had killer shows. That's how I met DOA. They took us to Europe the first time. We played with DOA and Sonic Youth in 1985, that was a lot of fun.

How did you first start playing your instruments?

Well, I had played violin and violin notes are the same as the bass guitar, so that was a pretty easy transition. We couldn't read music. Those skills became kind of buried. Mia had played music, so she was self-taught. We were in the music scene and all these guys were playing. We watched them, and thought it's not that hard. I didn't like playing guitar; I thought it was too hard. But then as the years went on I realized the guitar would have been much easier than playing bass, in terms of energy put out. But I loved playing bass; I think it's from all the years of playing violin. Cecilia was raised playing piano; she was always taking classes and learning. Susan Miller was raised playing music; she came from a musical family. She was brilliant. Rebecca was excellent also, I mean she came from a musical family too, played extremely well, but played a different style from Mia or Susan, so we went through all these kind of weird transformations. I'd say more than half of us were educated. Then I'd say a couple of us, Mia and I, just kind of slammed it out. But I think that was one of the things that made our music unique.

How was Frightwig formed?

Mia and I met while working at a movie theatre on Market Street, at the Electric Theatre when it was a rep house. All of the employees played in bands, so it was a little hotbed of music. She was sixteen and I was about twenty-three. We just started playing. I got this really crappy bass from someone. She had a guitar from Steve Demartis and we just started playing at their warehouse. We would play every day. We had our sad songs, our tales of woe. That's how it started. Then we started looking for a drummer. We had a drummer named Tana who had a little speed problem, so we had to fire her finally. She didn't want to play a show, like she would practice, and when we had our first show and were trying to move our equipment, she says: "I can't play, I won't play." So we're like, "You are fired!" Then we played with Rachel, who played in Mudwimmin. That was a lot of fun. Rachel's great, she had this song "Cow for You" which was so hot and sleazy, it's really a fun song. But Rachel didn't want to move her equipment and was always late to shows. Cecilia was coming around and moving Rachel's drums, just right there, the eager beaver. She was this six-foot-tall blonde, so hot. After a show that Rachel was hardly there for, we moved her equipment and then told her that we're going to play with Cecilia. Then Cecilia, Mia, and I formed a pretty tight unit. That was almost the best time for Frightwig. We were offered a lot of shows because we were a novelty act, really, being an all-female band. We were well-known in the scene too, Cecilia was the girlfriend of the drummer from MDC and we knew a lot of music people.

We had a lot of support from male bands like Snakefinger, they were great to us, and DOA always treated us with the utmost respect. And Black Flag—Chuck Duchowski and I were good friends, and SST booked some of our tours. They were great because they could get night after night shows for us. I didn't care if it was a café, but you had a show going across the country. I can remember him saying, "Okay, here's the itinerary, this city, this city, it's going to be eighteen hours to get to the next city. Do you think you can do it?" I said, "Is it humanly possible?" We loved to play night after night. We met a lot of great people on tour. We did several national tours, in 1983, '84, '85. In New York City we kind of became the toast of the town, with Courtney Love dragging along, making me go into nightclubs and saying we're on the list when we weren't on the list, and her screaming at me to go up and tell them, "I'm in Frightwig, let us in right now." I'm like, "Fuck you, I'm going home."

Cecilia, myself, and Mia, that was the best. Then when we were in NY the first summer, Susan Miller had moved to the East Coast and Bruce Loose from Flipper had moved. That was after one of Flipper's first big bust ups. So Susan and Bruce were living down on 3rd Avenue, on the Hell's Angels' block on the Lower East Side. They were in a basement apartment, and we came and stayed. The Hell's Angels were really nice to us. I wanted Susan to be in the band to make the sound bigger because it was pretty harsh with just a three piece. She joined and added this beautiful dimension; we were so great at that point, in '84. She left NY and came to the West Coast with us. We had a lot of things going on, we were offered a tour to Europe, our first album [was] out, *Cat Farm Faboo*, the first full-color album that Subterranean did. I remember talking to Steve Tupper and saying, "I feel strongly about this!" [the color]. So he said, "Well, okay then."

So Susan's with us, it's all going great. We're getting ready to record our second album and Mia gets married in Reno after one of our shows in 1984. They spend their wedding night in the back of the van between the equipment, riding back because they didn't want to stay in Reno. We go to New York and we're getting ready to go to Europe. It's four months away, and Mia tells me she's gonna quit after we get back from Europe and that on the tour in Europe, she and Bosco are going to be on a motorcycle behind us. Mia and I were so close. We love each other, we're like sisters, and she left me for him. I told her if that's the case then you can just leave now because it will be too hard in Europe. So she left the band and we were leaving the next night to play down in Atlanta with Sonic Youth. We had been invited down because we played two months before and had this huge riot with skinheads out front of the club, so we got all this press.

When we came back to the West Coast after Europe, it was Susan, Cecilia, and myself. Our friend in Celebrity Skin, Tim, had this friend, Rebecca Tucker from Montreal, and she was quite different than Mia and I. We wore '50s dresses and work boots or cowboy boots (or fabulous costumes!) and Rebecca was like this metal woman with thigh-high boots and black eyeliner, always made up, she was really hot. Rebecca is so brilliant; she made a lot Frightwig t-shirts. She brought a lot of creativity and art to the band. It really kind of changed our sound, but she was following Susan's lead at that point. We had finished recording our album, produced by Eric Drew Feldman—he played with Captain Beefheart and later Snakefinger, then solo'd and played with P.J. Harvey for years, he's well respected. So we take off on this tour with Rebecca, Susan, Cecilia, and myself, and Frightwig was still pretty good at this time, but there wasn't the passion that Mia and I had because we would fight before shows and then put on these brilliant shows, with our white-hot anger, like *arr, I'll outplay you!* Because maybe I missed a note the night before. We had this intense chemistry. So then we were on tour and Susan was sleeping all the time, and she's not wanting to drink but she's wanting to eat a lot. We find out she's pregnant, so she leaves the band, our album's out and we're back to a three piece. Then Cecilia quit in 1986, so it's just me and Rebecca. We keep on playing, we record *Phonesexy* with Lynn Perko, which was a piece of crap in my opinion. That's what happened to Frightwig. It's like what happened to "I'm going to make my living off my music"? Yeah, right.

So we start playing with Lynn and that was fabulous, but that was short-term, she had other things on her plate, but we love each other and it was fun playing together. Then we get this drummer Dana, who was a glitter rock lesbian who wore stonewashed jeans and sequined vests. Rebecca and I, we're like, "This is not cool," so we bought her some black jeans for her birthday, but the thing is she's this six-foot tall blonde, so between Cecilia and Dana, no one is going to notice. (Laughs) Except they want to hear "Punk Rock Jailbait." So we go on this national tour and she bought us a motor home to tour in, we get to the town and she would leave us at the club and go to the lesbian bars. So on this tour I'm like, "I'm sick of this, I don't want to do this anymore, and I feel like a monkey. This is fucked."

So then I was hanging out with Steve Blush, who introduced me to Stephen Chirazi, the music journalist on the West Coast. He introduced me to the world of heavy metal, which was an interesting ride, and I ended up marrying him later. We had come back from the Suckass tour after people in New York like Carlo McCormick was telling me at CBGBs that Dana was there wearing aqua blue dolphin shorts at our show in CBGBs, he was laughing, saying, "This is your drummer?" I was like, "I don't care, I don't care anymore," it was such a Spinal Tap kind of tour, it was just horrible. Our popularity was going down. L7 was coming on the scene and they were hot, I mean we had them play their first show with us when *Phonesexy* came out, they came up from LA and opened for us at the Kennel Club. Then we played with them up in Seattle, and we were both on tour, we were so happy to see our girlfriends in L7. We're hanging out before the show starts, they go up to play, and out comes Jennifer with her top off, with just a little bit of duct tape on her nipples. I mean, we had spent years in Frightwig wearing clothes and not using our sexuality in that way, and that was just kind of "You're old hags and this is the next level." I thought, "Okay, I have huge breasts, if I went out there I'd blow you off the stage, but I don't chose to show myself in that way." But I was just happy to see women find their place in the music scene because why shouldn't we? And today it's 50/50 women to men in music.

It's been brilliant watching in the earlier stage. The last of the '80s we would play a little bit, I had my son in '92, and we had this offer from Electra Records for a $250 signing bonus to get back together. We had this Southern offer to put out our first two records on a CD, *Wild Women Never Die, They Just Dye Their Hair*. One of the women who used to work at Rough Trade in San Francisco worked at Southern and she loved Frightwig. She wanted to do this project, she put in a lot of effort and time and made a really nice piece of work on Frightwig. But in the States it didn't sell, it wasn't marketed. So at Southern Studios in Chicago, my friend who worked there called me and said, "They're going to destroy your CDs and your cassettes for tax purposes." I was like, "That's my baby! They can't do that! You have to send them to me, and don't send them C.O.D., fuck Southern—they didn't promote this."

What other bands had you performed with, and at which venues?

We starting playing at the Mab, we were really excited to play our first Mab show. We played the Mabuhay with Flipper many, many times. We played with everyone. We played with Dead Kennedys. We weren't in the early music scene that I watched; the Nuns were done, Crime was done. All these bands were burnt up at that point, there was a whole new wave, it was hardcore, that's how you would classify it, then there would be Flipper. (Laughs) We played at the Tool and Die. We played wherever we could get a show. Paul Rat, when he was booking the On Broadway, upstairs from Dirk booking the Mab, he had us play almost every Friday night. He would have bands from LA come up. We played with Christian Death, Lydia Lunch, she was always nice. If there was a show, he would have us open for a hundred dollars on Friday nights. At our shows we would sometimes wear matching outfits, like waitress outfits, we would sometimes dress up glam rock and wear platforms, or just wear our '50s dresses, we weren't really punk rockers. We put on make up and eyelashes, we were really into makeup. I was putting glitter on my eyes and just being colorful. We were not [about] punk rock spikes and chains.

How did Frightwig decide on this name for the band?

Bruno D'Smartass—Steve Demartis, bassist in Flipper, currently in Goofball—was Mia's boyfriend in the early '80s. He would come in from work, we would be playing in the studio, and he would tell us how bad we sounded. He started calling us Frightwigs. Frightwig is a slang term from the '50s describing a woman whose hair is a mess, tights ripped, not a proper lady, if you will. Mia and I loved that name. We felt it conveyed our true selves.

What type of fan base had you accumulated: male compared to female?

We had a lot of male fans, but we had a lot of female fans, too. We inspired a lot of young females across the country. Young girls would come up to us really excited, we would always talk to everyone and hang out. A large male fan base too, a lot of sexual attention in that way from the males. We were part of the music scene so like Red Hot Chili Peppers and TSOL, bands on tour, whatever town you were in, whoever was in town, you'd go to their show or they'd go to yours. So we had a great base of people around us, good solid people, and were treated well. We were watched out for. Sometimes we had a lot of heckling, like "Show us your tits!" We did not like that, we would always say, "Show us your dicks, come up here and show us your dicks, strip for us!" back. We have this song, "A Man's Gotta Do What a Man's Gotta Do," and that became the strip song. It was funny, they were jumping around, falling over because they couldn't get their pants over their boots, a lot of time they just had their underwear on. It wasn't really about showing their penises, it was more of a thumbing your nose at sexism. We were playing up in Vancouver with some old spiky, haired, heavy English band and we were getting spit on. This was in 1982, our first time there, and we were getting spit on. DOA was on the bill. So DOA says, "Here, have a beer before we play." So we have a beer, then another one, then we have a buzz because the beer is much stronger up there. So we've got this buzz going, oh my god, we go out to play and we're getting these hardcore calls and getting spit on because it was popular at that time. It was a big a raised stage, so we would back up to our amps and get out of the way. Mia had bronchitis. I can spit far, we used to do that with guy bands on tour to kill time, go outside in the parking lot and have a spitting contest. So we'd go up to the corner of the stage and point at somebody and Mia would spit on them. We held our own and we put on a good show, that's one thing I'll say about Frightwig, we did not play boring shows. We would have people come up and play with us. We would have dancers, acrobats, whoever we would find around town. Just generally have a good time. The less people there, the better the show you put on.

Frightwig played mid-tempo to slow punk rock in the era of hardcore, where many punk bands were trying to outdo each other by playing as fast as possible. What inspired the band's distinctive sound? How were you received by the punk scene at that the time?

We didn't really have a problem with that. First of all, we could not have played fast and accurately with our 'talent.' We weren't really interested in exerting that much energy. The most important thing is, we were really into our songs. I love slow dirgy stuff, Mia liked faster stuff, like "Vagabondage" is pretty fast. Generally we did have mid tempo or slow, but we always did have a couple of fast songs. We liked playing slower music, we didn't generally get booed or anything, I mean it was a largely male audience in the early days, generally a male scene, but I think because we had breasts and buttocks we were tolerated a lot more than if we were a guy band. Flipper had it all worked out, they were like this huge wall of sound, but they were slower. It was Ted Falconi's guitar and his amps, and then the bass. Steve was a great drummer and he held the mess together. It was simple notes but it would always sound so big through Ted's guitar wizardry and foot peddles. I think that filled in the fast guitars. They would let us borrow their equipment. Unfortunately, they didn't really go out on tours, they just couldn't get over their egos and get out there and work the road like a lot of bands did.

The lyrics to songs like "A Man's Gotta Do What a Man's Gotta Do" and "My Crotch Does Not Say Go" were strong assertions of female power and anger. What reactions did the band get from female punks early on?

Girls liked it, we were pretty popular with the women's movement, if you will. Going up to the West Coast in the early days, a lot of lesbians would come and assume we were all sisters under the sun together. We love women but we loved men, we all had boyfriends. But we had a strong following in the women's scene. Cecilia's song "My Crotch Does Not Say Go"—all of her songs—were about her fucked up relationships. My songs were all about saving the world kind of stuff. Mia's were about her relationships and her self-destructiveness. Rebecca's were about comic books and Hollywood. People liked our songs or didn't like them, but we had a wide variety so there were a lot to choose from.

Did you see Frightwig as a radically feminist band?

One particular tour we were being asked a lot of questions about feminism. The thing with us was we just wanted to rock and have fun. I mean, we liked to dress up, we weren't really that socially 'let's change the world,' we were just enjoying being in a rock band. So the serious feminists who want you to pay attention and go to a protest, you know, we'd play benefits, women's benefits, AIDS benefits, any benefits to help the children, but we didn't really want to be classified and boxed that way. So it was a conscious decision not to join the brigade, I mean, we love women obviously, and we hate any oppression of women.

We saw it as our right to play. We naturally had a strong, powerful spirit, so that would be your feminism right there, and being free. Being free to take off and drive across the country to play your music, not to conform. That was very powerful. But we didn't make it with all of the west coast feminist crowd because we sometimes played with bands they didn't like. Like the Mentors, boy we heard about that. What some of the women didn't understand was, we were making fun of these guys, taking the piss out of them. Feminism in general... love it, practice it, raising a teenage boy to respect women. In regards to Frightwig, the fact that we played instruments, wrote the music, moved the equipment, drove ourselves without a man on national tours, printed our t-shirts, booked our own tours... [all] made us, in essence, feminists. Freedom. I think of feminism as being free to do and act how one wants. I feel strongly for women, as we do get the shit end of the deal, still. However, as a woman, I feel lucky to be an American woman. I think of women globally who are beaten, raped, [have their] genitals cut out, women who are today, yes *today*, in July 2007, somewhere right now a young woman is being stoned to death. Imagine that. Rise up, women! As a woman who is approaching fifty, I do not see the passion for women's rights with a lot of young people. What is up with that? Rise up, women!

Can you tell the story with your band the Tormentors?

Oh yes, we saw the Mentors play in LA and loved them, they were funny as shit—*so* offensive to women. I decided they had to pay for their sins against women. So I start telling El Duce how much Frightwig wants to play with his band, how much we love him. We go home to SF and I start calling him, telling him we need to book a show together and we love you. We book the show, and for two months before the show I called him almost every day and stroked his ego. We went to LA as the Tormentors. We stopped in Tijuana for some wrestling masks and a fifth of Mescal. At the show, we were very sweet to the Mentors before we played. We come out on the stage—the Clash were there, and lots of LA's music illuminati—with the wrestling masks on, with the bottle of Mescal, drinking it, passing it around. I kept on calling El Duce "El Douche Bag" and ripping his band apart. What pigs, ha! Then we started into our twenty-minute version of Fleetwood Mac's "Dreams"—really slow. We were so ugly that it was beautiful. El Duce was running around the club screaming, trying to have the PA turned off on us. He was yelling in a microphone for us to get off the stage. Great fun. At the after party, El Duce passed out standing up—yes, on his feet—and we used this big indelible black ink marker and wrote on his forehead and his big round tummy "Frightwig loves you, baby"! I saw him at a party the next evening and he looked kinda pink on his forehead, he told me someone wrote on him and he had to scrub really hard to get it out. Ah, sorry about that. The Mentors were fun, El Duce was the soul of that project, he was a clown with demons. I am sorry he has passed.

What was most gratifying about being in Frightwig?

Well, it's really self-gratification; I loved playing music, being on stage, playing with my band. We had this really wild ride. The first couple of years, our first summer in NY in '83 people got to see us, but then in '84 it was like we were the toast of the town. We played the Ritz for twenty minutes for a thousand dollars. That's like twenty dollars a minute! That was all great. But that was all ego... ego stroking, you know? We played a John Waters video release party at the Cat Club, which had been a church before, it's beautiful and the stage has a stairway that ascends down to the main floor. He had all these plastic pink pigs all over the place and Divine was there, all the NY underground elite. We had some really hot times, playing in Europe opening for DOA in Rotterdam, we come back and play the last night of the tour and word had spread about Frightwig, we come out on this big stage and the whole front of the stage was full of cameras and flashbulbs, and the audience was huge, with hundreds, almost thousands of people. We had this energy that we could really do this, be a touring band. I wanted to play Europe a lot, they loved us, we had all this attention. So then we go back to San Francisco and another one left for pregnancy. Mia was not pregnant when she left but she was married, and [because of] Mother Nature, she got pregnant immediately. So I've always felt like two women left for pregnancy. Cecilia would just quit when she got sick of it—she quit three times. We actually started to play again in 2002, Cecilia called me up after eight years. I feel like I'm at a place in my life where I'm really settled and I've fulfilled my motherly needs, got this cool thing going on and had some time, so I say yeah, I'd do that again. So we started to play, but it turned out Cecilia was going through big life changes and needed shoulders, Mia and I both had two hours on Monday and Friday to play because we had kids, etc. It just kind of fizzled and I quit, which was great because they both quit on me three times. I didn't even want to do that music because they just want to hear you play those songs from the first few albums. I realized also that I'm done. They want this little scene from back then, this little picture. As far as being a musician, it's not like we have a large audience, let's be honest. It's not rewarding.

Will you talk about your favorite shows with Frightwig?

Playing the Danceteria with Redd Kross in NYC, 1984. Wild clothes, put makeup on them, I wore platforms, we partied. Jeff and Steve McDonald, nice men, cute as hell. They were so funny, so LA, they are sweethearts. Playing in Rotterdam, opening for DOA in 1985. We opened the tour in Rotterdam and closed the tour there also. Last show of the tour, we came out on the stage and the front of the stage was lined with photographers and writers and people. Bulbs were going off. It was a huge turnout for Frightwig. Oh my god, that was fabulous. If we could have only kept that momentum... Playing in Zurich in 1995 with Team Dresch and Bikini Kill, and being billed as the grandmothers of riot grrrl. Didn't really like that as much, it was a lesson as to how we were seen at that point. I loved hanging out with the girls in the bands and talking shop, one more time.

How did your early music and shows differ from your later ones?

I like the earlier [ones] better, because it *was* better,—musically, the chemistry, and relationship-wise.

What do you think when you hear that Frightwig is credited with influencing the third wave riot grrrl movement?

Well, um, that's a little bit much, don't you think? I feel like we did show some girls it was okay to rock out, even if you didn't look like a Barbie doll. I know we inspired some of the more popular female bands from the mid-'80s—L7, Bikini Kill, Babes in Toyland, etc. I loved it. I loved seeing these girls playing music. L7 was great, I was envious watching their rise, but at the same time so happy for them, understand? I love seeing women rock, it's freedom.

How did the band release Cat Farm Faboo *on Subterranean Records?*

We recorded it at Hyde Street Studios in three nights, from midnight till 8:00 am, with Gary Creiman. God bless Gary Creiman. He's still in San Francisco, we still get together once in a blue moon. We paid $2,000. The album was co-produced by Steve Demartis—Bruno is his name these days—he and Philip Lithman from Snakefinger co-produced the album. We recorded it, took off on tour to NY, following the Butthole Surfers. We get to NY, we go to the club we're supposed to be playing at, and they were like "Who are you?" They said we weren't booked to play and they called Gibby to see if it was true. He was like, "You're really here? You came?" We actually played at the 8BC Club every week for food money, hanging out. We became good friends with Dennis and Cornelius from the 8BC Club (8th Street between Avenue B and C). So we're in NY, we don't have any money, we're trying to get shows, making connections, hanging out with Susan and Bruce while our album is being mixed in SF, and we're concerned about the money, we want it done. Those guys spent two months mixing the album. You can imagine what was going on. I've heard that there was a lot of money spent on things to make you stay up and tweak on this, and that was *my* album. We left it in their hands and it sounded really good, but if one had to pay for that bill, one would not be able to ever play music again. It was disappointing, but I do love that album and the second.

The band's second album, Faster Frightwig, Kill! Kill!, *has a decidedly more melodic sound than your debut record. What prompted the band to go in this particular direction?*

That was Eric Feldman. He produced the second album and he's the keyboard wizard, he played with Captain Beefheart when he was a teenager in LA, he played with Snakefinger. Philip Lithman was one of the Residents, he's the one who died, this lovely man from England. We toured with Snakefinger and he produced the second album, that's his keyboard flavor, which we really loved, like on "American Express." On "Freedom," I got to sing in my country voice and have all the backup singers, all my girlfriends, in the studio.

Will you explain the evolution of the routine during your live performances of the song "A Man's Gotta Do What a Man's Gotta Do" that involved inviting a male member on stage to dance?

Well, we'd get cat calls, so we'd say "Get up here and strip for us!" We'd have them singing backup with their pants down. We were in Switzerland, Mia, Bambi, and I, doing "A Man's Gotta Do," of course everybody knows about the stripping, and this really drunk skinhead with a Dead Kennedys shirt standing there with his girlfriend, he comes up on stage so fucked up, and he's stumbling around trying to get his belt off. So I say into the microphone, "He's too drunk to fuck!" Then his girlfriend runs up on stage and pushes me, because I've insulted her boyfriend's masculinity. We did have a few violent interactions over it, but generally it was all in good fun, it wasn't just like a nasty "We hate you, strip for us." It was good-natured, it wasn't really a routine. There was this guy Ford, who went on to play in DOA, he was one of the teenagers with this fanzine in Edmonton, they're interviewing us in the band before the show, so they ask if they can strip for us that night. It's four teenagers, they're like little punk buds, so they're dancing around in their underwear, and at the end of the song they turn around to the audience and pull their underwear down and have Frightwig written across their butt cheeks. It was so cute.

Strong echoes of Frightwig can be heard in bands like L7, Babes in Toyland, or Bikini Kill. Have latter-day bands cited you as an influence?

Well, on the *Wild Women* reissue, in the booklet, there's a comment in there from Courtney Love. Courtney says that Frightwig—now here's a backhanded compliment if I ever saw one—are the true *Grandmothers* of riot grrrl, without them there would never be Bikini Kill, L7, Hole. So we were acknowledged. We played with Bikini Kill on that tour in Switzerland with Kathleen Hannah and Team Dresch, Donna Dresch's band. I'm sure she's still playing, she was the bass player in Black Flag for awhile, the blond lesbian, she's part of the grrrl movement. We played with those bands, they opened for us. So it was obvious, they're coming up and we're the grandmothers of riot grrrl. And if we wanted we could be playing that tune, but there's so much beauty in life and so much music to play. (Laughs) I personally liked the girl bands, and seeing women rise up and play. There wasn't really a lot of snootiness, a lot of dissension, I feel like there was a lot of support over the years. I kind of missed the boat with all of that because we were before it. L7, we did play with them, kind of interfaced with them a bit, and I watched them go to heights I never achieved. But I also feel I opened some doors, and that makes me really happy. You know, my son is going to do a bit better than I did in life, in his own way. It won't be through rocking, unfortunately.

What other bands have you and the other members been part of?

I was in Frightwig for the duration. I started to play music with my husband a few years ago and came up with Greywig. Yeah, I get to just sing, no bass playing. We have a lap steel, piano, drums, stand up bass, harmonica, backup singer, life is good. Mia Levin played in Mudwimmin, ADSR, and lots of other projects. Cecilia Koon plays music today with accordion people, in the woods or something. Susan Miller left the band to have her beautiful daughter Jolene, and went to school, I saw her graduate from Berkeley in Women's Studies, she was the valedictorian. She is a professor for Women's Studies in Southern California. Rebecca Tucker moved to LA, she plays with her husband in Cockfight. Rebecca makes leather costumes for rock and porno stars. Rebecca was the most fabulous peacock Frightwig ever had [and a] bitchin' guitar player. We briefly played with Rachel Thoele and Bambi Nonymous, they both played with lots of other bands. My favorite was the Mudwimmin. We played with Lynn Perko for a short stint on drums. Lynn's hot. Oh yeah,

I always forget, we played with Paula Frazer for a short while. She was a very talented musician and songwriter. Our first drummer, Tana, she was a sweet girl but the one who didn't want to play on stage. She later died of a drug overdose, sad story.

Will you talk about your life now?

Coming from my rock past, which was wild, I have had ample time to honestly contemplate why I would behave in such a way. Why did I want this kind of attention? Basically, I was raised by wolves, I was in psychic pain. Don't get me wrong, I do not regret almost anything, but jeez, some of the stuff. I participated in a lot of things as a young teen that I would not have if someone was watching my back, understand? I didn't have the love and care, so I have made sure my son has had that attention from me. He is lucky; I am remarried and so is his father, he has four loving and relentless parents. He is enveloped in love and care. I worked hard to be a good mother. I wrote him a song, "Little baby sucking on my breast, those were the times I loved best." I so enjoyed being a rock chick, I really believed in what I was doing and I loved playing in the band. However, having Zak was the very best thing that happened in my life. It made me whole. I took it seriously, and stayed at home with my baby and had a ball. I feel like I have had this really unique ride in life. I have rocked out so hard and I have loved and been loved well. I am fortunate, I know that. I have poured my time and attention into Zak, my boy who is fifteen. He is great, he is kind, gentle, smart, and a great soccer player. He has bad taste in music, but we'll let him live.

I have raised him to respect all people, women especially. Following your heart in your creative endeavors, learning, studying, and gaining knowledge in whatever you do. Most importantly, loving well. These are the keys to a happier existence.

Mary Huff was born in Roanoke, Virginia in 1967 and is bass player and vocalist for Southern Culture on the Skids. The band formed in 1985 in Chapel Hill, North Carolina, playing flawless instrumentals with harmonizing vocals in the cross-genres of surf, country, rockabilly, blues, honky tonk, and swamp pop. Since Mary joined in 1986, they have been a three-piece band consisting of Rick Miller, lyricist, singer, and guitar player; Mary Huff Miller, bass player and vocals; and Dave Hartman on drums. Their lyrics and sound are described as dirty, rough and wild.

Their music has been described by *Filter* Magazine as "Dick Dale meets Hank Thompson." While their original material consists of clever and humorous takes on low brow culture, they also create new renditions of old country and rock classics. Rick describes their songs as 'party music', which is especially true when they perform live. They are the only band that captures the raunchy punk edge of the Cramps but with a genuine Southern hillbilly sensibility circa 1960s Nashville.

The songs are all about dancing, sex, and fried chicken with titles like "Camel Walk," "Cheap Motel," "69 El Camino," "Deja Varoom," "Carve the Possum," and "Come and Get It." At their shows expect to participate, whether it's being covered in banana pudding, the limbo contest, or eating the fried chicken. The theme of the band, as evident in their name, seems to be poking fun at white trailer trash culture while lovingly embracing it and all its endearing ways.

Notable albums they've released to date include their first, *Southern Culture on the Skids* (1986), *Too Much Pork for Just One Fork* (1991), *For Lovers Only* (1992), *Ditch Diggin'* (1994), *Dirt Track Date* (1995), *Plastic Seat Sweat* (1997), *Liquored Up, Lacquered Down* (2000), *Mojo Box* (2005), *Doublewide and Live* (2006) and *Countrypolitan* (2007), a masterpiece of Americana pop culture.

How and where did you all meet?

I met Southern Culture when my band the Phantoms opened for them in Richmond, Virginia in 1986, while I was attending college at Virginia Commonwealth University.

Have you had any musical training? Do you play other instruments?

I started piano lessons around the age of seven and went with that until about thirteen. The cello I started around nine and went till I left college at nineteen. I can play guitar, enough to make it through some drunken Neil Young tunes. I am good with percussion. I have played a lot of maracas, tambourine, cowbell, and pots and pans on our records over the years. I am Mary Huff, Queen of the Rhythm Egg. I have a violin I can sort of play if I hold it between my knees—ya know, like a cello.

You're known not only for amazing bass playing but for your vocal talent as well. What about your singing, any vocal lessons?

Thanks for the compliment. The only vocal lessons I have had were from a speech pathologist a few years back. She taught me about how to warm up and preserve my voice on the road, after I was diagnosed with a small cyst on my vocal chord. It's like a little callus. I earned it by singing too hard over crappy PAs, then drinking and socializing long into the night, for years and years. Talking over loud music when you already have bronchitis or a bad cold is hell on your throat. Screaming at band members doesn't help either.

How do you feel about doing more vocals on the later albums?

I'm fine with it. I do like to sing, especially in the studio. The band has a nice studio now, and we had all year to mess around with overdubs on this last record of cover tunes. It was fun. I am always gung ho about doing harmonies: I hear the third, now lemme do a fifth, now a seventh, let's double track, I can sing a better lead, let me sing this one, and so on. Then they hand you a tour schedule and it's like "Oh crap, what have I just done to myself here?"

Who were your influences while growing up and currently?

I was influenced by anything I heard in my house, which was everything! Between the radio (AM and FM), Lawrence Welk's TV Show, and my mom's record collection... She had some rad stuff for being a mom with three small kids, everything from Iron Butterfly to Otis Redding, the Rolling Stones, Jesus Christ Superstar, Elvis, the whole gamut. Tons of Beatles, I learned how to sing harmonies from listening to the Beatles non-stop. "Life is very short and there's not time..."

Eventually, by the time I got to high school, I had a good hard rock and metal schooling, and then it was new wave, punk rock, and hardcore that pretty much ruled my life. All this while I was a cellist playing classical music in school and in the Roanoke Youth Symphony. When I joined Southern Culture I immersed myself in a whole new world of music, the blues, R&B, soul, rockabilly, '60s psychedelia, go-go, country, and surf music. I listened to all of them and borrowed heavily to contribute to the SCOTS song pot.

Who inspires you? Did you have any mentors or idols growing up?

My mom and dad inspired me first to pursue music and express my individuality. My dad was an awesome boogie-woogie piano player and could play anything by ear, and Mom did musical theater for years. She bought me my first bass and amp, and hauled me and all of the band equipment around to my band gigs. For the record, my idol growing up was definitely Chrissie Hynde. Good lord, I worshipped that woman! I covered a bunch of Pretenders songs in my first band. I just wanted to be a badass, awesome singer and performer just like her. She really put me on the sure path to what I wanted to do for the rest of my life.

What type of environment did you have growing up?

Well, I grew up in Roanoke, a city in the Blue Ridge Mountains of Virginia. My dad ran the local Royal Crown (RC) Cola and Nehi Bottling Company. So as a kid I got to drink free RC with my Moon Pies. That's pretty darn 'countrypolitan,' and I guess you could say it came full circle to the Southern joke about an RC and Moon Pie.

Will you talk about the formation of the band?

Rick and his buddies formed the band in an Art Lab at UNC, Chapel Hill, in 1984. The band's gig was opening for the movie *Café Flesh* at a theater that showed porn movies on the weekends. I hear they went over pretty well with the raincoat crowd. About 1987, there was a restructuring of the band, with the exception of Rick Miller. That's when I joined, and a year later was when we recruited my old drummer, Dave Hartman, to join the band. We have been the three core pieces ever since.

How did SCOTS make themselves known in the beginning?

Back in those days it was all word of mouth. You only got to know bands by going to clubs and checking them out, except for a few spins on college radio stations here and there or if you made it to a spot on your buddy's cool mix tapes. When Dave came along, we decided to get on a three-year plan so we could quit our day jobs and do the band full time. So we started making our own demo tapes, sent them out, and started playing in a wider and wider circle. In 1991, we put out *Too Much Pork for Just One Fork* on Moist Records, gave our bosses the finger, and haven't looked back since.

Who writes most of the lyrics? Has this changed over the years?

Rick writes all the lyrics and all the tunes in SCOTS. I am mainly an arranger and in charge of crackin' the whip when stuff starts falling apart. Not to say that I don't hit a few clams now and then myself.

How do you really feel about the band's hillbilly/trashy element?

Well, it's a tradition that goes back to jug bands, the Grand Ole Opry, on up to *Hee Haw* and then eventually Southern Culture on the Skids. In a way we're a part of a long-standing tradition of satire on people in the South. It's Southern culture! It's not mean-spirited at all, we celebrate it by poking fun at it, but we enjoy ourselves immensely and so does our crowd. Southerners have a great sense of humor. I think that is a large part of what we do, but we consider ourselves entertainers as well as musicians and that well may be what confuses people at times. I mean, the vaudeville guys had their shtick, the grunge guys had their shtick, and the metal bands have their thing, and we have ours. It's not just music; it's entertainment!

Who does your fan base consist of, for the band and for you personally?

Well, that is what makes Southern Culture unique. We appeal to all types and ages. We have people tell us about their little kids dancin' to "Banana Puddin'" and their grandparents jukin' to "Put Your Teeth on the Windowsill." If it's an all-ages show, you will see from three to eighty getting their groove on. At any given show it can stretch over three generations. We have had sons, fathers, and grandfathers at the show at the same time. Last weekend, a father and son came up to us after the show and told us that we are the only band that they can listen to in the car together, so it's played everywhere they go. We have great fans, and lots of them have become really great friends over the years. Our fan base is one of the things I'm most proud of.

SCOTS combines highbrow art with lowbrow culture. How do you do it?

I have no idea, but it seems to work. I think Picasso said something like, "Good taste is the enemy of art."

What inspires your ideas for songs and albums?

Where I live and the people that live around me. You can drive fifteen minutes in any direction and have enough material for a record. Traveling through the Southern landscape is very inspiring.

What's the process for making a SCOTS album, from beginning to end?

It starts with rehearsing full-time every day and night until the riffs and ideas start to gel and the picture starts getting clearer of where the songs are going. Then we end up with twenty or thirty songs that we whittle down to an eventual thirteen or fourteen songs that survive the test of being good enough to make the final cut. Now that we have our own studio over-dubs and mixes, it can go on for weeks, sometimes months. It's more satisfying that way, knowing that you have tried things different ways so you don't question yourself as much later on. Mastering has gotten a bit trickier since we have gotten pickier ourselves. The artwork is always up to Rick's approval. He has the ideas and vision of how the theme of our records end up. Rick will come up with some songs and then I will work closely with him on arrangements. Then we get Dave to come over and [we] start rehearsing as a band. We will do a few secret shows locally so we can test the songs live in front of people. That usually helps weed out the decisions of what songs to put on the record. We have played under the names the Gruesome Twosome, the Three Pigs of the Aporkalypse, Green Bean Casserole, the Pine Cones, and one of our favorites, King Smoothie and the Top Shelf Art Ensemble. If we can play the tunes live, it gives us more confidence to get into the studio and knock them out. That's about the gist of it.

What are the influences on SCOTS?

SCOTS' influences are far and wide and it would be hard to nail it down. Any popular music from the 1920s on has inspired us. Individually I'd say I listen to more popular music, old standards, hard rock, and newer artists. Rick's thing is definitely surf and garage, and Dave is probably more Stax and Muscle Shoals and '70s soul. But all three of us like all of those anyway, so between the different genres, we each can bring our own vibe to making a records.

Some say you're the musical equivalent of John Waters, would you agree?

I love John Waters! I wouldn't say we are the equivalent, but he is definitely an inspiration. We all love his movies. The first time I ever heard a Link Ray song was accompanying the dancing asshole scene in *Pink Flamingos*. That really stuck with me. We have a good friend, Mr. Gene Mendez, who knew Edith Massey for years. "Oh, Mr. Egg Man!!"

Will you talk about more of your favorite music?

I like all genres of music—jazz, rockabilly, blues, country, mental, punk, classical, and everything in between. Pretty much the only thing I don't really like is what I hear on the radio. I think some douche bag termed it "modern rock."

Will you talk about your experiences with the great Hasil Adkins?

Oh man, I loved Hasil, the Hillbilly Huncher! What a sweet, beautiful guy he was. He sent us like ten reels of tape. It just showed up in the mail one day. We lovingly cleaned all of the peanut butter and cracker crumbs off of them and listened to over a hundred songs. We picked around seventeen songs, enough for a record and a single, mastered them, and had it ready to go, but the record label we were working with at the time went out of business. So we sent them back to Hasil and later on it ended up coming out as *Moon Over Madison* on Norton Records. That record was mostly his country stuff, which not too many people had heard before. He was mainly known as the Rockabilly Wildman from West Virginia up until then. We did some touring with the Haze, whew! That was crazy. Sometimes he would stay with us at my house. In the mornings we would sit on the porch and he would tell us how to eat everything in our front yard, from the squirrels and turtles to the weeds. We made a live recording with him in Atlanta called *The Hub Cap Hunch*. If anyone out there has a copy, let me know since I lost mine. There is nobody like Hasil, and everybody misses him.

Is the lifestyle portrayed as SCOTS how you really live on a daily basis?

Unfortunately, it's pretty damn close.

What is a typical day for you? Who or what are you passionate about?

I am a hillbilly vampire! That song "Midnight to Six" by the Pretty Things sums me up well. A typical day is getting up in the afternoon and watching TV, *Buffy the Vampire Slayer, Angel, Guiding Light,* or *Viva La Bam.* Then I usually rock out to some records and then get ready to drive a good way out to Rick's studio. We usually work on songs all night and goof around with his son Jack and Queenie Beans, the dog. Then I get home pretty late, around 1:00 a.m. or so, and I'll crack a brew, strum a guitar—in other words, "drink and think"—unless we are on tour, and that's a whole 'nother can of worms. I live in a little wood house surrounded by big woods. I have possums, and raccoons have babies in my chimney, deer in my front yard all the time, the occasional black snake in my basement, cicadas in stereo, fireflies blazin' and owls a-hootin'. It's pretty awesome, really. My home is packed with spoils from the road, vintage clothes and thrift store gold, lots of vinyl and wigs out of control! Yep, that's my house. My passion these days is to get juiced up and try to learn Neil Young's songs on my acoustic guitar. I could just sit here and try to figure out all the instruments that I have acquired over the years: accordion, mandolin, violin, harmonicas, and some other weird cheap instruments like my trombone, and a drum set which I'm not too shabby on.

How did you decide whose music to cover for the album Countrypolitan?

They were some of our favorite songs dating back to when we were kids. A lot of them from our parents' record collections.

Do you or SCOTS as a whole have a certain era you base your work on?

I would say the '60s definitely are the period that we draw the most from. I'm really into that tough go-go country look that Loretta, Jeannie C. Riley, and Tammy had going on. I love that look! We all dig horror movies, grade B to Z, preferably. We did the soundtrack for a Herschell Gordon Lewis flick, *Blood Feast 2... All You Can Eat*. That was a big honor for us. I was raised on horror flicks. I love those chicks in the *Hammer Vampire* movies with the bouffants and eyeliner and heaving bosoms. Fuck Paris Hilton, I want to look more like those babes!

What venues did you perform in when you first started? What is your ideal venue?

We started anywhere they'd let us play. Everything from coffee shops to parking lots, shopping malls, and prisons. We did a prison tour of the North Carolina Men's and Women's Medium Correctional and a couple of Maximum Security Prisons in N.C. They liked us, too. They were a captive audience. As far as the ideal venue to perform in, I guess I would put on top of my list: one with good monitors.

What was the strangest thing that has happened at one?

So much weird stuff has happened to us that it is almost impossible to narrow it down. We flew all the way to Anchorage, Alaska, for one show. We pull up to the Community Civic Center and noticed a Little Debbie truck parked outside, which sort of raised an eyebrow. The show was packed full of fun drunk Alaskans and the sun was still up even though it was eleven o'clock at night. We started playing and there was a spirited round of midget tossing off the stage into the crowd. Towards the end of the show we launched into "Camel Walk," and unbeknownst to us, two thousand Little Debbie snack cakes had been handed out to every person in the crowd, and they had been squishing them up for at least an hour. They started hurling them at the stage and when they made contact it was like getting pelted with granite rocks! Rick and I finally ran behind the PA speakers, but kept playing of course, and all poor Dave could do was bob and weave as they soared by his head. I went on my first fishing trip for king salmon about six hours later, and I was the only one to catch anything. We headed for the airport and promptly got a phone call from Chapel Hill saying that Dave's house had been destroyed and mine damaged by Hurricane Fran. That was a weird trip!

There was also a biker chick in Wichita who pleasured herself onstage with a spicy hot chicken wing, whilst in a full leg cast. The two naked Santas on stage with us at Roskilde Festival 97 in Denmark, seeing a dude get stabbed with a butter knife while we rocked a seafood/antiques emporium on the Outer Banks during an emergency hurricane evacuation. You know, stuff like that. The list goes on and on. I could fill a phone book with all the strange things that have happened.

How did your shows develop? Will you talk about the Bucket of Chicken?

Our shows just seem to have developed organically over the years. We enjoy playing, so stuff happens naturally. The Bucket of Chicken started one night at a pub in Harrisonburg, Virginia in the early '90s. The owner gave us a bucket of chicken as our dinner, and it was sitting on the side of the stage while we were playing. A homeless guy wandered in and started eating it and we said, "Hey, man, that's our dinner, and if you want some of it, you at least have to get up here and dance with us." The crowd went wild. We figured we would do it again at the next show but with some cute girls, and it just kinda stuck after that. It's good to feed a hungry crowd.

What other fun things have you done during a show?

We used to give out pots and pans, hubcaps and metal spatulas for the audience to beat on during the shows. We did that for years, but when they started coming back with blood on them we decided to nix that to avoid a lawsuit. People really got into it. Dave used to wear a hard hat and invite people to do a 'Wipe Out' type of drum solo on his head. I saw that one go wrong a few times. We started a garage punk and surf festival called Sleazefest where bands would play for three days and nights. We filled up a baby pool with banana pudding and would get girls to wrestle in it, guys too. That was a fun mess.

How did your romantic involvement with Rick come about?

We had been together for eleven years and I've seen the SOB almost every day for the last twenty years, but even though we are not romantically involved [anymore], we actually get along better now than we did back then. It's kind of a Fleetwood Mac thing. It was the hardest thing I've ever done to stay in the band after we split up, but damn if I didn't get through it. Now we are just one big happy dysfunctional family.

What are the band's touring schedules like?

We used to tour virtually nonstop for years. We have come to our senses and cut back considerably since then. When we were on [record label] Geffen and supported those releases, we worked really hard. When *Dirt Track Date* came out I think we played like 330 shows that year. That was hell. We keep it reasonable now, and Baby Jack and Mamma Sarah come along for the ride.

With whom have you toured? ?

We have toured with a lot of great bands. To name a few: Reverend Horton Heat, the Paybacks, Neko Case, the Greenhorns, Throwrag and the 45s. These days we like to tour with our friends' bands if possible, so that we have a good time on the road.

Do you feel your band is appreciated enough?

Yeah, we get a good amount of appreciation. I suppose it's important what the critics think. Every band likes to get a good review, and we usually get good reviews, but some critics hate us. In the end, it's really all about the fans because they are the ones that actually buy the records. They are the people that allow us to do what we do. Without them there wouldn't be the SCOTS.

What was the greatest moment for you personally in your SCOTS career?

To tell you the truth, it was probably during the Conan O'Brien show. I have been such a fan of his for so long that I thought I was going to pass out when I finally met him. He is the coolest. We actually have done that show three times so far. Playing at the base of Mt. Fuji for 20,000 [people] tops the list!

When we hit the 100,000 sales mark on *Dirt Track Date*, Geffen whisked us away to a surprise dinner party at Spago's in LA. I was wearing hot rollers and torn overalls, since we were soundchecking for a show at the Roxy that night. I wasn't expecting it at all. Being served by a French waiter at Spago while I was wearing hot rollers was a hoot!

Which album did you have the greatest pleasure making?

Personally, I think *Dirt Track Date* was my favorite album to make. It was our major label debut and our first big-budget record. We worked really hard making that album and it paid off, so that felt pretty good. I also like all of the records that we have self-produced and recorded in our studios: *Zombified, Liquored Up and Lacquered Down, Mojo Box,* and *Countrypolitan.* They were all done that way.

Do you have any other side projects you've worked on?

I don't have any side projects per se, but I have done vocals and instrumental work on a number of other people's recordings. Two Dollar Pistols, Demolition String Band, Sean Kennedy, the Moander, the Fleshtones, Mark Lanegan, and more. It's fun to work on other people's music.

Who are some of your favorite contemporaries?

I really like the Brian Jonestown Massacre, Roky Erickson, Queens of the Stone Age, HIM, Dead Moon. I have hundreds of favorites in all different genres.

How long do you see the band making music for?

I'd be lying if I said that I didn't want the band to go on forever. In the future I see more records, more movies, more TV shows, more money, and more adventures. Perhaps a solo record, who knows?

Sean Yseult, born Shauna Reynolds in June 1966 in North Carolina, was the bass player for surreal horror/punk/metal band White Zombie. The band was founded in New York City in 1985 by Sean and Rob Zombie, with roots in punk rock and metal until garnering mainstream superstardom in the 1990s. White Zombie infused metal with dark psychedelia and the new sounds of grunge, combining tongue-in-cheek sarcasm with psychotic sex, gory horror, and satanic sci-fi fantasy. The music was slower and harder than anything since the early '70s.

White Zombie chose their name from the 1932 film starring Bela Lugosi. Their albums are cult classics, recorded from the mid-'80s to the late '90s: *Gods of Voodoo Moon and Pig Heaven* (1985), *Psychotic Blowout* (1986), *Soul Crusher* (1987), *Make Them Die Slowly* (1989), *La Sexorcisto: Devil Music Vol 1* (1992), *Astro Creep: 2000* (1995)—these last two albums went platinum—and *Super Sexy Swingin Sounds* (1996). In 1998 White Zombie broke up, and Rob Zombie went on to a successful solo career as a musician and filmmaker.

After White Zombie disbanded, Sean continued on to her own infamy. Voted one of the top bass players in metal history, Sean has fulfilled her own artistic goals with many successful projects. In 1995, she founded the band Famous Monsters, a surf rock trio featuring Sean as Devil Doll on bass, Kate Campell as Vampire Girl on guitar, and Carol Cutshall as She Zilla on drums. They put out two albums in 1998, *In the Night!!!* and *Around the World in 80 Bikinis*. Sean also participated in the 1996 Germs tribute album, *A Small Circle of Friends: A Germs Tribute*.

Sean opened her own bar, The Saint, in New Orleans and in 2002 founded the band Rock City Morgue, which blends punk, classic rock, and blues. She also joined the Cramps for their 2006 Halloween tour. Sean has now embarked on a successful design career, utilizing her BFA in Graphic Design from Parsons School of Design. She is the founder of the clothing company Yseult Designs, and also creates visual art with Louis St. Lewis. The artwork is very much in the spirit of White Zombie, featuring a '60s psychedelic distinctiveness, and can be found in many galleries across the US. In 2008, Sean married Chris Lee in New Orleans.

Growing up, did you have any intention of being in a band? What were you listening to in your formative years?

Well actually, growing up I *was* in bands. When I was really little I would play piano and my parents' friends had kids about [my] age, who were all musical and grew up watching *The Partridge Family*. (Laughs) All of our parents listened to the Beatles and Rolling Stones, lots of rock bands, so we were surrounded by music. I can remember as far back as six years old, playing in fake bands with our friends, but they were real, our friends really played instruments, and we'd get together and play. I remember playing in nightclubs, actually as early as six or seven. My piano teacher would take me to do blues and jazz improv with real old bluesmen, and I was this little kid on the piano. My parents let her do that, which was strange, in retrospect. Also, the friends I had from when I was little, when they grew up to about twelve or thirteen, actually had a band that I played in, still around nightclubs. I was around ten years old at the time. It wasn't that I was thinking I wanted to be in bands, I just already kinda was when I was little. As far as playing bass, I started picking that up in high school, just getting obsessed with punk bands. I would say the Cramps were a big influence. Also, not that I loved early hardcore bands, but that was kind of what was happening when I was in high school. So, you know, hearing Black Flag and Dead Kennedys was punk for me, because I wasn't old enough at the time when punk first started to get influenced by all that. With hardcore bands it was kind of like, "I can do this." (Laughs) The same attitude, I would just pick up an instrument and start playing.

While attending design school, what were your aspirations?

I went to a performing arts school in North Carolina. I was actually there for ballet, then I switched to visual arts. I always knew I wanted to move up to New York and I wanted to get through design school, but by my senior year in [high] school I knew I wanted to move up to New York and be in a band. That was definitely a goal, even though I was going to be in design school. The real plan was to get in a band actually *at* school. That happened at school with White Zombie—three out of four of us went there—the other guy was still in high school. So that's how we met, in design school, Rob and Tom our second guitarist. We were all at Parsons at the time.

How did you first meet Rob Zombie and how was White Zombie created?

Rob and I started the band, and Tom was our second guitarist. We kind of went through a few guitarists quickly in the first couple years. So it was pretty much me and Rob. We were both—obviously, by the way we looked and what we were into—we were, I hate to say "goth," but I loved the Cramps and Birthday Party and he loved the Misfits. We were both at all the hardcore matinees at CBGBs and seeing Black Flag, so we definitely had that in common and wanted to start a band, but we just wanted it to be really different. We knew we wanted it to be heavy, dark, and different. We were a little obsessed with Birthday Party, Black Sabbath, and Black Flag. Everything from Greg Ginn's crazy solo work to the Butthole Surfers, who were just coming out around that time, and all that seemed like it might be cool to try and mix up. Our second guitarist was in the band for quite a while, and he really embodied that. It was hard, Rob was the frontman and I was the bassist, so it was hard fulfilling whatever vision we had with neither of us being a guitarist. So we kept going through guitarists, trying to get it right. It worked out really well with Tom for quite a while, but we kind of wanted to take it to the next level and get a little heavier, get a little more professional, and he was into the more damaged guitar style. Which is great, he's a great guitarist, I still admire his playing a lot, but it just wasn't working with what we wanted to do. So then we got Jay in the band and the rest is pretty much history. It worked out pretty well.

What type of music did you intend for White Zombie? What predecessors directly influenced its direction?

I think all the things I mentioned, like Sabbath, even Black Flag, but that wasn't something we were listening to a lot. The Misfits, of course, that was a big influence for Rob. Even the Cramps, the Birthday Party for me a lot, just those driving tribal bass lines; same with the Butthole Surfers, I loved the bass lines they had going. Our drummer Ivan was this high school kid from Brooklyn, total metalhead, and that actually ended up being a big influence because he was constantly blasting Slayer and Metallica, stuff we weren't really into. We were more in this underground world and that was a little 'from another planet' for us, but we kind of started getting into it and incorporating that into whatever we were doing, too. I have to say that was influential, the early Slayer and all that.

How much was your part in developing the White Zombie sound?

The music and songwriting was me and whoever the guitarist was at the time, and Rob would act like a conductor and be like, "I hate it, I like it, OK I hate it, OK that's good, that will work" ... comments like that. (Laughs) We'd piece things together accordingly, but I wrote a good chunk of the rest in the early days. From then on, it was 50/50 between me and Jay. Rob, of course, did all the lyrics: he would piece together riffs of what he liked and didn't like, but he didn't play guitar or bass, so Jay and I would write all the riffs.

Did being female in this band ever become difficult?

No, not at all, it wasn't ever a factor.

What made you change to playing bass from piano? Had you considered playing guitar for White Zombie?

Yeah, you know, actually, when Rob and I met, I had a guitar and I was trying to learn, but I just knew a few chords. It's not like I could solo or really play very well, and it just seemed more realistic to speed things along [and] pick up a bass. The bass was really easy to play because I grew up playing violin also, so it's like the violin was a cheat sheet as far as the frets and everything. It was pretty easy to jump on the bass. I loved playing piano, but I never wanted to play piano in a band. I always wanted to play guitar or bass, it wasn't even an option. It just didn't seem very cool at the time. Not that I have a problem with it now, but at the time I definitely had an issue with it. You know, if you're going to be in a heavy band it's gotta be guitar or bass. I made that switch pretty quick.

To what extent did your ideas differ from Rob's?

He was more into the Misfits and more into... not mainstream rock, but he liked the Doors. We both liked Sabbath, we both liked some heavy stuff, but it was pretty much a mutual vision at first. We like a lot of the same things and had the same goals, but it was kind of later, just before we broke up, that Rob got more into stuff that was a little techno, the preprogrammed kind of thing, a mixer and all that. It made sense as a direction we could have gone, because in a way he kind of invented using all the original sound clips we used to throw in our early records, recordings from horror movies and *Taxi Driver* and stuff like that. It was like his movie obsession and him holding a microphone up to the TV with a cassette player and recording, then somehow trying to mix it into the recordings we were doing for ten bucks an hour at the cheapest studio we could find. So starting off with that and then getting more and more obsessed with layers and overlaying things, I can understand him wanting to go in that direction, but I was getting more into bands that were just bands without any extra prerecorded crap and all that, and Jay [was] also. We were getting pulled apart towards the end as far as what direction we wanted to go, like any band. I guess that's why people break up, right? (Laughs) I liked a lot of those bands, like Ministry and Nine Inch Nails, they were doing some cool stuff, but it just wasn't what I wanted to do.

When White Zombie fist started, what were your shows like?

Oh man, they were pretty crazy. We lived on the Lower East Side in New York way back in the day when there was the Love Club, which was in the basement of this Latin club. We played with Dinosaur before they were Dinosaur Jr., and just a weird mix of very cool underground people. There was CBGBs, we might have even played the Pyramid and a few other of the really small clubs—really small, you know, not even usually a stage. You know, you're playing on the floor with people in front of you. Maybe twenty to fifty people max, it was crazy. We would do really funny things, too. I remember once we made these Gene Simmons masks on a Xerox machine and passed them out and made the whole audience wear Gene Simmons masks while we were covering "Dr. Love." People thought it was total irony that we covered Kiss songs, I guess because we were so bizarre at the time. We actually really liked Kiss, but these people thought it was a joke. I guess our fans were like the bands we would play with: Honeymoon Killers, Pussy Galore, people like that and fans of those bands. That was the scene we started out in, on the Lower East Side.

How did the shows change as your fan base began to grow?

It was really strange, but somehow the band Biohazard from Brooklyn took a liking to us, and also the Cro-Mags. Harley saw us one day and we thought he was going to beat us up, but instead he said he liked our band. Slowly we started infiltrating L'amours, the big metal club in Brooklyn, playing with these bands. We always thought people were gonna hate us but they liked it, so that was kind of a transition, playing L'amours. Then we got asked to do a few Northeast dates with Slayer, and those shows went great. Most bands get booed offstage with Slayer [but] we totally won their audience over each date and we thought *wow, maybe this is where we belong.* That was really the turning point, the shows at L'amours and Slayer. We got to open up for Pantera at L'amours and we ended up being great friends with them. We ended up with their management and doing tours with Pantera. That's when we really started getting in to bigger stage settings and bigger crowds, so we definitely owe a lot to Pantera.

What were some of the most memorable White Zombie shows?

There were a few. One would have to be playing this huge festival called Rock in Rio that was down in Rio de Janeiro in front of 30,000 people, which was pretty insane, one of those soccer stadiums. We played with Page and Plant, Smashing Pumpkins, and Black Crowes, it was just a huge, huge thing. It was crazy to see a sea of people that huge, it just looks like a wave, it doesn't even look like humans at that point.

On the opposite end of that we played this place in Kansas, it was in the middle of a cornfield, called the Out House. It's kind of a famous place, but it's literally like this cinderblock shack in the middle of a cornfield and you'd have to drive about a half an hour just to find it and you [can] probably fit like fifty people in there. It was packed and there were people surrounding it, out in the cornfields trying to listen. Some of the most insane shows were the smaller ones. There were kids hanging from the ceiling, you know, just going nuts. We played this huge club called Harpo's, in Detroit, which was a big rock/metal club, and winning over all those metalheads. Those fans were unbelievable, showering us with gifts. I think we played that same club four times. I have so many things still from all these Detroit fans. They kept wanting us back. I have this stack of the coolest VHS tapes of early Kiss footage and early Sabbath playing a club in Paris, and they knew I liked *Casper* and *Hot Stuff* paraphernalia. I don't know how they found this out. As far as White Zombie really breaking through and getting these die hard fans, that was pretty amazing.

Did Timothy Leary and Forrest J. Ackerman really attend your shows?

I actually met Timothy Leary through Al Jorgensen of Ministry, and when we first met we went up to Timothy's house. Al was really good friends with him. We ended going up there many times and just hanging out. He was like this cool dad or uncle that you wish you had, but I had a cool dad so I can't complain. I guess it was like this crazy old uncle. We'd hang out with him quite a bit. We would stay the night many times, it was so great, he was such an amazing person. He'd set up dinners with us and some Congresspeople and some filmmakers. He'd love mixing it up to see what happened. I really admired him.

With Forrest Ackerman, I love him, and when I had my band Famous Monsters, he not only came to our show (and he never goes out at nighttime), but that afternoon he took us up to his house and took us on an entire tour of his house. We got to see his entire collection, like Dracula's cape, monsters and set designs that Ray Harryhausen built, just incredible things.

What were White Zombie shows like, and how did they evolve?

We were always trying to make things as visual and over-the-top as possible, even though we were playing CBGBs. I remember we made this homemade pyro with gun powder, completely illegal, but anything we could do to make it like a Kiss show. We'd go to the cheesy stores in New York down on Canal Street and buy mini cop lights, strobe lights, and rope lights, whatever we could, and wrap them around our amps and drums. Anything we could do to make it a crazy insane show, we would do. As we got bigger, of course, all that became a little easier to do on a professional level, with a real pyro guy and, of course, big light shows. Towards the end when we were doing arenas, headlining, we had a really amazing show with a montage on movie screens behind us of horror movies collaged together. I actually just had to go through a lot of old bootleg live performance tapes, we're getting ready to finally do a box set of all our early recordings with a DVD. When I saw the footage I thought, *wow*. I was always onstage, so I never really got to watch it. Watching these bootlegs was kind of amazing, you don't know whether to watch the band or the movie. It was definitely pretty spectacular.

How much of your audience was female?

Because of the music being so heavy, it was mostly male. But I think because there was a girl in the band, it brought girls in there, too. Also, we weren't bludgeoning, beat-you-over-the-head metal. I think we always kind of had a good groove to our music, I think that helped bring girls in there, not just a bunch of headbanging dudes.

What kind of feedback did you get from female fans?

I would get great feedback, definitely, girls even to this day still come up, and especially when we are playing, tell me they [started playing] the bass because of me. That's always really flattering. I know back when I wanted to be in a band and picked up a bass I only had Ivy and Joan Jett to look up to. It's nice to hear that, because I've been in that position myself. What actually was more—well, I wouldn't say *more*—but equally impressive was the super metalhead guys that had never seen a girl on stage. They would come up to me and say I was their favorite bass player next to [Metallica's] Cliff Burton. That was a monumental compliment. They wouldn't say, "Oh, you play good for a girl." In some of the metal magazines I got voted Best Bass Player. I wasn't ever best female bass player, it was just best bass player in a metal band.

How did you manage to escape that stereotype?

Well, first of all, I worked hard and I enjoy playing, but I always wanted to avoid that stigma of 'girl musician' or 'good for a girl,' whatever. I just wanted to make sure I was equal, not just the girl in the band. To be honest, I'd be wearing torn-off hot pants jeans and engineer boots a lot of times, and people still thought I was a guy. I kinda always enjoyed the androgyny, and with my name being Sean people didn't really know. A lot of people thought I was a guy, which I was fine with. We all dressed pretty much the same in the band. I was never trying to be sexy or dress like a girl, that's never been a part of my agenda. I just had to make sure I wasn't seen as a woman first. I wanted to be seen as part of the band and a bass player first. I guess it worked.

How did being romantically involved with Rob affect things?

When we met, we started the band and starting going out at the same time, almost for the whole duration of the band. I don't think it affected it one way or the other. But definitely towards the end, when we broke up, that complicated things a bit. It's definitely hard to be in a band with an ex. It shouldn't have been, really, I mean, we were still friends, but you know, it just always does [make it hard] for some reason.

What led to the demise of White Zombie?

Partially our breaking up, and partially Rob just wanting to go in the techno direction as far as prerecorded tracks and things, those two things, definitely.

Will you talk about some of the bands White Zombie played with?

We toured with Kyuss when they were all still in high school. That was pretty amazing. Way pre–Queens of the Stone Age. All those guys are just amazing musicians, Brant Bjork, the whole band is just great. It was quite an experience getting to watch them every night. We got to tour with the Ramones around '95, it was a little awkward for me because they were opening up for us. But every night they were like, "Thank you so much for taking us on tour." Joey would say this every night, "Oh, you guys are so cool for taking us out," but our audience didn't fully appreciate them. It was lame. I was totally in awe to be on tour with the Ramones, and I was almost embarrassed that we were having to play after them. I mean, they're gods in my book. It was just a little awkward but they were so nice and so thankful. They said, "Nobody ever asks us to go on tour, you guys and Pearl Jam are the only bands that ever asked us out." I was like, "Well ,there's a reason! People are probably too scared to ask one of the greatest bands on earth to open for them."

Whose idea was that?

It wasn't mine. I don't know, I guess it must have been Rob's. That takes a lot of balls to ask a legend to open up. But they were totally into it, we got to be good friends with them all. They were so cool. Really an amazing experience, and I was actually dumbfounded [that] our audience didn't know who they were or get it. I thought, "Really? Is there anyone on this planet who doesn't worship the Ramones?" I couldn't believe it. Now they have all this fame, like everyone wears a Ramones t-shirt, they can get them at the mall. Still I just think, you know .. I hope some of our fans discovered them. I felt bad, but it was great having them out.

Will you talk about the formation of Famous Monsters?

You know, the last couple years of White Zombie got to be a bit grueling, just constantly on tour. It was always fun playing, that one hour that you're onstage, but the rest of it... we were starting to come apart as a band. It wasn't that fun. So I had this idea to do this completely silly band as a release and just for fun. I had a friend in New York and I went to go visit her for the weekend and I said, "Okay, I have these songs and I can't really play guitar, but here they are." I showed them to her and she played guitar. She was friends with Bob Bert, who played with Sonic Youth and Pussy Galore, he was around then. A day or two later, over that weekend, they said, "Oh, well, there's this 8-track studio," and we just went in and recorded the songs. I did a photo shoot with them. I know it sounds ridiculous, but it really did all happen over a four-day weekend. We found all these silly costumes and wigs and found a Frankenstein mask for Bob and were like "Here, let's just do this photo shoot." We did it and I went back on tour with White Zombie and got started on this cassette and I mailed it to Estrus because I just always loved the garage bands, everything, on Estrus. I always loved a really good theme band with full costumes, like the Mummies, the Phantom Surfers, all the stuff they had on Estrus. So I mailed it in anonymously and he wrote back and said, "Yeah, I definitely want to put this out." We had a 7-inch on Estrus [and] we didn't even really exist. We kind of kept it secret, I never even told David Estrus who I was, even for a while. There were no real names on it, just Devil Doll, Vampire Girl, and Frankie Stein. They didn't know who we really were, no one did.

It was just fun and also because in White Zombie, we had always said no one is allowed to do any side projects. So it was like doing a side project without using my name or saying who I was. Then we took a year off and during that year Rob did a side project, he started his solo band. So I thought "Fuck it, the cat's out of the bag now. I'm going to have some more fun and do some more Famous Monsters." I also moved to New Orleans during that year off, which turned into us breaking up anyway. I just found some girls there: Katie Campbell, who turned into Vampire Girl, was a bass player like me, she didn't know how to play guitar. So I gave her a guitar and showed her some bar chords. Carol Cutshall, who was She-Zilla, replaced Frankie Stein. She was a set and costume designer and [had] never played an instrument in her life, especially not drums. I was like, "Here's a couple drums, here's a guitar, let's do this." We were friends, so I thought that it would be fun to hop in a van and play shows.

We ended up having a really good time. It was extremely punk as far as none of us really knowing our instruments. I think a lot of people were shocked that I would do something so totally underground and amateur. But it was really fun and we didn't care. To be honest, it was supposed to be kept underground who [the] members were, it was never supposed to be announced that anybody from White Zombie was in the band. It was just this silly thing. They ended up putting a sticker on the record, so a few people would come out to the shows expecting to hear heavy music and they'd hear this lightweight surf stuff, get mad, and leave. I felt bad because, you know, I didn't even want my name attached to the band, it was just going to be this secret second identity I could have for a little while. That's the kind of music I was really listening to a lot of the time. I always loved Link Ray, even the Ventures. I was into a lot of surf music obviously or I wouldn't come up with all those riffs.

What inspired the surf B-movie horror theme of Famous Monsters?

Musically, ever since high school, I got into the Estrus label. Especially I love the shitty recordings, one-track garage recordings. There's something about the sound of them. I know a lot of White Zombie fans listened to that record and thought it was crap. It's like, it was intentional, it wasn't supposed to be this fancy recording, but it's hard to explain to some people. Also, from my early childhood, I have a distinct memory of the cartoon the *Groovie Goolies*, and I would talk about it for years and no one knew what I was talking about. They had a band: there was Frankenstein who played the xylophone, there was Wolfie. I finally found a video with all the early episodes and thought, "Oh my god, here it is!" It was all the stuff from my childhood—*The Munsters, Josie and the Pussycats*—it was really kind of like about being a monster cartoon band come to life.

People would ask me, "What are your goals with this band?" I said, "Well, tour Japan and turn into a cartoon." And I wasn't joking! That was the goal for this band. I actually got to tour Japan twice and I actually met with all the major cartoon networks and I got to pitch it as a cartoon. One of the top animators in Hollywood, Mike Moon, loved the band and did a whole treatment and did all these amazing drawings of us and we had storylines and everything. I don't know, for some reason it didn't get picked up, but it's amazing and I think it's timeless so hopefully we'll pitch it again one day. We were more tied in with outer space: we would be in our private little jets in outer space, we'd each have our little matching different colored jets traveling around from planet to planet, and of course something wacky would ensue, and we'd have to end with a song on each planet. Something in that manner. (Laughs)

What were favorite horror/sci-fi movies that inspired Famous Monsters?

I always loved Harryhausen films, those were my favorite. I love the ridiculous fake animatronic, bizarre, stop-animation monsters, it just looked so cool. The horror I like is a lot of the campier films than the classics, of course. My earliest memory is waking up when I was little, at six in the morning, and turning on *Sunrise Theatre*—that was hosted by a werewolf or something—and seeing *The Creature from the Black Lagoon* on Saturday morning and then seeing *Frankenstein Conquers the World*, which is such an amazing movie. It took me so long to find it again because I couldn't remember the title since I was five or six years old when I saw it. But now that I've found it, I think it's a Toho film, the filmmakers of *Godzilla*. It's this teenage kid that had a radiation effect from Hiroshima that made him grow and grow, so he turned into this, like, fifty-foot Frankenstein teenage Japanese kid, and he's battling this lizard that's kind of like Godzilla but not. There's *Mad Monster Party*, I love that, the stop-motion film. There's so many amazing things out there, I could talk for hours.

If you could have recorded any soundtrack or script, what would it be?

I love lots of Coffin Joe movies. I just love the absurdity of mixing in a few classic monsters and graveyards. I love when there's absurd things grouped together, like that movie *The Incredibly Strange Creatures That Stopped Living and Became Mixed-Up Monsters*, like a Steckler. Especially when there's gimmicks involved with the releases, like using Emergo-Vision, like *House on Haunted Hill* when the skeletons come out at you from behind the curtain. They had it here in New York at the New Art, a William Castle Fest here. I saw *The Tingler*, *House on Haunted Hill*, *Cat Woman on the Moon* in 3-D, *House of Wax* in 3-D, too. I love anything campy and twisted. As far as horror movie soundtracks, I love *Goblin*, all the Argento films. I did start writing a lot of soundtrack stuff, but getting into the reality of it and the business was really unappealing to me. It's something maybe down the road I might get into later. It's a whole other world.

What brought Famous Monsters to an end?

I guess it did come to an end. I hate to think of it being over, but our drummer, She Zilla, moved out to Los Angeles, and she works on a lot of movies doing costume and wardrobe design. Our other guitarist, Katie, ended up joining Nashville Pussy for a while playing bass. Now she's in a band in Canada called C'mon. That's pretty much what happened. Everyone just had to follow their lives, and we ended up in three different cities. We still say that if we got some amazing offer, we'd pull it together and fly out.

You have a coffin bass that you designed, will you talk about that?

I actually have two of them now. When White Zombie was at its peak, I had every guitar company offering me free basses, and this one company said, "Hey, if you ever want to design something different, we'll build it for you." I was like, "Well, I do have this idea." I drew it out and they built it. They made me one that's black with silver trim and another one that's silver metal flake with black trim. It's pretty over-the-top.

So which female musicians do you admire?

Joan Jett is a big role model for me. The first time I saw her I was underage. I got a fake ID and snuck into this little club. I thought, "Wow, she's just like a Ramone, she's a chick but she's like a Ramone." It was a turning point. As far as more recent girls I've seen on stage that really blew me away, [there] was Melanie from Burning Brides—they're amazing, like Black Sabbath meets Cheap Trick, real melodic. The singer looks like a young Marc Bolan, she's just this amazing, hard rocking, cute little girl, and the bass is almost as big as she is. She's all over it, headbanging and going nuts. They're a trio that sounds like there's ten people, it's amazing. About a year ago I saw this band out of New York called Earl Greyhound, their bass player, her name is Kamara. They're heavy rock, they sound really new, though. I can't quite explain their sound, but she's a great bass player.

How did Rock City Morgue come about?

Rock City Morgue came about when I moved to New Orleans and after Famous Monsters were not playing anymore. This guy, Rick Slave, I knew from New York days, he always had really cool bands here. He had a band called Kretons back when we started White Zombie. I was a huge fan. They were a perfect blend of the Ramones and the Cramps. I was friends and a fan, so we ran into him on the street in New Orleans. He's such a great singer and frontman, so we decided, let's do a band. I started getting back on piano, and wrote some songs on piano that were along the lines of Nick Cave. Rick immediately had vocal lines and lyrics that fit with them. Even when we play the heavier stuff, I usually play on piano. It's just a different sound we've developed. We got to play with X down there, and with the Cramps. We got to tour Europe. It's worked really well and [we] had some amazing shows.

Is doing a different project a conscious decision, or does it reflect your changing tastes?

It just kind of happens as a band member. Like if you're the lead singer and lead guitarist you can form the whole thing yourself and hire a few lackeys to complete your vision. But if you're a band member and enjoy being in a band and collaborating and writing with people, things kind of mutate, turn and twist and become other things, which is what I enjoy. Some of the songs I write entirely, and some the songs our guitarist Johnny Brashear, writes but a lot of times he'll play a riff and I'll come up with something and we collaborate. Just to be able to write songs on the piano that turn into songs for this band is a really cool thing. I've always like playing dark sounds with the piano. And then to hear it with a full band...

When did you open your bar, The Saint?

The Saint has been open for more than five years now, and been doing really well. It's been another thing that's been keeping me busy. When we first started the bar, my boyfriend and I were totally in there all the time, every day and every night. We're still a big part of it as far as the look of the bar, the jukebox, what goes on, the feel of the place. But there comes a point where you can't be in a bar every night, you'll kill yourself. Jay, our guitarist from White Zombie, joined on and is a partner now. He helps run it when we're both out of town.

What made you decide to start designing clothing accessories?

Inadvertently I did these graphics and thought they'd look cool on silk, so I had them printed on silk scarves, and it turned into being a part of the fashion world. But I'm trying to branch out into other things, like home furnishings, dishes, books... different things now. It's going really well. I've got showrooms now in NY, Los Angeles, London, and I've got boutiques from here to Tokyo, so it happened pretty quick. People compare the graphics to Pucci or Peter Max, which I guess are childhood influences that I can't help. It's basically from sketchbooks I fill up, these drawings, and then I color them in Photoshop and do color separations, then silkscreen. I had always planned on getting back into design after being in bands, so I'm trying to make that happen now. I've been in a few different shows and I've done some photographs that were in the Rock Show of Fine Art in Texas.

What was it like to play with the Cramps?

That was amazing. I've gotten to be friends with Lux and Ivy over the years, and like the Ramones, [the Cramps] were a band that White Zombie actually took on tour, which was again really weird because I worship them as much as the Ramones. I got to be friends with them on that tour, and later they just called me up to see if I could fill in on bass for this West Coast Halloween tour. Like I said, it was really an adventure, I totally worship them, but I'm friends with them, so there's a weird fine line between [playing and] geeking out as a fan. It was a huge honor.

We played with the Groovie Ghoulies, too. When I very first wanted to be in a band, before I moved up to New York and was still in high school, I met Dexter Romweber of Flat Duo Jets and I Married a Monster from Outer Space. Before I moved up there for a couple weeks, I was playing in a band with him and his sister Sara Romweber and the original singer of COC. The four of us were going to be in a band and call ourselves the Groovie Ghoulies. That's when I didn't even have a bass yet, I'd had a Farfisa [organ]. It was fun but very short lived. You know, I realized there already is a band called the Groovie Ghoulies. The Demolition Doll Rods were on that tour, too. I love that band.

Looking forward, what are your future plans for any music projects?

I think just playing with Rock City Morgue is enough right now. I'm trying to focus on my design work. And sometimes things come up. I got offered, the day of the show, to play bass for Andre Williams when I was in New Orleans. I had to learn fifteen songs in an hour. That was pretty amazing. I'm always up for any weird one-off thing that comes my way.

DANIELLE STAMPE GWAR

Danielle Stampe AKA Slymenstra Hymen, born November 1967 in San Diego, California, was the best known female character in the infamous punk / art rock / thrash metal band Gwar. As social satirists addressing every taboo subject matter, their themes are saturated with sci-fi and horror, using instruments and elaborate costumes that resemble battle armor and large weapons to execute their point (literally). Gwar's characters depict aspects of mythology, war, violence, and sex, and include Oderus Urungus, Slymenstra Hymen, Flattus Maximus, Balsac the Jaws of Death, Beefcake the Mighty, Jizmak Da Gusha, the Sexecutioner, Sleazy P. Martini (Gwar's manager), and many others.

Gwar's basic mythology is that billions of years ago a bored Master/ Creator of the Universe made death, destruction and war with its crowning achievement: battle god-creatures known as Gwar. Desiring supremacy, Gwar tried to overthrow the Master, who then puts them in the Death Pod and banishes them to Earth. After making Earth their playground and destroying the dinosaurs, the Master felt they had too much freedom and encases them in an Antarctica iceberg. In the 1980s, they are freed by gamma rays melting the iceberg (a result of excessive hairspray use by bands causing a hole in the ozone layer above Antarctica). Sleazy P. Martini discovers them and returns to America, where they become the greatest band in the universe.

Since 1985, they've released 15 albums and numerous videos. The albums include *Hell-O* (1988), *Scumdogs of the Universe* (1990), *America Must Be Destroyed* (1992), and *This Toilet Earth* (1994).

Stampe left the band to pursue other projects in the '90s. Danielle created Girly Freakshow in 2000 doing circus sideshow acts including the Miss Spidora illusion. She also performs with the Brothers Grim Sideshow and Lucha VaVoom. She holds the world's record for human endurance of high voltage electricity and is in the *Guinness Book of World Records* for fire breathing (distance and duration). She is educated in Women's Studies and Sociology, and speaks at many universities about feminism, women in mythology, her character Slymenstra (which she created), music and performing. Her latest character is Ms. Electra, who shoots lightning bolts from her fingers. Slymenstra rejoined Gwar for the 2002 Bitch is Back tour.

When Gwar began, were you involved in the original group?

I came along a little bit later. Gwar started as early as 1984 in Richmond, Virginia; everybody in Gwar was in college. There was a building called the Milk Bottle, an old dairy factory. All these artists lived there. Hunter Jackson made all these costumes and was making a B-movie in Richmond, a sci-fi thing. Then they decided to throw the costumes on Dave Brockie's band, Death Piggie. Gwar was sort of hatched out of that.

There were a lot more artists involved. For instance, one of my friends, Collette Miller, was the first Gwar woman, but she wasn't even called "Gwar woman," she was called "Gwar girl." There were two of them: Hunter Jackson's girlfriend, Heather, and Collette, she was Dave Brockie's girlfriend. They did a show or two, maybe three. In the old, old days of Gwar, they would do one or two shows a year. It wasn't like they had toured yet. In 1988, when I showed up on the scene, I was friends with all those people first. Later, Lisa Harrelson was the Gwar girl because Collete and Heather had both left or been kicked out. It was sort of a boys' club; you know, hard for girls to infiltrate. A few tried, but I'm the one who conquered them. (Laughs)

In what the public knows as Gwar, yes, I was an original member. But in the eyes of the original members of Gwar, which numbered probably fifty by the time I got there, they all feel they are the original members. In a way they're not, because they weren't the ones that toured and that the fans know. As far as Gwar is concerned—the stockholders, people that owned Gwar—[that's] the group that I was in, starting in 1988. That's when we became a corporation, that's when we became a business, that's when we got a record deal a couple years later. If you ask someone in Gwar if Danielle is an original member, they'll say yes. If you ask older members of Gwar, like my friend Collette, she considers herself the first Gwar woman. It's just who you ask, I guess. I consider myself the one and only Gwar woman, because I was the only one who put up with those people as long as I did.

And you became an icon...

Yeah, so basically the earlier girls sorta forged the way for the Gwar woman character, but they weren't really into the character as much. Maybe it just hadn't gotten to that point in development in Gwar with any character. So I come along and I was this crazy dancer and I'd go to these free jazz shows, these jazz shows that happened in Richmond were sorta like punk rock jazz, like that whole math rock thing was coming out of Richmond and I was bouncing off the walls, dancing all over the place, doing this—I don't know what you'd call it—punk rock noodling. (Laughs) It was kind of like hippie noodle dancing, but also angry and pissed off. Gwar saw me there.

Then Lisa Harrelson, the drummer's girlfriend, broke up [with him] as they were getting ready to go to a show in New York at the Ritz, I think opening for Danzig. No, we opened for the Butthole Surfers. That was '87 or '88. The Ritz is now Webster Hall. Since I was making the costumes for Lisa Harrelson—I was an artist as well, not just a dancer—when she flaked, they came to my house in the middle of the night and asked if I wanted to go. Actually, they had to do a show in Shafer Court in Richmond and I did that as my try-out for going to New York the following night. So I threw the costume on, I did the show, and they thought it was great. There I was, going off to play before the Butthole Surfers. So that's how I joined Gwar.

I didn't really know I wanted to be in a rock band. It wasn't my dream or anything like that. I was more towards the art side, you know, painting and sculpting and interested in clay. I didn't really know where my path was going. In fact, at first in college I took Fashion Design. I did that for a year. Then I switched over to Fine Arts.

In the beginning of Gwar, we started touring, we started doing the Eastern seaboard, developing grassroots markets, going up north to New York, New Jersey, and doing Trenton City Gardens [New Jersey]. We did a couple colleges—Vassar College, Princeton—getting smaller clubs, and doing the South, too. We were developing those two areas simultaneously. In 1988, Gwar started leaving home to play shows out of town for the first time, and I was there for those.

At the time our fans were super uber-cool punk rockers. People in the know. We weren't in magazines yet, it was just all word of mouth, grassroots-type style. We put a record out that year called *Hell-O*.

Did you start touring before you put an album out?

We did a few weekends here and there outside of town, and then the record came out. Gwar met Kramer—do you remember the band Bongwater, with Ann Magnuson? Well, we did our first Gwar record with Kramer. He was Ann's partner in Bongwater. He put out the first Gwar record on Shimmy Disc Records, which has now been bought by Metal Blade and redistributed. In the early days, when it was on vinyl and it was the punk rock do-it-yourself days... it was those days in rock and roll when Gwar was started. That was kinda fun, to see all that happen.

Why did characters like the Sexecutioner and Sleazy P. Martini leave?.

A lot of people were working on Gwar, about twenty of us, and some people just got older and grew away. Sleazy P. Martini was the first to leave; he had done the touring thing, had his fun with it, but was more of a homebody and didn't enjoy the touring part of Gwar. So he always just stayed at home and did sculpting and built Gwar props and stuff. He's still involved in Gwar today, but just behind the scenes.

For instance, the Sexecutioner, Chuck Varga, ended up moving to New York, just to continue his art, his passion in art, his path in it. He had done Gwar, was now over forty and just done with it.

I was the last one to leave... well, me and Hunter left at the same time. Hunter was more forced out of the band. Unfortunately, because he was the inventor, it was very hard for him. He and I are still friends, and he lives here in Los Angeles as well. For me, I had moved to Los Angeles and had still kept coming home for a tour or two, but Gwar was having a really hard time at that point, too. We had just been beating ourselves to death for years trying to make this thing happen that never quite seemed to go all the way. It was an idea that was partially realized, but I wouldn't say realized, because we certainly didn't have the success we hoped for. I don't want it to sound wrong, but we just beat ourselves up. We had these crazy touring cycles that were nine months long, we would come home, then the guys would make a record. While they were making records, we would build a new show and then make a video. We made all these videos and movies ourselves, and that was a wonderful experience as a young artist because we were able to experiment with so many different forms of media.

I came out of it thinking I didn't really do that much art when I was in Gwar, but I did. I mean, I know how to do latex, plaster, or RTB molds for latex, whatever the material. All the different things I learned just building my props and helping people build their props... Recently I've applied this experience while working with the LA Opera, and a lot in group projects. Especially doing the scenic thing, painting and creating backgrounds in the movies when I moved out here to LA. It was a real strong card, because I actually had hands-on experience with so many different mediums. I feel like in the film industry a lot of people just know one thing, like "I'm a mold maker," "I'm a model maker," "I'm a painter."

Since I have also worn the props, I've revolutionized some of the props so that they were more actor-friendly, and people loved it. I think that's because I've been acting on stage with props for years and since normal sculptors haven't, I have an advantage.

You've contributed so much people may not have been aware of...

My whole art experience with Gwar, the whole scope of it, was with the performance angle and the writing angle, as far as developing my character, and all the research that I did. I did years of feminist theology research developing my character. Oh my god, I was obsessed. I always had like six books at my side. Jennifer Finch from L7 gave me this book called *When God Was a Woman* by Merlin Stone, and it talks about the goddess religion. So I was in the middle of building this character and I was in freshmen year of college, and you're taking all those Art History Study 101s. Then I took a Women's Studies class and that's sort of the direction I went with Slymenstra, as far as the development of her character. I wanted to basically turn her into every female icon in the history of man, because Gwar was telling the history of man in all their comic books and stuff. So what I did was assume the characters of Kali, Medusa, the Virgin Mary, all the different icons. You know, the evil yet fascinating woman. (Laughs)

I also played upon a lot of man's fear of woman and how they've depicted it in art—woman as half-woman/half-lion, woman as half-woman/half-snake—as a feminist punk rocker, 'cause that whole vibe was going on... like "women of rock!" That was a fun era because women were pissed off for no reason. I have no idea now what I was mad about back then. Boy, was I pissed! (Laughs) That was my age I guess, I've grown out of it a bit. It's fun to look back on. I had the uppity women/man-haters club, Slymenstra Hymen-style, because the guys were such sexist characters on stage. I did that with the women's side to balance the scale. Like run onstage and chop Oderus Urungus's penis off and bask in my glory of doing something to manhood or whatever. It was silly but fun.

How did Gwar come up with enough money to get the props?

In the old days, the early days, Gwar would make a whole bunch of stuff and it would be practically papier-mâché, but made really strong because it was done with cloth instead of paper and with wood glue instead of white glue, and sometimes we put some fiberglass resin over it. So in the early days the costumes really hurt, they were pretty uncomfortable and cruder. We all worked hard in the very beginning: when you wanted a costume piece you would try and get something really together. We'd basically put in our time for free for many years. But then later on when we would do shows, as the funding for Gwar got bigger and bigger, the shows would raise the money to pay our rent for the art studio we had. We always had an art studio for years and years, since the mid-'80s. We combined all our tools there and resources and just started doing it. The same for the Slave Pit, which was always a great one, the Slave Pit—"Don't talk about it, do it!" That's why we called it the Slave Pit, we were all just slaves to this idea. We would just do bong hits, take acid, and just stay in the Slave Pit all the time, making shit. There was nothing else to do in Richmond, Virginia, you know? I think it was a real breeding ground because it was such a creative college, it was a big art school. There was just a lot of real fun people around us, at the right times.

There's a lot of humor in Gwar: the giant acid cube, the World Maggot...

Yeah, there used to be, there's not as much anymore. We had the big acid cube; the World Maggot is the doom character. That's an old Indian legend. All of our stuff, if you really were to sit down with a scholar and look at early Gwar, you would see there are a certain amount of archetypes, like Joseph Campbell's *Hero with a Thousand Faces*. There are all these stories that are shared throughout the world, and Gwar is one of those. What I'm talking about is what I consider the real Gwar, before I left. The whole mythos in the comic books is that we were all from other planets that were banished here on this insignificant mudball planet. I was put here so that Gwar could mate with me and create a super-race, but I wouldn't put out so Gwar was forced to fuck the monkeys and thus the human race was created. The comic was based on what Hunter Jackson drew at six years old.

After I left, Gwar changed a lot. I was the last original to leave, now we still have original members in the band. It's Dave Brockie, Brad Roberts the drummer, and Dirk on guitar, then we have Bobby and Matt, who are longtime slaves. They were not original members because they were too young—they were in junior high when we formed in '88. But Bobby's been around Gwar forever, even when he was still in high school. I consider them originals because they've been around for twenty years. So there are five of them, and then there are some Elders. We call everybody that's older in Gwar, even before me, who were still with the group "the Elders." And there's Elders around that still are involved, like Don Drakulich's friend that still makes props. In a way, I feel like Gwar is a lifelong thing that you're involved with, because I know we'll be doing books later. I want to still be a part of all that but I just don't want to tour anymore. I put in seventeen years. I'm still active in Gwar even though I'm not always on tour with them, I bring Gwar things to the table; I get them TV shows. I still try and bring them business when I can. I'm still friends with them now. I certainly was ready to get out of there, and I wouldn't say that I wasn't bitter, but it wasn't a bitter departing. I was just at a point in my life as an artist where I felt like it was time for me to move on to my next project. And they've taken another direction, they went more the evil route, they thought that the silly route wasn't working.

That's too bad, because that's one of the best parts of the band.

Yeah, I agree, there's a lot of contention about the new Gwar, like whether people like it or not. Some people love it. Some people are just getting exposed to Gwar for the first time, so that's what they know as Gwar, and the Elders are all grumbling. All of us that have been in Gwar forever are like, "We liked it better before." So, you know, things change and things grow. Honestly, to make Gwar even still exist they probably had to pare down and not have as many people around to pay, just to make the project work. Maybe that's why we never really worked, because we never really had enough money. We made a lot of money, Gwar was like a big huge oven that was burning, like the *Titanic*, and you were just taking money and throwing it in there never to be seen again. Because we just constantly tried to outdo ourselves and up the ante: make a bigger dinosaur; a newer, better Oderus.

Each tour would be more elaborate and bigger, with more characters?

We really did that for a long time, then after a while people were like, "Oh my god, I've got to make some money." We all lived in that studio that we had, we went from a smaller studio to a big humongous... what we called "the Gwar compound." The Gwar compound was incredible.

Did it become like a cult? Did you have followers, people camping out?

No, not that really, but *we* were camping out. (Laughing) We had this attic that we converted into little bedrooms. It was sort of like living in the dorms after college—the Gwar dorms—and you had like twenty-five kinds of athlete's foot living there. It was disgusting, you know.

As soon as we got older, we all got little apartments. Gwar is living better now, now that they've pared the numbers down. People are actually making real salaries. I'm not saying I didn't make a real salary with Gwar, I certainly did towards the end of my career. The only reason I'm saying this stuff is not to be negative, it's just that Gwar asked a lot of people to participate, and after a while we were just kind of worn out by it.

How many people in total were in the band?

Well, there were twenty people in the band actively at one point. That was sort of our heyday and that was the most. We'd have two tour buses on the road, with tractor-trailers with our stuff in it. Other years it would be more like twelve or thirteen. I think they're at about that now. The numbers of how many people have worked on Gwar are astronomical. There, of course, was our core group of twenty that never really changed. Gwar didn't have a lot of switching around of people. The only people that really switched around a lot were slaves, and Mike Bonner was the original slave, he was the funniest one. He was like a monkey jumping around. Just so fun to play with and interact with onstage; he was really, really good. When he left, he just wanted to get on with his life. He and his wife got married, they bought a house, he had a mortgage, he started a construction business that was really successful. One thing I love about Gwar is you don't hear these horror stories about so-and-so left Gwar and now they're a crack addict. Everybody from Gwar is successful. Well, not everybody, there are about two or three tragic stories, but considering the circumstances... It's pretty neat to hear what everybody's doing. So I really enjoy that part of it, that people didn't turn into rock stars and just kept doing art.

What about Oderus, what's going on with him?

Oderus is basically running Gwar, and doing his thing touring. I believe he still paints some. He's the one who really wanted to take the direction of the band into a more serious thing, because he just thought that's what the fans wanted. Maybe that's what *he* wanted, I don't know, but he was such a funny guy. He's hysterical.

He was on mainstream talk shows, like Jerry Springer *and* Joan Rivers?

I loved him on Joan Rivers. Yeah, he was great on Jerry Springer when he was telling parents, "Look, it's not the responsibility of artists to raise your children." And then he was saying stuff about the government blowing up stuff and what's more obscene, etc., etc. He just went off about how humanity has fucked themselves with war, forever. He said it so eloquently.

Does Gwar consider itself punk or metal?

In the early days I would say we were a punk rock band, and then the whole thrash metal/everything, kind of combining things, era was going on, and Gwar was just developing as musicians anyway, and we had better musicians at that point that could play their instruments and not just play punk rock. At that point, we were more of a thrash punk metal band, and then as time progressed we became what we were joking about, we became that Kiss band. We became the metal rock stars that we were joking about. I think *America Must Be Destroyed* was, I swear, my favorite record. I don't know if it was the least sold, but I thought that record was genius. And that one is kind of on the metal side. After that it went way metal, way more metal each time.

Were there any particular comic books or novels that influenced Gwar?

Most of the people in Gwar were sci-fi junkies. Dave Brockie has a fascination with WWII and Nazis, not from a prospective that he idolizes them, I think he studied it to understand why this happened again and again. That's why he studied war, I feel. He was also into Tolkien, Moorecock, and all those sci-fi writers. Philip K. Dick, all that type of stuff. Him, Hunter, Scott Krahl, pretty much all of them, and me too, because I got influenced by what they were into and what was around me all the time... all the horror movies they were watching.

So it's like gore mixed with sci-fi?

Yeah, gore mixed with sci-fi mixed with war. And because we are from Virginia, most of us (not all of us) come from some sort of military or government family. My father was Navy, I know Don Drakulich's were CIA and FBI, and then somebody else's dad was FBI, and somebody else's was a federal judge or something.

What did they think about their kids being in Gwar? Did they care?

Brockie's mom was a WWII nurse, went through WWII. I think most of us came from pretty strict upbringings. There were definitely people from [intact] families; there weren't a lot of people from broken homes.

Was this traditional upbringing fodder for parody in Gwar?

We were all just thinking about stuff like that then, too, in the late '80s, early '90s. People were screaming a little more. Like the Million Man March. The thing I did with L7, I went to DC with them one time and did a Fugazi show, and then we all went and did the march for abortion rights. Then we did this whole performance with Debbie Harry, L7, and me on the Capital lawn. That was pretty neat.

Are you a feminist? Your character has such a masculine element.

Yes, I was sexual but masculine at the same time, because I had to be in the boys' club and be tough, superhero tough. I felt like I had to compete.

You had to be as balls-out as the guys. Or be bossy. That's something I learned that you don't need to be like, after Gwar. Channeling Slymenstra through me for so long, it really affected my personality after a while. I feel like [even] after leaving her behind me as a character, that I'm playing her all the time, practically. I mean, I knew how to turn her off when I got offstage, I didn't have to be Courtney Love twenty-four hours a day. But in a way, Slymenstra seeped into my true personality, and that's something that I had to work through after leaving her behind. I was doing things in my real life like bossing my boyfriends around, you know, doing these bad behaviors that Slymenstra was doing. You know, expecting guys to get fucked up the ass. No, I'm just kidding, [that] didn't work in real life. (Laughs)

You got away with a lot of amazing things on stage.

It's so funny. I hit Jello Biafra over the head with a bloody tampon, how cool is that? If you think about all the metaphoric things I did, I just can't believe I got away with it all. The way that I would present things at Gwar meetings, because I was the girl I always felt like, "Hey, you guys,

I've got this great idea for a theme, we'll have this and that and the aliens will impregnate me, I'll be the Virgin Mary, we'll do this whole thing!" If I went in and said that—absolutely no, vetoed, we're not doing it. If I went around to each artist in Gwar and was doing my art project near them, I'd be like, "Oh man, wouldn't it be cool if we had this alien and it came down, abducted me, and impregnated me?" So in the course of coming up with an idea, you would tell someone else about it, they would come up with ideas. So, at a meeting, I'd go, "Hey, what about that idea Bobby had for that alien cum gun? That was really funny." Then the next thing I knew, my whole idea was getting produced, because that's how I had to do it.

I figured it out pretty early, that if I just said "Hey, what about this idea?" if it had anything to do with demeaning Oderus, bumming one of them out to get my little kick in, like "I get to kick you in the balls!"—if I said that, it wouldn't happen. But if I let it develop the right way, then I'd get my way. I had to do all this... I called it "creative manipulation." Later they knew, because I would talk about it like how I'm talking about it with you. And Hunter would be like, "A little more creative manipulation." It was like a joke after awhile. Because in Gwar you would have an idea, and someone else would be like, "And I thought of this great idea!" Then it would be theirs, you just had to be used to saying, "Whatever, as long as it gets done."

How did Gwar come up with ideas? Did you have meetings?

Yeah, we did; Gwar had weekly meetings. In heavy production times, we would have two meetings where everybody in Gwar was in the same room at the same time. Two a week. Monday night meeting was the big meeting. Thursday night meeting, if we needed to have one. If we were in production cycle where we're doing movies, we would have Monday night meetings and we'd set the meetings for the rest of the week. Like script meeting Tuesday night from 10 to 2, on Tuesday we would be doing this if anybody wants to be there. We would have heads of different departments, sort of corralling things, to make things happen. The whole scripting process and writing process was a Monday night meeting. If we were having an idea session, we would just start writing all these ideas down and arguing and talking and arguing, then everybody would get sick of it, we would leave and come back again. Do it again, weed it out, and then put it in some kind of order. Then we would come up with a production plan: "Okay, we need to build a new Gor-Gor, we need Gor-Gor's head to be able to do this." Then we would start planning everything out and budgeting it, then handing out projects to people. Like, "Scott Krahl, you're going to do Gor-Gor; Matt Maguire, you're going to build Captain America (or whoever the character is), Grambo, and Morality Squad; Hunter, you're going to draw it, and then these three are going build it, you guys are all going to work together." Stuff like that.

Recording the music came first, and then the meetings for the live shows?

It all actually happened simultaneously. Gwar was broken into two factions: the artists and the musicians. It almost became a bad thing in the end, because the two sides were at war with each other. That was just the dynamic of being with people for twenty years really, in retrospect. So the musicians would be writing records, etc., and Dave was a big idea man. He was Gwar's leader and still is. He was a force, had the loudest voice and biggest head, and was able to point everybody in the right direction somehow and orchestrate the whole thing. Not that he was the mastermind behind all of it, because it takes more than one person to run Gwar, especially in the old-fashioned manner. That's why I think Gwar was so wonderful back then. Because it was so multi-layered, there were so many smart people involved and that's what made it so juicy. There were a lot of different areas to bite into, like, for instance, the female fans could bite into my character and really get into it. Now I feel sad for them because there's no female character.

I kind of weighed out the male/female you need for any good drama or any good production. You have to have something that creates conflict; the male/female struggle is the biggest one. Without Gwar having that, sometimes I have felt after going to see them since I've left the band, [that] it's just too boyish in a way.

In critics' reviews, was Gwar taken seriously as musicians?

I think that it was really sad what happened to Gwar. Our second record, *The Scum Dogs of the Universe*, was put out by Bluebeat Records, an English label. It was Buster Bloodvessel from Bad Manners and English Beat, that whole ska crowd. So they did the whole English press thing with our first record and made it a real big splash. But you know how the English press is so critical, they were like, (in a snooty English voice) "Well, the show was wonderful but the muuusic..." So for some reason that stuck, and I know that, in the beginning, Gwar's music wasn't exactly up to par just because it was punk rock, whatever, mayhem. But then as Gwar was taking themselves more seriously, Gwar got excellent musicians; I will never let anybody say anything else about them but that.

I always thought the musical angle was great.

Yeah, but for some reason the press just never did. Now they really are trying to put the music in the front seat and that's sort of why they have toned the show down, and they feel that they are getting more acclaim for that. I feel they've always deserved it. Yeah sure, *Hell-O* was a little crappy, so what? It was our first record, and it was a punk rock album. So, I mean, technically what the critics say doesn't really matter anyways. If it's true punk, it doesn't matter. It's if the fans like it. Gwar has been around for twenty years now. If any band lasts twenty years, there's something to it.

How did the fans react to you, males vs. females?

I had some stalkers and I got some really great crazy sex fan letters. I got really great letters from women and girls. One of the fun things about being Slymenstra was I felt like I was getting young boys to fall in love with a strong female icon. And that just really lit my fire because I just loved to feel—I know this sound silly—that I was making some sort of difference in the world.

Would you say that 80% of the audience at your shows were males?

Yeah, 80/20 probably, and I think more women came when I was there. I think the numbers have dropped a little bit, because I know that I did have a fan base of some sort that was showing up just to see me. When I first put my MySpace site up, wow, I got a big huge response. I was really surprised, I really haven't toured with Gwar since around 2000 and I did one little thing in 2001 or 2002. I mean, for being out of the game for five years... And when I left Gwar, I left. I didn't leave a Slymenstra goodbye letter or anything, I was just like *done*. I walked away from the project and didn't keep putting out Slymenstra t-shirts or any of that stuff. I did use Slymenstra to do Girly Freakshow, and that sort of let me know that fans still wanted to see Slymenstra. That's one of the reasons I went back to Gwar a second time, just to do one little thing. It was more for the fans. Everybody was like, "We miss Slymenstra. We miss Slymenstra," so I just had to do it one more time.

At live performances these guys show up ready to have good time, they have a sense of humor, they're more light-hearted about stuff, but then there's macho posturing that goes on in the pit. Then there's you up there, this female presence that's dominating the whole show. It's funny to see them stop what they're doing and just stare in awe.

Yeah, the fire shows, the fire dances, were really great. They were like primeval, and I felt like that brought the bacchic element into Gwar, where it was just like this orgy of spirit and anger and emotion. That fire thing I was doing was like a sex dance in a way, but it was really raw.

They were seduced and terrified at the same time?

Yeah. I swear, back in the day when I was really into my character and I was really into Gwar, I felt like I really did have a demi-goddess living through me. I would work out really hard before the shows. Henry Rollins inspired me to do that.

I felt like I was conjuring up this spirit that would go jump into me and I would literally bounce off the walls. I just had this spirit that was volcano-ing and bubbling out of me. I really did feel that. I remember in my later years in Gwar, when I finally did decide that I was done, it was because I was imitating my former feelings, that it wasn't really there anymore. I felt like I was acting, like "back in '96, what were my dance moves?" It turned more into an acting job rather than this whole religious experience.

Well, Gwar shows looked honestly exhausting...

Yeah, most of us would be setting up all day. Not only that, but in the daytime Gwar worked real hard because we did our own PA, our own sound, our own lights. Lugging our own gear in and out, we'd get our own load-ins and load-outs, we did not hire roadies. We had a guitar tech and maybe two roadies, but it wasn't like we had a crew that just put everything up for us and we walked in and put our costumes up and got to perform, like most bands got to that were on our level. We were spending all the money on latex rubber or fiberglass. We didn't have that luxury. Beyond that, we did comic book stores every day or radio stations. Gwar was a real hard job; it was definitely show biz.

I feel like my involvement in the group definitely formed me into a super-worker. Now I'll be on set fourteen hours a day and it won't be that bad. Most people aren't used to working that way. When I'm with the circus, same thing. I had a real discipline that gave me an advantage. I think they were expecting, because I was a rock star, that I was gonna be this real prima donna, that I wasn't going to be able to hack the work and training schedules, the physical training schedule. I did it, you know, and that meant a lot, because I got involved in Gwar at such a young age.

How old were you when you started?

I think I was seventeen. I had finished high school and just started college. I started it right as I left high school.

Who were your inspirations growing up?

Exene Cervenka from X. I loved her. As far as music goes, Madonna and Exene. I just loved that Madonna can put things together so well with her team. She's a really good example of a modern artist and how they realize they can't do it all themselves. The art of it is putting the right team together. And the fact that she's still going so strong, more power to her. I just felt like she was the first female musician who just really took charge of her career. Everything about her is calculated, you know. You've got to admire her discipline even if you don't love everything she does. I just admire her discipline.

She uses oxygen backstage because she exerts herself so much on stage...

Gwar did that too, a lot of bands do that—Ozzy Osborne does that. You have to, because with all the smoke on the stage and a Gwar show can be two hours long. With Madonna, she's a dancer first and a musician second at her shows. She dances so incredibly hard and she never looks likes she's tired when she's on stage. That's physically taxing. When you run offstage to do a costume change, people will shove oxygen on your face when you're changing. It really helps. And then you can go right back out there with that same energy.

Has anyone else inspired you?

Oh god, there are so many. When I was younger, I was so into Frida Kahlo, Georgia O'Keefe; I was really into a lot of women. Billie Holiday, Sarah Vaughn, Ella Fitzgerald. All the jazz singers, I loved that type of stuff. I was into the circus the whole time, too. There's all the circus people

I love, Annie Oakley is probably my favorite, she was a Wild West star. I also like Calamity Jane and cowgirls.

Gwar used so much stage blood, what was it made of? Corn syrup?

Uh-uh, that stuff is awful. The blood that was pressurized through the tanks—the stuff that got sprayed on the audience—that was concentrated powdered food dye with water. The stuff on us that was thicker was a special Gwar recipe; we used an ingredient called carrageen, it's a seaweed emollient, it's used in everything: lotion, milk, ice cream. We got it in its raw form and boiled it down, made these big tubs and vats of it. Later we found where we could get it already made. So that was an invention of Don Drakulich. His parents had gone to Belize and found about this super drug, carrageen. And we were boiling it up and putting it in all kinds of foods, we realized how thickening it was. So we would make thick batches, cut that with water and then put the food coloring in it. So that's where it all started. And it's healthy for you, too! Karo syrup, man, I don't know if you've ever used it, but if you get it on your leg and your knees sticks together, it's so uncomfortable. If it dries a little, it can actually rip your skin off.

Didn't you break a world record for electric shock?

Yes, while I was in Gwar I started working with these people who were developing this Tesla stunt where you shoot lightening out of your fingers. Nikola Tesla was an inventor who made this machine called the Tesla Coil, which sends electricity through the air without wires. He worked with Edison and that whole shebang. He invented AC/DC power, the microwave oven, the radio, the light bulb—a lot of them Edison took credit for. This machine, the patent was stomped out because the powers that be wouldn't have made any money. Nikola Tesla had done this stunt a long time ago. There have been a few people who have done it throughout time. But nobody had done it in a really long time, so I thought that would be the coolest thing for Slymenstra to do.

So I hooked up with these people here in Los Angeles called KVA Effects, and they do all Tesla-type things for the film industry like create lightning on set or whatever. They had been looking for a long time for a girl to do this stunt. They had these old scientist guys who could do it, but they thought with a girl they could sell it more. So here I come walking along and I had already been doing smaller Tesla stuff and I'm like, "I've been wanting to do that stunt where you shoot lightning out of your fingers for forever." They were like, "Oh my god, we've found her!" So basically they taught me how to do the stunt, built a coil—a really big coil—with Brent Turner, he was the creator of the coil. I just helped a bit and put together this act called "Miss Electra."

First I tried to get Gwar to let me do it onstage, but they didn't want to pay for it, or Dave didn't want to be upstaged, or the band was afraid, I could give you a hundred excuses as to why I wasn't allowed to. I was already getting tired of Gwar at that time, and I just felt like, "God, here I come up with this great visual effect and they don't even want to use it? What am I doing here? This is a waste of time." I kept feeling held back. I just wasn't allowed to do as much as I could have done.

So I set out to do Girly Freakshow that summer, and Gwar was sort of on a two-year hiatus. I put that Girly Freakshow together, though it had already existed for years around '98 or '99, but had never really done a national tour, except Lollapalooza. Girly Freakshow was myself, Ula, and Sharka of the Painproof Rubber Girls, who were out of Coney Island, New York. Sharka is now in San Francisco and is a tattoo artist.

They actually started Girly Freakshow. We used to do Jackie 60, and have girls all over the venue cracking bullwhips, eating fire, laying on a bed of nails, contorting. So I asked the girls if they wanted to do a national tour. They weren't interested because they were off doing different things. I was going to use the Gwar name to launch the Girly Freakshow and I wanted the lightning stunt to be the big shebang. So we set it up for this thing called DragonCon—a comic book, sci-fi, gamer convention—one of the biggest ones. Twenty or thirty thousand people show up. Gwar was friends with these guys, Gwar was even playing there. At that event, we had TV come out, *Ripley's Believe It or Not* and *Guinness Book of World Records* were both invited. I set a world record that night: I did 175,000 volts. Then, later on for the TV show *Ripley's Believe It or Not* and *Guinness Book of World Records* I broke my record. It's for "Human Endurance of Electrical Current."

How does it work exactly, for those who don't know?

I don't really tell how it works, but basically I use a Tesla Coil, I sit on top of a table, the electricity runs through the table, I'm sitting on a piece of metal in water, then the electricity travels through my body and out my hands. It will travel out the highest point in my body, so if I were to lower my hands it would come out my head, but that would hurt too much. I put little metal rings on my fingers so that it comes out there. Basically what electricity will do is travel the path of least resistance. So since I put metal on my hands, it goes right to it. There's quite a sensation. I've had a couple accidents where I've really felt the electricity. It's almost like what tattooing would feel like, basically, in my ass and my hands, where it's coming in and going out. It also feels like when you lay on your leg all day, it's like that, but a little stronger. Pins and needles.

What happened with the cuttlefish incident, the confiscation of the penis?

I think we were in Raleigh, North Carolina. We were doing a show at a small venue. It looked like there were undercover cops in the audience because there were like mom and dads there with Bart Simpson shirts on—they were really obvious. So we sorta knew we were going to get in trouble, but we didn't know for what. Basically, they came in and said we were disseminating a sex act in front of minors, even though it was a fake penis. They said something got fucked, so they confiscated Oderus's penis, which we never got back. Hello Nazi Germany.

It was some kind of undercover sting, like North Carolina didn't want us in their state. We got popped, they took the penis, they arrested Dave Brockie. They couldn't find my vagina because I had hidden it, so I didn't get arrested. Neither did anybody else, because they didn't have genitalia hanging off. They had like little slave things, loincloths. We ended up making a movie about it called *Phallus in Wonderland*. Here's the funniest part—guess what the judge's name in North Carolina was? Richard Boner, Dick E. Boner. We used that in the movie. That is his real name, the judge who presided over the case. Truth is often funnier than fiction. Isn't that hysterical? It wasn't fun for Dave because he's a Canadian citizen and we didn't know whether he was going to get thrown out of the country, whether he was going to get some sex crime. So we were banned from North Carolina for a certain amount of time. We've played there a lot since, and nothing has ever happened again. The only other place we were banned from was London, England. I was a Page Three girl as Slymenstra in *The Sun*, in '89 or '90. I had this fake foam head in my hand and a sign that read: *Bring your mom's head to the show and get a dollar off.* It caused such a stink that Parliament wouldn't let us come to England.

What happened with the North Carolina court case? Was the penis sitting there as evidence? How did you keep a straight face during the trial?

He was in jail overnight and released on bail. A year later we had to go down there for court. But we had to get a lawyer, pay all this money. The ACLU helped defend our case. I wasn't there. They had his penis there, and Gwar was like, "No! It's a fish, it's the Cuttlefish of Cthulhu!" It was a really serious matter because Dave could have been kicked out of the country. It could have ended our band. Dave says it was the worst night of his life. I still don't know what happened in jail. The final decision was us being banned from North Carolina, and we might have got fined. We never saw [the penis] again, but we made a new one. He called it the Cuttlefish of Cthulhu before the case, it was around since the beginning of Gwar; I think it was a Moorecock thing. We named all of our things—we had silly little names for everything. We wanted to make a whole Gwar dictionary at one time, but it never happened. We had our own little language. My vagina was called the Clam Slam, which was also my signature wrestling move. I would throw a man to his knees, and then I would grab him from behind the head and start slamming his face into my clam, hence the Clam Slam. It was the most powerful move in all of Gwar! Followed by the Dick Whip, which was this little whip I had with a huge penis on the end of it. I'd put it down to my crotch and pretend it connected itself and then it would run me around the room like it had control, and I'd be running around going *Ahhh!!* like it had power. Then it would start raping all the slaves. That was Dick-Whipped instead of pussy-whipped.

So what are you mainly doing now?

Miss Electra has worked with the Torture King at Not Scary Farm every year for a month at Knott's Berry Farm's Halloween event. There are thousands of people a night there. She's performed in Lucha VaVoom, a burlesque Mexican wrestling event. I've wrestled in the show and done Miss Electra. I've worked in the Velvet Hammer run by Michelle Carr and Rita. They broke off into two halves and Lucha VaVoom was born, but I've done both of those shows. She's also done an international magician competition with Mr. Marrick in Japan. I ended up winning. I got that event through an agent named Chuck Harris, who represents all the 'weirdos.' He was a burlesque comedian back in the day. Right now there's a play on Broadway being written about the story of his life. He's an incredible person. My image now on stage is a 1950s' Russ Meyer bombshell—the whole drag queen, pin-up star look. So my career after Gwar has been pretty much Miss Electra and the set painting business.

PHOEBE LEGERE

Phoebe Legere, born 1963 in Lexington, Massachusetts, is an interdisciplinary performer, composer, and visual artist based in New York. She emerged from the '80s Lower East Side punk/performance art scene and appears in the 1998 documentary *Mondo New York*. In the early '80s, Legere was best known for her song "Marilyn Monroe," performing in Chanel-style minisuits with an accordion, singing in a four-and-a-half octave voice ranging from ethereal to operatic. She not only plays the accordion, but also piano, synthesizer, and many other instruments. She has built electronic circuits for performance by hand, commenting, "Ecology, electricity and gender equality are my primary themes. I feel that I will fulfill the Fluxus dream of total Intermedia Immersion if I don't electrocute myself first."

Phoebe is also multilingual and has written songs spanning many genres, including new wave, classical, and avant garde. She was invited to perform with David Bowie for his *Glass Spider* tour in 1987. In the '80s and '90s she released *Meet the Monad* (1984), *Trust Me* (1985), *Blond Fox* (1987), *Marilyn Monroe* (1989), *Phoebe Legere* (1992), *Six Flights Up* (1994), *1000 Kisses* (1995), and *4 Nurses of the Apocalypse* (1996). Her more recent eclectic works include *Last Tango in Bubbleland* (pop and Celtic soul; 1997), *Swingalicious* (swing covers with the Brooklyn Bums; 1999), *Blue Curtain* (2000), *Children of the Dawn* (2001), *Passion Flower* (2002), *Trillions of Electrons* (2003), *Salmon Singer* (2004), *Sonification* and *Midnight and Ultra Romantic Parallel Universe* (2007). Phoebe's work in 2000 with the Tone Road Ramblers led to a Pulitzer Prize in Music nomination that same year for her work, *WaterClown*.

Phoebe has also appeared in eleven films, and has received grants and awards as a playwright. She has been an artist-in-residence at the School of Visual Arts and the University of Victoria Graduate School of Engineering and Music, in addition to volunteering in New York City public schools. She is the host and writer for *Roulette TV*, a show dedicated to experimental art and music. Phoebe also ran for Governor of New York in 2006 with the Integrity Party. In addition, she co-founded and an archivist for the New York Underground Museum, a virtual museum attempting to catalogue the works of the world's greatest bohemians.

How did you first become interested in the arts, and how old were you?

My mother and father are genius artists; we are creative people. In our household, nothing was more important than art: there was constant drawing, painting, singing, beauty, proportion, laughter, costumes, dancing. I started playing the piano before age three, I wrote my first song at six, and did my first oil painting at about five. I started playing professionally in the church at age nine.

My parents taught life-drawing classes. I never had any idea that people were ashamed of the naked human body. All I knew was, "The thumb of the right hand is on the left side," or "The bone of the inner ankle is a little higher than the bone of the outer ankle," "The ears line up with the nose," "Draw the space between the figures..." that kind of thing. I was raised differently.

When I went into the world and I learned that people in America have contempt for artists, nature, the female body, and beauty, I was mortified! It still shocks me, every day. How can people cut into the earth and poison her? How can people do something as vulgar and grisly as war, mutilating each other? Or for entertainment? Give me a break!

And how is it that men can say cutting things to women, still judging them only on their looks, unable to see the soul of the woman, the real essence of a woman, which is love, creativity, and life?

How is it that people will not acknowledge the obvious fact that the human body is one of the most beautiful things ever created? It should not be hidden, or concealed, or made an object of shame, or sold by the mafia in topless bars and on the internet, or dismissed as unimportant in church. The human body is as sacred as anything else in the Universe—an expression of the holy mystery. That is my truth. My voice comes out of my body. My body is beautiful. I was born that way and I was raised that way by my mother and father, who were both beautiful and gifted. And they suffered for it, too. They were too cool.

Have you had any formal training before singing?

I have never had a voice lessons. My parents said, "Why should we spend money on voice lessons? You can already sing." This was not cheapness. I mean, of course they are cheap, you have to be cunning and thrifty to be an artist. But they didn't like the phony, artificial sound of opera singers. They liked the jazz sound. I have a natural sound. That is why people say quite often it is angelic. The angels don't take voice lessons. They just sing.

Of course, I am a music freak. I listened to records constantly and picked up tips from geniuses God put in my path along the way. For instance, a guy who said he was Rod Stewart used to come to my apartment and play me amazing tapes, like Janis Joplin singing in a small club, or *Plinth* (which is early Rod singing with Jeff Beck.) This guy said, "Frank Sinatra once told me just open up your throat as if you are giving a blowjob." That was very good advice. Try it.

Later, Rod's manager, Arnold S., called me and said, "You don't know Rod Stewart. Stop telling people you know him." Well, if that guy wasn't Rod Stewart, he certainly gave me some great advice about singing, which I have never forgotten. And note: the guy who said he was Rod Stewart and looked like Rod also picked up quite a bit of his standard jazz repertoire from me, at One Fifth Avenue, which was my jazz gig throughout the '80s and '90s.

One thing that may have contributed to my extraordinary strength and staying power is that I studied Yoga from a very young age. I learned it at 18, when I was with the Wooster Group. I was the resident composer there. I would be doing headstands and look through my legs and there would be Willem Dafoe and Spaulding Gray looking at me upside down. We had a yogi who taught us how to breathe. Breath is the most important thing. The lungs are the interface with the external world. The mitochondria are there, and they are also in the brain. Listen to my work *The Common Root of All Organisms* to learn about these cells and others, and how they evolved.

How were you introduced to the performance art world?

There was a magazine called *Avalanche*, published by Willoughby Sharp. I read that magazine avidly. I listened to late Beethoven quartets, I read Proust, I loved art. I was into New Music I loved it: dissonance, noise. That is who I am. When I found out that there was a new art form that combined art and music, I was on it immediately. I felt that performance art was the answer.

I wanted to combine performance art with rock and roll, and that is how I formed MONAD in 1980. Our first gig was at the Performing Garage, the home of the Wooster Group. I played a Moog Liberation, the first handheld synthesizer. There were only seven made. Sun Ra had one. I had one. We played with Sonic Youth, John Zorn, Tom Cora, and Ethyl Eichelberger. It was like a never-ending carnival of highly intellectual entertainment. You could do anything on stage. Everything was permitted. I did *Follies Legere*, which was a sort of Crazy Horse-Origin of the Species with atonal new wave funk, and I did *The Big Bacchanal of Avenue B*, starring Jack Smith as Tiresias.

Punk had become a new kind of rock by the time I hit the scene. We lived for it and we also were fully expecting to die for it. I wanted to combine classical music, electronics, and new wave. I named my band MONAD for Liebnitz's concept of the Monad. Liebnitz invented the computer, or actually the adding machine. We rehearsed on Cortland Alley in Soho in a loft with no windows. Hence the windowless Monad. We did theater in between songs. I had Micky O. wear a gorgeous lavender penis costume and Luli, who now plays with Ikue Morie, wore a beautiful sparkly vagina costume. We performed in front of a huge painting of Madonna nursing a child. Droplets were flying out of her breasts toward the baby's mouth, and her vagina was lined in feathers. This was in 1982. Madonna attended my concert and I guess it changed the course of her life. Her manager came to me the next year and said, "I will manage you and make you a star if you will get rid of your band. You don't need a band. We have machines to do all that for you." I said, "My band is my family. Music is a collaborative art form. If we let machines make the music, what's the point?" Camille Sasser said, "Have it your way."

How lucky I was that I met Arleen who ran A's Performance Loft! She is my mentor and my friend. We have founded the New York Underground Museum to try to preserve, curate, and present some of the work from that era.

When did you decide to integrate music with performance art?

My dream is Total Art Synthesis. I have always been multimedia. Because artistic hierarchies are so rigidly gendered, no one remembers that I was one of the very first out of the box with this shit, but as Aram Avakian once said, "You tell the pioneers by the arrows in their backs."

Did you realize early on how truly gifted you are?

Everyone always treated me like a genius. I tested very high on the IQ tests. The kids always copied me, and followed me. I was funny, always making jokes. But on the other hand, many folks hate a gifted person.

Going back up to the Underground, in other cultures people value their artists as healers and shamans. In America, they hate you and root for your downfall. If all else fails, they steal your ideas, and then discredit you by sticking a camera up your skirt when you aren't looking. Like *Mondo* fucking *New York*, the movie that killed downtown, and many careers.

Why did Mondo New York *become such a tragedy for you?*

Mondo New York was all my idea. Well, Nile Southern and I came up with it. We used to think as one person in those days, Nile and I. We were very big thinkers. The producer came to me and said, "We want to do a movie about the East Village." The producer, Stuart somebody, said, "Will you meet with our writer?" I said, "Sure."

I so wanted someone to document what was going on in our neighborhood because I knew how special it was—a real renaissance. So I cooperated, and brought Nile Southern, my boyfriend at the time. We went to Di Roberti's on 9th Street. Nile and I had a cappuccino and we were very innocent. We said to this creepy little writer, "Okay, use these people, like Dean Johnson, Joey Arias, Lydia Lunch, and John Sex, because they are the best people." And here is the idea: It's like a modern *Candy* (which Nile's father wrote), a young girl comes to town and we see it all fresh, through the eyes of someone from the outside. They took our idea and in return they promised they would "Get me a record contract on Island Records." I worked night and day. I was paid $200 in all. Then the creepy little writer started to fall for me or something. He called me up and said, "Come to my hotel room and bring some drugs." I said, "Huh? I don't have any drugs." He said, "Okay, you come to such and such a hotel." I said, "No way. I'm busy." I thought this was quite an affront. I knew what he wanted. I guess that was a mistake, like the many pricks I have turned down. There is no fury like a prick scorned, right?

So then we went in to shoot. I had just seen Prince, so I was kind of making fun of Prince and what I saw as his corny macho antics—like everyone, I adore Prince, but I am like a joker, it was all good fun. Humping the guitar and stuff. It was such a ridiculous time, the late '80s, with all this stupid iconic macho posturing and the heavy metal scene. So I was just having a good time making a big joke out of the heavy metal scene, and while I was doing this, the cameraman came and shot up between my legs. I was wearing a mini spandex Chanel suit designed by my friend Belle McIntyre, and I had on some kind of little thong panties. They shot between my legs! I was so caught up with the performance, I had no idea what was going on. When I saw the movie, I vomited. When that movie came out I went to see it with my family. I had no idea what it was going to be!

My career was over. I was blacklisted from every club because everyone thought that was what my act was, a sex act or something. This was a blatant distortion and sendup of me because I would not fuck that fucking little writer. And of course, the producers did this to make money, to exploit us, to make an easy buck. They killed my career. Island did not sign me. "Marilyn Monroe," my song, was a real hit on college radio, and I was unsigned, so I took a meeting with Lou Maglia [Island Records' president] and he said, I quote, "Yeah, people like the song but it just doesn't *knock my dick in the dirt*." Okay, that is how they treated women in the music business. I mean, this thing is breaking out of college radio, and I wrote it and arranged it and paid most of the *Playboy* money to get it recorded, and I hand it to them and they are talking about their dick. It was like an extreme nightmare of poverty and bad faith and public humiliation unfolding, and I could not stop it.

Did you have any mentors in your early years?

Larry Rivers, Allen Ginsberg, Terry Southern, Spaulding Gray, and Hunter S. Thompson.

Over the last few decades, what inspired your music?

Love is always my inspiration. Music is about love, you just move out from the core of it. My mother says I am like Pollyanna because I try to see the good in people and I like to put them on a pedestal and make a big deal out of them. This was one thing that made me not quite a punk.

You're extremely intelligent and it shows in your work. Do you see yourself as an artist in the Dadaist vein?

Thanks for the compliment. I don't think I am special at all. Because of my upbringing, I was not socialized into acting normal. I refuse to diminish myself, or my gifts, in order to be accepted and fit in. To me, my work is highly logical and makes perfect sense. I do what the culture calls for. I kick culture in the teeth, I spit on it, I urinate on it, and I hug it to death and wait for it tell me it loves me. Being in the underground means you don't take the easy way, you take the true way. It is a political choice, it is the politics of perfect freedom.

Will you talk about your work with Roulette TV?

Jim Staley is the head of Einstein Records, my record company. He said, "Phoebe, I think we are going to do a TV show." I said, "Jim, I think I should be the host." He said, "Who will write it? I said, "I will write it." So there you go. That's how life works. Just tell people what you want. *Roulette TV* is about the extreme frontier edge of art and music.

I am constantly trying to figure out how I can tenderly and lovingly get experimental artists to open up. I know how they have been hurt, I know how sensitive they are, and how wounded, because of the nature of our materialistic and celebrity-driven culture. The questions interviewers ask on TV and in the newspapers seem brutal and insensitive.

You don't have to be that way to get to the truth out of someone. Just make a safe place for them, let them conjure themselves out of the mute matter we've been given to live in. Coax them out of their bodies, their space suits, for a few minutes. Let the soul bloom.

Who are some of the performers you've had on the show?

Laetitia Sonami inspired me to create my *Rap Shoes.* Pauline Oliveros gives me strength to be strong and be a mature female composer and not get hung up on that stupid *am I beautiful, am I rich, am I cute enough?* crap. All I am trying to say is that women waste their money and ruin their lives obsessing over their looks. None of that matters, even men don't care. They just want a confident broad who smiles and has fun and fulfills her own dreams. The record companies, starting maybe with Blondie, only signed girls who a) gave good head, b) would have sex with multiple executives, or c) looked like models or strippers. There are exceptions, maybe three that I can think of, and those three women are very attractive, very good, and had to wait decades for their success.

But all that matters is music. That's all. My last night with Marilyn Crispell and Lotte Anker was unbelievable. They are true improvisers, very brave. As Nadia Boulanger once said, "Mastery of one's technique gives perfect freedom."

In the experimental vein, which musicians have you collaborated with?

I have an ongoing collaboration with Morgan Powell and the Tone Road Ramblers. We are a "composing collective." With that group I do works that combine science with music. Our first work, *The Waterclown,* was about the formative movements of fluid, vortices, spirals, eddies. Then I did *The Common Root of All Organisms*. Eight years of earth history. You can see a video I did of it with the music online and work samples in my New York Underground Museum.

Then I did *Dark Energy*, about astrophysics and "Lambda, the God equation," and next *The Prairie*, about the ecological and phylogenetic interrelations of the Tall Grass Prairie, which is where man first appeared. *The Savannah* is a critically endangered biome, and I was able to incorporate prairie cocks and giant sloths into my work. These works are many-layered, with symbols, meanings, and metaphors, and the music is deep. I write them in a state of feverish meditation at an artist's colony called Ragdale.

Do you write all your own music, both lyrics and compositions?

I hear both the lyrics and music coming at once. I have written almost a thousand songs, two operas, three musicals, and many shorter works for small ensembles. I write, for the most part, alone. But I think my collaborations are very strong. I have one with Eno and Leo Abrahams. Oh, it is good! It's about astrophysics, love, and sex. Leo is a great composer. He is now the guitarist for Bryan Ferry and Brian Eno. He is a genius. It's rather a nice story with a happy ending.

Did you have trouble being taken seriously because of your sexy persona?

Who doesn't take me seriously? Anyone who witnesses me playing or my painting or my poetry or my videos would have to take me seriously. My photograph was printed because I am photogenic, and many people came to conclusions about me without knowing anything about my art. Just because you have good hair does not mean you are stupid. I have a curvy, long-legged body, and I have good hair because I am part Native American. That's not a persona. That's how I was born. I bleach my hair because it's fun, but underneath I am still a very smart brunette.

With your vocal talent, you could have become a pop or classical music star, yet you chose to stay in the underground. Why?

Why? Because I am an artist. Pop is for dummies, the underground is for the smart.

After many performances and rave reviews as an artist, you posed for Playboy. *What influenced this decision? How did it affect your career?*

[*Playboy*] came to me and wanted to publish my paintings of women. I was thrilled! I always loved the art in *Playboy*. When they visited my studio they started to offer me money to pose. Oh, I was scared. They wooed me for months and months. They wore me down. They offered me so much money and I was so broke from the lawyers and the recordings and what it cost to do rock and roll in those pre-digital days. And in 1988 I knew my career was over—that is, in the old days, once you were off a major label, you were damaged goods. I had been signed to Epic at a very young age, and that is another story of sexual harassment to the point of depravity; the Epic contract alone cost me $20,000 in legal fees altogether, and I was eighteen with artist parents. After Epic, I knew I would never make any money. [*Playboy*] offered me so much, it was stupid to turn it down. I was able to live, and develop my art. I lived very frugally for ten years on that money. Artists need time. They need to just sit and think, and do their art. Why doesn't this government understand that they should be helping artists instead of sending young men to their deaths?

Actually, it's the only national publicity I ever got and was great for my career. Guys loved me for it. And girls were glad too, because now they could feel superior to me. "Oh, she did *Playboy*." Fuck them. Are they so pure? What's wrong with naked women? I like naked women.

How did you get involved in acting and Troma's Toxic Avenger?

I thought Troma was going to use my music. They lied, since my career was over and I knew it. I was only about twenty-three. That's the way it was in those days when the record companies ruled the earth.

Do you have any regrets from your early years?

Only one. There was someone I loved and I should have just gone and camped out on their doorstep until they let me in, because this person was the absolute best and the perfect lover for me. I always wanted to give artists their space, so out of respect I kept my distance. But if you love, love, *love* someone, perhaps it is alright to just go and join them, because life is so short and you never know when someone is going to get so sad they just shoot themselves in the mouth.

Kembra Pfahler, born August 1961 in Hermosa Beach, California, is founder and vocalist of theatrical performance art band the Voluptuous Horror of Karen Black (TVHKB), a cult phenomenon. In 1990, she created the band—described as part high fashion glamour, part cult horror film archetypes—with its name a homage to B-movie scream queen Karen Black. Kembra developed the conceptualized philosophies of *Antinaturalism, Availabism,* and is now working towards what she calls *Precognitive Folklore* in her work. Before forming her band, Kembra spent time in the '80s working both in front of and behind the camera as both model/actor and director, especially with a Super-8 camera.

In performance, Kembra and dancers appear on stage in full body paint, usually in metallic or polka-dot bikinis, towering frightwigs, and stiletto black thigh-high boots, with makeup reminiscent of Linda Blair's in *The Exorcist.* With each song, the performers carry enormous theatrical props. They not only play music as a rock band but perform rituals and ceremonies of baptism intended to purify and indoctrinate the audience into Kembra's founded religion Blatholisism, the dancers acting as clergy or Voluptuaries.

Their first album in 1993 was *A National Health Care,* followed by *AntiNaturalists* ('95), *Black Date* ('98), and several limited edition 12-inch vinyl picture disks. She released a TVHKB video, *Voluptuous Horror,* in 1995 and has contributed to compilations including *Virgin Voices: A Tribute to Madonna* (2005). Kembra appeared as Sharon Tate in Geoff Cordner's photo illustrations which accompanied Legs McNeil/Gillian McCain's article, "These Children that Come at You with Knives," about the Manson family, published in *Pop Smear* (1999).

Kembra has appeared in films including *Surf Gang* (2006) and *Gang Girls* (2000) directed by Katrina del Mar; *War is Menstrual Envy* (1992) directed by Nick Zedd; and *The Sewing Circle,* a 7-minute documentary by Richard Kern in which her vagina was stitched shut.

In addition to launching a couture clothing line in 2003 based on the band's aesthetic, her art is currently being shown at Rove Gallery and is part of Deitch Projects. In 2008, her performances at the Whitney Biennial included *Actressocracy* and *Whitney Live.* She also released the book, *Beautalism,* a photographic catalog of her work, in 2009.

What was young Kembra like?

I grew up in Los Angeles, California. I was born into a family of Southern California surfers and my parents took me up and down the coast on surfing trips. They gave me this name and always said to me, "Oh, you're very special, you're very different, you're going to grow up to be very creative." They were always very artistically nurturing. My mother used to make clothes for me when I was a child, like mostly black and white houndstooth check schoolgirl dresses. She always put me in black and white saddle shoes, with a strange, very severe pageboy haircut. I had kind of a strange couture high-fashion childhood on the beach that I always used to feel very uncomfortable walking around in. I would always walk home from school peeling off my clothes, taking my saddles shoes off.

My mother used to also make costumes for the school pageants. My earliest memories of her costumes were big flower heads that she made that we all put on. I later used those flower heads in a Voluptuous Horror of Karen Black song. She made a lot of decoupage, a lot of collages. She used to make me read one book a day. I was a big fan of Dr. Seuss, of course, the great writer from San Diego. I used to watch *Star Trek* all the time, and I used to sit on the beach and just look at the tides. That was about it. I don't remember participating in school whatsoever. The California school system is not really very inspiring. I ditched a lot. I started smoking marijuana, of course, as early as I possibly could—like most kids from the beach.

How early was that?

Oh, you know, fifth or sixth grade. I also went to another West Coast institution called the Virginia McMartin School, which was later found out to be, allegedly, a school for satanic cult activities and child pornography. There was a big law case, a legal case against Victoria McMartin, who owned the nursery school. I don't recall anything like that ever happening. As an adult I remember seeing the TV movie of my nursery school, sort of like a witch-hunt that occurred in my Southern California haven. Mostly I just grew up, just California dreamin', as they say... I loved classic horror films, like the Universal monsters, Frankenstein and Godzilla. I like mutated monster movies like Bigfoot legend-type films. I like monsters, and *Jaws,* of course.

How did you first get interested in performance art?

Mostly when I moved to New York in 1979, I didn't have, well... just to backtrack a little bit, I had grown up in high school listening to the first wave of West Coast punk rockers like X, the Cramps, the Germs, and the Mau Maus. When I left Southern California for New York, I kind of had a feeling that I did not want to start a band, you know, I felt like they had all done it so well on the West Coast and that I wanted to do something different. I didn't really know what I wanted to do, but I sort of started from nothing. I just remember walking around the neighborhood in the Lower East Side—you know, there was a smaller artistic community at that time. Like Klaus Nomi was still around, John Sex, and these older NY performers that were always doing events, weekly performance events, and I was just this kid sort of hanging around.

One of the older artists said, "Hey, do you want to do a performance art piece?"

I said, "Okay, sure." I remember getting booked into this place called Armageddon near the West Side Highway in NY. I remember going home and trying to figure out what I could possibly do for a performance art piece. I didn't have any training in acting. I had no desire to really be that. So in the spirit of Availabism, which is making the best of what's available, I remember going home to my apartment, I had some eggs in the refrigerator. I just thought to myself, "I'll just take my clothes off, stand on my head, and crack eggs on my vagina, and that will be effective."

Sometimes we have this sort of collective unconscious of our imagination. You know, the egg is a common thread in many different mythologies, and it was available to me and so I just did it—it's taken years to figure out why I did that stuff. So that was one of the first performance art pieces that I did. It was very minimal. It was without music and was less than three minutes. That was when I first started employing the use of Availabism. The best use of what's available: my body, which was available. I didn't have any musical instruments. The invitation was there, so I had to come up with something. In those days, that kind of artistic communication, it was more or less creating something that was stories worth the retelling of. In other words, I didn't quite know what I was doing, but I knew in the aftermath that would be quite a nice story to retell, "Oh yeah, she stood on her head and cracked an egg on her vagina." Very simple.

To what extent had you been introduced to the New York Lower East Side art scene? What other artists inspired you?

I got here in 1979 and I was lucky enough to learn about the legends who still were alive in my neighborhood, like the filmmaker Jack Smith was on 1st Avenue, the Living Theatre headquarters was still on 4th Street, Allen Ginsberg was still around, all the '60s people were lingering. The new punk rock people were here as well, though I don't know how much I was a part of that, although I was somehow included in it. I was a bit younger than the '80s wave of art. I felt like I was the seventh grader and they were the twelfth graders.

Did you see them as mentors? Any memories of specific artists?

Well, definitely. Ethyl Eichelberger from the Pyramid Club always impressed me. Ethyl Eichelberger was an amazing performer who's now passed away. Most of the people are no longer alive. But they were so prolific. There was a healthy competitiveness amongst the Lower East Side residents to just sort of try to do more, create more, change the paradigm of what was currently in existence in NY.

I got exposed to filmmakers like Kenneth Anger and the Kuchar brothers, Mike and George Kuchar. When I was a young girl there was this place called the Millennium Film Archives. That's how I met Mike Kuchar, who kind of named the band the Voluptuous Horror of Karen Black. I had done a performance art piece with a Super 8 film that I had made, and Mike said I looked voluptuously horrific because of my body paint and wigs and stuff. I was very influenced at that time by the Viennese—the Vienna Actionists Group: Rudolf Schwarzkogler, Günter Brus, Otto Muehl, Hermann Nitsch. I was interested in them because they were doing something that I hadn't ever been exposed to in California. I thought their images were outrageous and terrifyingly beautiful. They did live performances and they documented with pictures, so the Vienna Action Group was very important to me.

I always listened to classic rock—mostly bands like Kiss, Mötley Crüe, Van Halen. I never really outgrew that. You know how some people never outgrow hot dogs or hamburgers? Growing up in California I had classic rock roots. I carried that with me to NY. I always used classic rock in my Super 8 movies. I used classic rock soundtracks for my live performances. That's eventually why I started my own rock band, because I got sort of tired of using other people's music for my own thing.

So how did the performance art morph into a live rock band?

Basically, it was a desire to not use other people's music anymore. I had met my partner, Samoa, who was from Hiroshima, Japan, and Samoa had a background in Butoh and Noh and all this strange Japanese theatre, but he also had a surrealistic temperament, he loved bands like Grand Funk Railroad, and I love that combination of influences. So we were partners, and he played guitar. I got to NY around 1979 and for ten years I just did Super 8 films and performance. Around 1990, we decided to form a rock band, the band Karen Black, which was just bass, guitar, and drums. It wasn't experimental music at all. We always had this intention: kind of *verse, chorus, verse, chorus, guitar solo, verse, chorus* band. Something very meat and potatoes—because the subject matter of our songs and the visuals that we used with our band were a little complex, so we wanted to have a plain piece of bread that the weird creamy butter could live on.

So that was an entertaining package that was a successful package for us. Also, I wanted to be able to go on tour, and in the '80s I had been invited to film houses and museums, but I didn't find that very appealing. It wasn't fun enough, and a driving force behind all of our artwork has been hedonism, enjoyment, pleasure, and fun. It was just a little bit too dreary to work in the academic world at the time. So we went on tour with Karen Black all across the country in a Winnebago. We were on tour for about ten years.

Did you and Samoa have a similar vision for the band's basic concept?

We did, definitely. Of course, we're not the Rolling Stones, but we had a Mick Jagger/Keith Richards type of relationship where Samoa would come up with guitar melodies and I would come up with the lyrics and the visuals. It was a very symbiotic relationship. I've since started Karen Black on my own in the past couple of years. I reformed the band without Samoa. It still seems to be effective, although I did enjoy playing with Samoa for a great deal of time. But Samoa sort of grew out of it. We had played music together for so long, it was so involved with going to band practice, that we started to get sort of good at being musicians.

At one point Samoa said, "We don't need these costumes and wigs, and Kembra, why are you standing there naked with body paint on?" I said, "Gosh, well, you know... hmmm, this *is* interesting." We sort of flew in different directions. He became a grassroots guitar player / country musician, which is also very interesting because he's the only grassroots musician from Hiroshima.

Did you design the costumes, props, and stage?

Yes, yes, I am guilty of committing all of those acts against inanimate objects. I am the one responsible for bringing a chest of drawers onto the stage so that I could sing songs called "Underwear Drawer." That was the number where we would pull undies out of the drawer. Essentially, all the theatrical illustrations on stage were very, very literal. In other words, we weren't displaying a dead chicken singing about rainbows. If there was a volcano on stage, I would be singing about baking or mothers. The props on stage were just basically to help illustrate a story behind the song. Sort of like what my mom used to do in the children's school pageants.

All the props are very low-tech; they are mostly made out of light foam and hot glue gun work. I made—and still make—all the props in my apartment. They are a little more refined, now I get to show my props in galleries and museums. But they're all very compact and low tech, I like a Luddite, low-tech approach. We're not like a fiber-optic type act; we're more like a papier-mâché type.

It was more about expedience and being able to travel. Mostly, reflecting back to the earliest egg piece, I'm always trying to strip things down to make them as potent as possible, simple as possible. I guess what I would say is a building up of a vocabulary of images. Sometimes it takes an artist their whole life to build up their little vocabulary of images. You know that thing that I do standing on my head and cracking eggs on my vagina? I had a friend ask me once: "When are you going to stop doing that?" I said, "Well, probably never because I'll need to just do it for the rest of my life." A really comfortable impression, but I'll include other things as well. Which is what happened. That's still in the vocabulary of images... but there's like fifty other things too.

Was Karen Black your first musical project?

Yeah, it was. I sang on GG Allin's record. I'm friends with other bands, I've sung on other people's records. I'm writing a song with Debbie Harry but Karen Black is my only musical project. Also I do work now with my friend Antony, from Antony and the Johnsons, who I like very much.

What was required to be one of the Voluptuaries?

Well, for the girls of Karen Black, their requirement was to really think through what they were going to do onstage, because there was some nudity involved but there was a very fine line between creating a sense of adult sexuality as opposed to just using our bodies as an illustrative tool. And that kind of underplayed exhibitionism takes—and took, if you could believe it—a lot of discipline and rehearsal, and a lot of discussion. Like some of the girls had been younger, I always ask them if they would be able to stand behind the project five years from now. If they were sitting around the Thanksgiving table with their aunt from the Midwest, would they feel comfortable discussing one of the more extreme pieces, like the *Wall of Vagina* where we stack up on top of each other, spread our legs, and have plain yogurt dripping down the center of our legs like a stack of pancakes? The process is for me to choose people, to make sure that they're clear about what my intention is with Karen Black. We're not doing a live sex show. Getting into that costume can make people want to behave a little campy. Camp is fine, but that doesn't really fit into the dynamic of Karen Black live on stage.

Some people haven't worked out, but a lot of the girls that do the most difficult things onstage I've known for over ten years. There are people that have been around for quite a long time. They went on tour with me, they have done shows in other contexts, like at my art galleries at American Fine Arts Company, and they've come to England with me. They've done a lot of thankless work, as well as a body of the more difficult work. It's fun to do shows and go on tour, especially the larger rock shows. I guess mostly the requirement for their participation is that they love classic rock and they realize that I'm trying to do something that I haven't seen before—that's the impetus for wanting to do this band. *I haven't ever seen this before, why don't we try this?* We don't have backing from major record companies; we do well on our live shows. There's a lot of perks that come from playing in the band.

What are those perks?

You know, dates and entrance. You get a little dull golden key to places that other people might want to go. You get a little dusty golden key into hell. It's fun playing in Karen Black. I haven't had any bad breakups with musicians in the band. I'm still friends with Samoa. We've always had a very good band. Something that I think has surprised people sometimes is that we don't play sloppy art rock.

Who have been memorable assistants in the rites of Blatholisism?

We started to do these ceremonies—at one point we were going to Las Vegas a lot—and we decided to do "Blatholosism," a sort of christening or blackening, in the parking lot of the Liberace Museum. There weren't actually any special guests but we could always get the band members involved. So that's what we were doing—we were doing the egg piece at the Liberace Museum parking lot in Las Vegas. Sort of like a baptism (or a take on that). It was just us, nothing too Jonestown, or too L. Ron Hubbard-ish, or celebrity-like. Tom Cruise was not there cracking eggs on my vagina... there were no known celebrities at all.

Can you name or give an example of an Antinatural Apostle?

Dolly Parton, of course, is an Antinaturalist that we admire. An Antinaturalist, meaning someone who is not a method type of actor, someone that is more embracing like the cartoonish element of behavior on stage or screen... someone who performs in a way that is markedly not real. That's what Antinaturalism is, like Frankenstein, Boris Karloff, Jack Smith the filmmaker, Carol Channing, Sweet Charity, Karen Finley, Diamanda Galás... who else? That's a little handful right there.

What inspired you to start your own religion of Blatholisism?

That was just a momentary tangent. I think it was at the time we started our own website... starting our own website the mid-'90s seemed very cultish, actually. We were doing things like incorporating, getting bank loans for our record company, so it just seemed like the time to start a religion, too. But we're really no longer doing that.

Have you ever met Karen Black?

She came to one of our earliest shows in Los Angeles and she introduced the band. She was very gracious and very funny. A few years ago I did a show with Hal Wilner and Lou Reed at UCLA's Royce Hall, we were reciting Edgar Allan Poe poems. We invited Karen Black to participate in that, too... so over the years we've had little visits, but we're not, like, buddies or anything. I find it really generous that she's never sued us or spoken of us too derogatorily. Our band is not about sarcasm or poking mean-spirited fun at her personally. It's never been about that. Mostly it's about the fact that our education was about watching movies, horror movies. The films that she had been in, like *Trilogy of Terror*, was more of like a reference point.

You've made art out of the mockery and destruction of 'traditional' beauty by making it terrifying. Was this your intent?

I don't qualify as an academic necessarily, although I have learned some things through the years about having been able to do things. I got invited to do a photo spread in *Penthouse* magazine when I did this piece where I sewed my vagina shut. I guess it's always been, like I said before, my goal was to put images into the world that hadn't necessarily been seen before. That sounds sort of pedestrian, but that's been my motive mostly. Had I seen someone else with a sewn vagina, black teeth, and huge wigs in *Penthouse*, I probably wouldn't have done that. I just wanted to present a different idea of female beauty. Maybe it had to do with my interest in the Japanese Butoh theatre as well. Having the body represent something strange, prehistoric almost. Any titillating imagery that I ever did was mostly to please myself, or my friends. We were never dressing for success—we were sort of dressing to get a snicker out of each other.

So as far as the images actually coming out to be beautiful, maybe my color palate, or my kind of art direction, has gotten a little bit more refined and pretty-ish. That's definitely been my intention, to make beautiful things... and I guess it's just debatable about what's beautiful or not. I love horror but I don't like slasher movies. I haven't really used blood or traditional, obvious violence. Although sewing your vagina shut is kind of violent how I did it looked more like stringing an instrument than butchering a vagina.

Will you talk about the Sewing Circle?

My two friends went over to Richard Kern's house. They were gifted nurses / nurse practitioners, and they just sewed my vagina shut. But I'm not really into the S&M piercing thing, it was mostly just done for that specific piece. Then we did it again with Richard [Metzger] for Richard's movie in black and white. Then I did it again for *Penthouse*. Michael Halsband took those pictures for *Penthouse*. That's one of my favorite pictures, too.

You have worked as a professional model, including the infamous Calvin Klein heroin-chic ads, yet you talk about high fashion being a disease?

I think that all of us, at one time or another, get the fashion bug. I definitely have it. I think that making clothes is an art form. At that time, when I was discovered to be a Calvin Klein model, I'd always been the ugly girl with black hair, an emaciated sort of rocker, and then all of a sudden I was on the side of buses. That got me mostly, like, accredited. Everyone was just astonished that I was on the buses. Since I've grown up to do so many pictures, to be able to work with these amazing high fashion people was just another fun thing to do. I'm not anti-fashion at all.

I love couture, and I make clothes now. It's a disease that you don't have to abstain from the drug that keeps you involved with this disease. You don't have to remain abstinent from the drug that keeps you in the high fashion disease. You can incorporate it happily into another medium. It's another medium, fashion.

For more than ten years you had a career as a domme in many BDSM films, such as Mistress Kembra. *How many have you done? What was your introduction, and were you working as a domme before the films?*

Well, how that occurred was a very famous man called Vince Benedetti ran a studio in Queens, and in the '80s I was hired to do art direction for him. Later, when some of the actors dropped out of the picture, they invited me and cast me as a dominatrix in some of their early S&M movies because of my appearance. I didn't have experience as a classically trained domme necessarily, but I had all of my Antinaturalist acting skills, which worked very well in that environment. Uncle Vince employed a lot of us from the rock scene, and it was just like a day job, essentially.

We'd have to go to the studio with some props and some equipment and sort of invent a scenario the day that we arrived. Sometimes we'd have to put out three to five films a day, and depending on the tools that were available, that determined the subject matter. I remember one day there was a blowdryer and some hair curlers, so we had a sadistic hair salon scene. It was all very not serious—it provided me with a good day job. I'm still friends with Vince Berdetti.

After doing many S&M films for him, like *Jaded Mistress* and *House of Pain*, this list upon list of films, I came to him with some ideas of my own and he let me do my own Karen Black work there in that studio, like *Punk Ladies of Wrestling*. I also did a film called *The Girls of Karen Black* with Mike Diana. That was an outrageous accomplishment because they were very traditional porno S&M, and we'd have all the Karen Black members there in full body paint performing crucifix masturbation. They weren't very bothered by adult sexuality in those films—mostly they were like B-movies.

From doing those S&M films I was able to do my own Karen Black films and remain friends with these amazing pornographers. They were some of the first porno people in NYC to do 35 mm. I met people like Annie Sprinkle around that time, and all these legendary sexual revolutionaries. The group of pornographers who made sex films because they wanted to were into sex not necessarily because they wanted to make money—they were into sex and they were interested in making pretty movies or funny movies as well. Films like *Deep Throat* portrayed that first wave of very political, outrageous pornographic films. Early Times Square people... Vince is part of that era. It's been a good relationship. I feel lucky that I know him.

Would you consider dominatrix work performance art?

Sure, absolutely. Although the imagery usually involved in the dominatrix work that I've done in the dungeon wasn't necessarily completely original. I could say, as opposed to the images that are presented, the vocabulary of images is a little bit already-written. The aesthetic was a little bit written. There's a performative element to being a dominatrix. I'm sure that I got a little more confident and could apply that kind of confidence. Being a domme or a submissive, doing domme acting or submissive acting, submissive behaviorism or domme behaviorism, has strengthened my ability to create a very strong wall of distance between myself and the audience—a very unnatural wall in a very un-casual kind of setting. So, certainly I learned how to do things that I probably would have learned in nursing school on those film sets, although I'm not a qualified nurse.

Did working as a domme have an effect on your art?

I remember doing one piece where I tied bowling balls to my feet, but that was more from medieval torture pictures I'd seen in Europe, like a Hans Baldung etching.

Can you briefly describe the film you starred in called Ferrum 5000?

That was by my friend, Steve Doughton. It was made in Super 8 and he used a lot of techniques that I love, like using a prism lens. There was a movie by Ed Wood Jr., *Take It Out in Trade*, a porno movie that used an incredible prism lens. Back then Steven Doughton had filmed all these natural wonders in Yosemite. He chose me to play the goddess of metal. I sort of erupted out of a pool of geological fumes. I was a little bit of an antinatural element. It's a beautiful movie. It's so incredible because it predates all the video toasters and CGI filmmaking. It was all very low-tech special effects and incredible looking Super 8 film work, and the subject was essentially about... outer space aliens. It was a beautiful film.

You've been directing films since 1996?

I started in the '80s, actually, with Super 8 movies, when I learned about places like the Anthology Film Archives and the Millennium. Before Karen Black we used Ektachrome 160 film, and we shared each other's cameras. We would make Super 8s and then play back the video footage on TV and re-shoot it with Super-8 cameras by pointing the camera at the TV and jacking up the colors—that's how we got a lot of special effects. I made a whole body of work in the '80s but I stopped when I began Karen Black. I did just a couple of my own movies at Uncle Vince's place. Now I've given all my '80s films to the Film Co-op of NYC and they're restoring everything. Filmmakers Bradly Eros and Aline Mare were very catalystic in facilitating younger people to make films. They showed us everything we needed to make movies, and shared their equipment. I have a whole hidden group of movies that exists from my young girlhood.

Will you talk about your experience in the Cinema of Transgression?

I was much younger than those guys—well, not that much younger, but essentially. Nick Zedd, Richard Kern, Tom Turner, and Lydia Lunch were the initial Cinema of Transgression filmmakers. They were very renegade. Tessa Hughes started showing films in the Lower East Side in the '80s as well, facilitating the first Cinema of Transgression films, like *Fingered*. I had the chance to meet Nick Zedd and Richard in the early '90s and I was able to make some movies with them. Towards the end of that era I made a movie with Nick Zedd called *War is Menstrual Envy*.

Yeah, I was lucky enough to have been able to meet those guys when they were still making a lot of Super 8 movies. I was mostly in my Karen Black costumes and I just appeared in his film as TVHOKB, Karen Stern.

What was your experience working on films with Ron Athey?

Ron asked me to be in a couple shows that he and Vaginal Creme Davis organized. Again, that was a meeting that occurred because of doing TVHOKB. That's one of the funnest reasons to start a rock band, because you get to travel around and meet so many different artists. I think I wouldn't have come into contact with all these outrageous genius savants without having been in this extreme rock band. If I had stayed on more of a Fine Arts path in the '80s I would have missed out.

How did you get into fundraising for St. James Infirmary?

My old childhood friend, Johanna, got me involved in that project. She runs the St. James Infirmary and is an activist in San Francisco. We grew up together—I used to babysit her. People like Annie Sprinkle were involved—SF is a little bit more advanced as far as being out of the closet with sex workers, prostitution, and health care for people that are in the business. The East Coast is quite a bit farther behind on that level.

We have PONY, Prostitutes of New York. I think NYC is still so married to the Midtown, suit and tie, john/trick image and the taboo of prostitution... the taboo of getting involved with sex workers. I think NY has too much money in mind to keep in the closet. This city is sort of a misogynist, patriarchal type of city still, that wants to keep sex workers as victims. We don't love our sex workers here, we don't give them parades or trophies or anything. So maybe one of the politicians may have fucked one forty times a night... it's really a shame. It's too bad because a lot of people get hurt from being in the closet. A lot of sex workers have to live with that double life and a sense of shame. They don't get to have a union; they don't get to have health care. It's weird. We're supposed to believe NYC is the most artistically advanced city in the world, but it's not. On a very grassroots level, on the level of what we actually do for our people here, we don't do anything here for our people.

Maybe the drastic state of the City since September 11th was consciousness-raising for everyone as a whole body of people. My dad is a West Coast pot-smoking intellectual. He's not an uninformed person and my father always says New York, or this country, is going to have to undergo something similar to the French Revolution. We're just going to have to revolt because things have gotten so bad here. One example is the difference between San Francisco and people like Johanna who gets grants for St. James Infirmary to run this kind of facility. There are places like that in New York but a little more defined; places like the Callen-Lorde Clinic.

I think that in NY there's a strange feeling, like "if you can make it here you can make it anywhere." So what happens is that people come here and they really have their eye on making it, where as the whole ethos of actually being an extreme artist is like you *better* be making it happen *now.*

There's a strange kind of *Sex in the City* / HBO / Donald Trump sort of distorted achievement. It's silly, very silly. Luckily, that's something I don't have to participate in, or my band. We can just dip into any genre or medium that we want. We're not marginalized into just one little neighborhood. We can really do whatever we want. It's a privilege. Thanks to a lot of tenacity and a lot of sacrifice too from our band members, it's going to stay that way. That's why I did that benefit for St. James Infirmary, because of having been a sex worker. I identified that I could be a sex worker if I wanted. I've done all sorts of things in the sex business, from the S&M movies to being in bands or being a domme. The kind of background I come from as a rock person lends to those kinds of jobs. A rock person did not go and get a corporate job working at VH1. A rock person's grind was part of the equation. A rock person from my background wasn't given (and we [still] aren't given) record contracts, so there had to be other avenues in order to fund the activities.

Being a sex worker was one of them—that's part of the rock lifestyle. Which doesn't really exist that much anymore, but that's cool too—a lot of the younger girls that I see in bands can maybe skip over that stage and become book publishers or presidents of companies. It's sometimes been a dangerous life, too. Some of the new young girls look at people my age and think, 'Okay, let's just skip over that part and become record company executives now, or let me just take this G4 movie equipment and be a movie director.' But skipping over the hard parts, I don't know…

I was having this discussion with a friend the other day, some of the new Nintendo generation and the new technology generations. They could be the ones that could save the world—the iPod listeners or the cell phone communicators. Who knows who's going to save the world? Could be an airhead American Apparel sock designer, we don't know how it's going to happen. So I try not to judge that genre, the Nintendo genre, I try not to judge too harshly. The people that came up in the '80s are quite different from the people that came up in the '90s, and then the people that came up after 2000... It's interesting—it's just quite different.

There's different access to information. While you had to go to New York to learn about people like Nick Zedd and Richard Kern, now anyone can just look them up on the internet.

Exactly. That's exactly it. There were only fanzines in circulations, there were hard copies, and there were fewer record companies. That makes for smarter kids today. I put somebody into a management position of my band that was sixteen years old—he was just a genius. But access to information is different. I guess it is what it is.

I got invited to teach a class at Columbia University, and one of these girls, an artist, was telling me that sometimes she just feels like she doesn't know where to begin. She was sitting in front of her computer, and it's almost too much for her to even process, and she just doesn't even know where to start her art project for that day. I told her to cover the computer—to put a black piece of fabric over the computer—and go do it. I love the book by Rainer Maria Rilke, *Letters to a Young Poet*, which is an excellent instruction manual. You can only really make artwork or the most powerful work when you are telling what you actually know about. Rilke encourages people. If you don't know what to do, go back to the far reaches of your mind, into your childhood or something... That has been an important book for me.

Do you have a maxim or motto you live by?

There was something that George Kuchar said that I always really liked: "You can do good or you can do bad or you can do nothing." That's one I always liked.

What does that mean to you?

That means that I have to just keep trying.

ABOUT THE AUTHOR

Zora von Burden is a poet, writer, and journalist who was raised and still resides in San Francisco. She is the author of four books of poetry: *Across Decades, The Hidden Chamber, The CF Hotel,* and *The Evening Hybrids*. For many years, her writing appeared in the *California Herald* and the *San Francisco Herald*. Additionally, her autobiographical writing narrates Geoff Cordner's feature-length film *Portraits from the Fringes*, featuring Iris Berry and Lydia Lunch. A segment of this film was adapted into a short entitled *Hotel Hopscotch*, which screened at international film festivals and aired on the BBC, as well as winning a Lucid Underground Film Festival award.

The author wishes to thank Jennifer Joseph, Michael Slavinsky, Ann Ameling, Richard Metzger, Adam Parfrey, Geoff Cordner, Dave Soldier, Mia d'Bruzzi, Stella Weir, Chris Carter, Wendell Goodman, Dave Vanian, Terry Button, Nalani Jensen, Kerri Welsh, Judith Peters, Mary Anne Huff, Rick Miller, Captain Sensible, Sid Terror, Aleix Martinez, Pamela Des Barres, Kitten DeVille, Patrick Bishop, Ray Jensen, Mark Cortale, Shirley O'Loughlin, Brad Hampton, Jennifer B, Maureen Turner, Eric Zassenhaus, Lisa P., Tiki Jim, and all of the women interviewed.